MANUAL OF
American English Pronunciation

FOURTH EDITION

Clifford H. Prator, Jr.
University of California, Los Angeles

Betty Wallace Robinett
University of Minnesota

92-1872

Harcourt Brace Jovanovich, Publishers

Orlando   San Diego   New York
Toronto   London   Sydney   Tokyo

Library of Congress Cataloging in Publication Data

Prator, Clifford H. (Clifford Holmes)
    Manual of American English pronunciation.

    Includes index.
        1. English language—United States—Pronunciation.
2. English language—Text-books for foreign speakers.
I. Robinett, Betty Wallace.   II. Title.
PE2815.P7   1985   428.1   84-25222

ISBN 0-03-000703-8

Printed in the United States of America

ISBN 0-03-000703-8

2 3 4 090 15 14 13 12 11 10 9

Harcourt Brace Jovanovich, Inc.
The Dryden Press
Saunders College Publishing

Contents

STUDENT'S NAME _____

COURSE AND SECTION _____

DATE OF RECORDING _____

Accent Inventory (Copy 1)

To the Student

This "Inventory" is to be used, preferably at the very beginning of the English course, so that you may have constantly at hand a diagnosis of the elements of foreign "accent" in your own individual speech. First, your voice will be recorded as you read the "Diagnostic Passage" on the next page. The reading should be done at normal speed, in a matter-of-fact tone, without unusual care in pronunciation; in other words, it should sound as much like natural conversation as possible. Then the instructor will listen to the recording many times, and make an analysis, on the following pages, of your speech difficulties. These pages will serve as a guide to the sections of the *Manual* that are of most importance to you, and show just what phases of English pronunciation should be of most concern to you.

The "Inventory" may be used again at the end of the course to measure the progress you have made.

SUGGESTED KEY TO CORRECTIONS

Phonetic symbols immediately under word: what you should have said. Second line of phonetic symbols under word: mispronunciation in your speech.

′ Over a syllable or word: you left this unstressed; it should be stressed.
(′) over a syllable or word: you stressed this; it should be unstressed.

Black line: normal intonation.
Colored line: your incorrect intonation.

/ unnatural pause you made.

ix

Diagnostic Passage

(1) When a student from another country comes to study in the United States, he has to find out for himself the answers to many questions, and he has many problems to think about. (2) Where should he live? (3) Would it be better if he looked for a private room off campus or if he stayed in a dormitory? (4) Should he spend all of his time just studying? (5) Shouldn't he try to take advantage of the many social and cultural activities which are offered? (6) At first it is not easy for him to be casual in dress, informal in manner, and

confident in speech. (7) Little by little he learns what

kind of clothing is usually worn here to be casually

dressed for classes. (8) He also learns to choose the

language and customs that are appropriate for informal

situations. (9) Finally he begins to feel sure of himself.

(10) But let me tell you, my friend, this long-awaited

feeling doesn't develop suddenly, does it. (11) All of

this takes will power.

Check List of Problems

I. STRESS AND RHYTHM

A. _____ Stress on wrong syllable of words of more than one syllable. (See Lesson 3, Section III, of manual.)

B. _____ Misplaced stress on nominal compounds. (L. 4, S. II.)

C. _____ Misplaced stress on two-word verbs. (L. 4, S. II.)

D. _____ Other improper sentence stress. (L. 4, S. II.)

E. _____ Improper division of sentences into thought groups. (L. 4, S. IV.)

F. _____ Failure to blend well, to make smooth transitions between words or syllables.

    1. _____ Improper insertion of /ə/ to break up difficult combinations of consonants. (L. 4, S. IV; L. 15, S. I.)

    2. _____ Insertion of /ə/ before initial s̲ followed by a consonant. (L. 15, S. III.)

    3. _____ Unnatural insertion of glottal stop. (L. 4, S. IV.)

II. INTONATION

A. _____ Unnatural intonation at end of statements. (L. 5, S. III.)

B. _____ In wh̲-questions. (L. 5, S. III.)

C. _____ In yes-no questions. (L. 6, S. I.)

D. _____ In series. (L. 6, S. II.)

E. _____ In questions with two alternatives. (L. 6, S. II.)

F. _____ In direct address. (L. 6, S. II.)

G. _____ In tag questions. (L. 6, S. II.)

H. _____ In other cases.

III. VOWELS

A. _____ Failure to obscure unstressed vowels in words of more than one syllable. (L. 3, S. II.)

B. _____ Failure to obscure the vowels of unstressed words. (L. 4, S. II and III.)

C. _____ Failure to lengthen stressed vowels before final voiced consonants. (L. 9, S. II.)

D. _____ Substitution of an improper vowel sound. (L. 2; 11; 12; 17; 18.)

1. ____ for /iy/. 5. ____ for /æ/. 9. ____ for /ʊ/. 13. ____ for /ay/.
2. ____ for /ɪ/. 6. ____ for /a/. 10. ____ for /uw/. 14. ____ for /aw/.
3. ____ for /ey/. 7. ____ for /ɔ/. 11. ____ for /ə/. 15. ____ for /ɔ/.
4. ____ for /ɛ/. 8. ____ for /ow/. 12. ____ for /ər/. 16. ____ for /yuw/.

IV. CONSONANTS

A. ____ Substitutions due to improper voicing. (L. 8, S. I.)

1. ____ /p/ for /b/.   5. ____ /ð/ for /θ/.   9. ____ /š/ for /ž/.
2. ____ /t/ for /d/.   6. ____ /f/ for /v/.   10. ____ /tš/ for /dž/.
3. ____ /k/ for /g/.   7. ____ /s/ for /z/.   11. ____ Others.
4. ____ /θ/ for /ð/.   8. ____ /z/ for /s/.

B. ____ Substitutions due to other causes, especially improper point of articulation.

1. ____ /r/ for /l/. (L. 10, S. I.)
2. ____ /l/ for /r/. (L. 10, S. I.)
3. ____ /ð/ for /d/. (L. 13, S. II.)
4. ____ /d/ for /ð/. (L. 13, S. II.)
5. ____ /z/ for /ð/. (L. 13, S. II.)
6. ____ /t/ for /θ/. (L. 13, S. II.)
7. ____ /s/ for /θ/. (L. 13, S. II.)
8. ____ /dž/ for /y/. (L. 13, S. III.)
9. ____ /y/ for /dž/. (L. 13, S. III.)
10. ____ /ž/ for /dž/. (L. 13, S. III.)
11. ____ /š/ for /tš/. (L. 13, S. IV.)
12. ____ /v/ for /b/. (L. 14, S. I.)
13. ____ /b/ for /v/. (L. 14, S. I.)
14. ____ /w/ for /v/. (L. 14, S. I.)
15. ____ /v/ for /w/. (L. 14, S. I.)
16. ____ /v/ for /hw/. (L. 14, S. I.)
17. ____ /p/ for /f/. (L. 14, S. II.)
18. ____ /hw/ for /f/. (L. 14, S. II.)
19. ____ /ŋ/ for /n/. (L. 14, S. III.)
20. ____ /n/ for /ŋ/. (L. 14, S. III.)
21. ____ /n/ for /m/. (L. 14, S. III.)
22. ____ Others.

C. ____ Improper point of articulation, resulting in abnormal sound but not substitution.

    1. ____ /d/. (L. 8, S. III.)

    2. ____ /t/. (L. 8, S. III.)

    3. ____ /r/. (L. 10, S. I.)

    4. ____ Others.

D. ____ Insufficient aspiration of initial voiceless consonants. (L. 9, S. I.)

E. ____ Excessive aspiration of final stops and voiced continuants. (L. 9, S. III.)

F. ____ Excessive aspiration of ''/d/-like'' medial /t/. (L. 9, S. I.)

G. ____ Improper addition of a consonant.

    1. ____ /ŋk/ for /ŋ/. (L. 14, S. III.)

    2. ____ /gw/ for /w/. (L. 14, S. I.)

    3. ____ /h/ inserted. (L. 14, S. IV.)

    4. ____ Others.

H. ____ Slighting or omission of a consonant.

    1. ____ /h/. (L. 14, S. IV.)

    2. ____ /s/. (L. 8, S. V.)

    3. ____ /z/. (L. 8, S. V.)

    4. ____ /t/. (L. 8, S. IV.)

    5. ____ /d/. (L. 8, S. IV.)

    6. ____ Others.

V. VOWELS AND CONSONANTS

A. ____ Confusion between the three usual ways of pronouncing the -ed ending. (L. 8, S. IV.)

B. ____ Confusion between the three usual ways of pronouncing the -s ending. (L. 8, S. V.)

C. ____ Syllabic consonants. (L. 10, S. III.)

    1. ____ Failure to pronounce the preceding consonant (for example, /wʊnt/ for /wʊdn̩t/).

    2. ____ Insertion of /ə/ (for example, /wʊdənt/ for /wʊdn̩t/).

D. ____ Failure to insert /ə/ between a front vowel and /l/ or /r/. (L. 10, S. II.)

VI. GENERAL COMMENTS

Introduction: to the Teacher

I. Differences in the Fourth Edition

This new edition of the *Manual of American English Pronunciation* differs substantially from its three predecessors, published respectively in 1951, 1957, and 1972. The most obvious change is the addition of two new lessons, numbered 7 and 16. The total number of lessons has thus been increased from 16 to 18.

The new Lesson 7, entitled "More about Intonation," is now the culmination of a sequence of five lessons that deal with the so-called "suprasegmental" features of spoken English which determine its rhythm and intonation. Lesson 7 permits treating several useful intonation patterns that were not discussed in earlier editions. It also provides room for a systematic inventory of patterns and a diagnostic passage for identifying the intonation problems of individual students.

Lesson 16, "The Sandhi of Spoken English," ensures more adequate treatment of the phonetic modifications that take place especially in informal types of connected speech. The two new lessons add up to a considerable shift in emphasis away from work on individual sounds and toward greater attention to the whole stream of speech. Years of experience in teaching pronunciation have led the authors to a deepening conviction that a diet made up principally of drill on minimal pairs of isolated words is not the best treatment for helping advanced students—the kind for whom the manual is primarily intended—to make their speech more widely intelligible.

In other lessons new sections and/or exercises have been added to deal with topics that had somehow been slighted or overlooked in earlier editions. These include words ending in -ate, whose pronunciation may vary depending on whether they are used as adjectives, nouns, or verbs (Lesson 3-III-4); "echo questions" (6-D); focus of meaning in questions and statements (7-I); adverbs ending in -edly (8-IV, 8-F-2); substitutions for /f/ (14-II, 14-D); phonotactic rules governing the positions in which consonants can be used (15-I); types of regularity in the spelling of sounds (18-I); and so on.

In other places the descriptions of sound production have been rewritten so as to update the theory on which they were based and to provide better practical advice regarding articulatory problems. Several figures have been re-drawn in order to achieve greater accuracy and clearer detail.

The authors have tried to eradicate traces of sexist attitudes wherever they were detected, and a definite attempt has been made to include female and male references in a nonsexist fashion in the exercises.

The most significant kind of change in the new edition, however, is the result of the effort we have made in various lessons to introduce more use of language for real communicative purposes in the learning activities suggested for students to carry out. The authors have always shared the belief among teachers that languages cannot really be learned unless they are used for pur-poses of communication. Without communicative intent, pronunciation is not true speech; it is no more than the manipulation of linguistic forms.

We believe that the basic process whereby one learns to pronounce En-glish, or any other language, is by imitating the pronunciation of those who speak the language natively (see Lesson 1, Section I, first sentence of all edi-tions). Direct imitation is most effective, but circumstances often make second-hand, indirect imitation necessary. And the imitation is also most effective if it takes place under conditions that approach as nearly as possible those of normal communication. Analyzing how sounds are produced is helpful but not basic.

We therefore conceive of learning to pronounce as a process that is nor-mally achieved in three steps:

1. Learning to hear and identify a sound or sound contrast when a native speaker produces it;
2. Learning to produce it when the learner's attention is focused on pro-nunciation;
3. Mastering it to the point of automatic production when attention is focused on meaning (our ad-hoc definition of *communication*).

Under some circumstances these three steps can no doubt be taken in quick succession, or even simultaneously. There is evidence that, in some cases, step two may precede step one. But there are advantages, when planning a course or writing a textbook, in thinking of them as taking place independently and in the order listed above.

Pronunciation exercises can be classified into three groups according to the three steps. An example of a step-one exercise would be listening to minimal pairs of words pronounced by the teacher and stating whether the word with a given meaning came first or second. Making as clear a distinction as possible between the italicized words in a sentence such as "He *slid* on the *sled*" would be a step-two exericise. A step-three exercise, involving the pronunciation of /dž/ for example, could be to read a discussion of jogging /dž́agiŋ/ and then answer the teacher's questions on the subject. (There is such an exercise in Lesson 13-I.)

The authors have become increasingly convinced that more attention should be paid to the third step in teaching pronunciation. Yet it is the step that has been largely ignored in typical pronunciation classes and that is absent from most existing materials for teaching pronunciation. How can we know that we have really helped our students improve their pronunciation unless we create frequent opportunities to hear how they pronounce when they are un-self-consciously communicating?

In the earlier versions of this manual some step-three activities were included at the end of the exercise section of most lessons. But one of our major preoccupations in preparing this new edition has been to increase the number of such communicative activities. We have added short dialogues that can be used in real-life situations, that have significant content, and that can be used as a basis for improvisation. Discussion questions and discovery procedures have been suggested, which should lead to substantial exchanges of ideas on appropriate topics. We have inserted poetry, limericks, jokes, and riddles where we judged they could be made relevant and useful. Contests and games have been included as conversational and motivational devices.

An innovation about whose possibilities we are particularly enthusiastic is the use of small-group activities that provide opportunities for pronunciation. Because a student in one small group can speak to the other members of that group at the same time as members of other groups speak to one another, the total opportunity for speaking communicatively in an environment favorable to good pronunciation is greatly increased. The possibilities for small-group activities are pointed out in a number of places in the new edition.

In other words, we have done what we could to enrich the general, nonlinguistic subject matter of the material which could give rise to un-self-conscious communication. And we have tried to do this without slighting the linguistic information and systematic drill that have always been the core of the manual.

II. How the Manual Is Put Together

This book is definitely *not* for beginners. Though an effort has been made to keep the English in which it is written as simple as possible, much of the subject matter is technical and requires the use of exact terminology. The manual focuses on only one aspect of English, its pronunciation, and treats that topic in considerably more detail than would be appropriate for students who do not already have a considerable command of the language. As has already been pointed out, it was prepared with the needs of advanced nonnative speakers of English in mind: to learn new speech rhythms and intonation patterns, to acquire a more natural and less bookish delivery, to strengthen the habit of weakening unstressed vowels, to concentrate on sounds that are not thoroughly familiar, and the like.

At a number of American universities it has also proven useful in courses designed to introduce native-English-speaking future teachers to the phonological system of American English and to methods of teaching pronunciation.

The manual is based on the kind of American English that can be heard, with some variation, from Ohio through the Middle West and on to the Pacific Coast. Living as they do in the region where the process of dialect mixing has gone furthest and where the language has achieved most uniformity, the people who speak this language undoubtedly constitute the present linguistic center of gravity of the English-speaking world,[1] both because of their numbers and their economic and cultural weight.

The original author of the book was born in Georgia but has spent most of his adult life in California. The second author has lived mostly in the Middle West. In order to avoid, in so far as possible, introducing our own favorite idiosyncrasies of speech into the text, we have agreed to accept Kenyon and Knott's *A Pronouncing Dictionary of American English* (G. and C. Merriam Co., 1953) as our authority for the pronunciation of individual words. We feel that it represents more closely than any other dictionary the type of speech, identified in the preceding paragraph, which used to be called General American English.

We do not accept, then, the oft-repeated cliché that a teacher can teach only his or her variety of English. While it may be true that most of us have to use the variety we are most familiar with when setting an oral model for our

---

[1]As indicated by its title, this manual deals primarily with American English. Readers should therefore understand that, when the authors speak of ''English'' without modification, we are referring primarily to the most general American variety. When there has been a need for greater precision, we have used more specific terms such as ''American English,'' ''British English,'' ''both American and British English,'' or ''the English-speaking world'' as above.

students to imitate, a partial solution to that problem can be found through the use of recorded tapes that provide a more widely standardized pronunciation. We can also use phonetic transcriptions and physiological descriptions that represent the most widely standardized form of English.

The authors would even suggest that professionally minded teachers might do, as we ourselves have tried to do over the years: that is, to learn how to avoid on appropriate occasions such features of regional dialect as we can identify in our own speech. We do our students no favor by flaunting in class the regionalisms—be they regionalisms of pronunciation or of grammar—that linger on in the speech of most of us. And a high degree of standardization is desirable and a source of strength for any language in this day of almost instantaneous worldwide communication.

We particularly recommend the use of tapes to provide a model when Lesson 16, dealing with the phonetic modifications that occur especially in informal types of connected speech, is being taught. Supplementary tapes of practice materials have been prepared especially for this text. If teachers have not had formal training in phonetics, they may encounter considerable difficulty in recognizing and identifying the sandhi in their own speech.

Since many of the difficulties nonnative speakers of English experience in pronouncing the language result from the interference of the speech habits they have internalized in using their mother tongue, it would have been advantageous to be able to organize the manual around a contrastive analysis of English and one other language. Because of the many diverse language backgrounds of our foreign students at American universities, however, it was not feasible to do this. Convinced that there are large categories of speech difficulties that all or most of our students have in common, we used a statistical approach to this problem. Our first task was to discover as accurately and objectively as we could what these areas of common weakness were. A check list of categories was set up in accordance with the phonetic systems of several languages that have been described by linguists and that were more or less known to us. We included, insofar as we could, all previously noted departures from the norms of the conversational pronunciation of educated native speakers of American English. We then recorded the speech, and analyzed and counted the "errors" of students at UCLA for three years. The result was a sort of frequency count of the pronunciation difficulties of a group of several thousand typical students from abroad. The manual was built around this count.

The largest linguistic groups among the students whose speech we analyzed were speakers of Spanish, Mandarin Chinese, Iranian, Arabic, German, French, and the Scandinavian languages, in that order. But there were representatives from all the major language areas of the globe.

We believe we have thus avoided two undesirable extremes: (1) a text organized solely in accordance with the subjective intuition of the authors, and

(2) one that logically and with equal emphasis treats all the elements of the English sound system without taking into consideration the special needs of the student group.

As the results of the frequency count became available, our next concern was to determine the order in which the various types of speech difficulty found to be prevalent in our mixed classes should be dealt with, and the relative amount of attention that should be devoted to each type. Our aim was to make the students' speech as completely intelligible as possible. Could this be best achieved by treating first and in most detail those difficulties which the count showed to be most common, by an arrangement based on simple numerical frequency? Or were there certain kinds of difficulty that were more serious than others, that affected intelligibility to a greater extent, and that consequently must be given greater emphasis?

We examined with considerable care the widely accepted assumption that "errors" involving the substitution of one phoneme[2] for another—pronouncing *that* as /θæt/ rather than /ðæt/, or *bit* as /biyt/ instead of /bɪt/—are necessarily those which most affect intelligibility, and are consequently those which must always be attacked first. As we gained experience, we were more and more forced to the conclusion that, while this theory might have some validity with reference to beginning students, it was of little value as a guide in our advanced classes. Our count revealed that the substitution of one phoneme for another was relatively infrequent in the speech of our students. Only a few such substitutions—/iy/ for /ɪ/, /ɪ/ for /iy/, /ɔ/ for /ow/, /a/ for /ɔ/, /s/ for /z/, /t/ for /d/, /d/ for /ð/, and so on—accounted for the great majority of cases. Most others, while theoretically possible or even likely, were actually quite uncommon and certainly could not be regarded as problems of major importance. We found our students having little trouble with /m/ or the diphthongs /ay/, /aw/, and /ɔy/.

We were also impressed by the fact that in almost all cases of phonemic substitution, even in those where the mispronunciation should have resulted in giving the word a different meaning—*bit* as /biyt/ (beat) instead of /bɪt/—the context made the intended meaning quite clear. In other words, the substitution seldom seemed to result in a misunderstanding. This impression was strengthened by the extreme difficulty we experienced in preparing drills made up of sentences in which either word of a minimal pair—*made, mate; time, dime; save, safe*—would be equally appropriate. Our students appeared simply to fail

---

[2]Sound which may be the sole feature whereby one word is distinguished in meaning from another: for example, *time* /taym/ and *dime* /daym/ are alike except for their initial sounds; therefore /t/ and /d/ are phonemes in English.

to understand a word much more often than they mistook it for some other word. We did not understand them a great deal more frequently than we misunderstood them.

On the other hand, certain nonphonemic "errors" proved in practice to be serious barriers to intelligibility, and were shown by our count to be extremely common. An Italian student had great difficulty in making himself understood because of his tendency to pronounce all final stops with a strong "finishing sound." For him and many others, the improper release and aspiration of stops was obviously a much more important problem than the substitution of, say, /š/ for /ž/.

We found that a knowledge of voicing alone did not enable our students to make a clear distinction between words like *plays* /pleyz/ and *place* /pleys/. Better results were obtained when we also pointed out and drilled the so-called secondary differences between /eyz/ and /eys/: vowel length and consonant release. These latter are not usually classified among the phonemic qualities of English sounds.

The senior author was at one time struck by two very fine examples of how nonphonemic differences in sounds may even cause misunderstanding. With another American professor and several Filipino educational officials he was traveling by car near Manila to visit a school in the village of Polo, province of Bulakan. The other American asked one of the officials to repeat the name of our destination, and understood the answer to be Bolo, Bulahan. In Pilipino, the native language of this particular Filipino, /p/ and /b/, /k/ and /h/ all exist as separate phonemes. Initial /p/ is unaspirated as well as unvoiced. In English, on the other hand, initial /p/ is strongly aspirated, and initial /b/ is not aspirated though it is voiced. The American, listening to a sentence in which the context gave him no clue, mistook the Filipino's unaspirated /p/ for a /b/. We have traditionally regarded voicing or the lack of it as the feature that distinguishes the phoneme /p/ from the phoneme /b/. But in this case aspiration was certainly the distinctive characteristic. The official had pronounced *Bulakan* with a perfectly normal Pilipino /k/, formed far back in the throat and with a very incomplete closure. In English this /k/ would have been made farther toward the front of the mouth and with a strong closure. Though these latter qualities are not usually thought of as essential to the /k/ -phoneme, their absence clearly made the American mistake /k/ for /h/.

When an individual begins the study of a foreign language, the new phonemes are often immediately obvious to him, and he therefore tends to learn them rather quickly. The American who takes up Pilipino cannot fail to become aware of the glottal stop /ʾ/ that distinguishes a word like *batà* /bátaʾ/ (child) from *bata* /báta/ (dressing gown). He will also, of necessity, learn very soon to use the phoneme /ŋ/ at the beginning of a word, as in *ngalan* /ŋálan/ (name), where it does not occur in English. But he may never notice or reproduce certain other features of the new sound system, such as the incomplete closure of /k/ or the lack of aspiration of initial /p/, unless these are pointed out to him. These latter are not obvious, though they may profoundly affect the ability of native speakers to understand the American's Pilipino.

We believe that any pronunciation text which devotes its attention almost exclusively to phonemic differences concentrates on what is most obvious and most easily acquired through simple imitation. It neglects precisely those phases of the phonetics of the language in which imitation is most likely to fail, and analytical knowledge and systematic drill are of greatest value.

Our own solution has been to regard unintelligibility not as the result of phonemic substitution, but as *the cumulative effect of many little departures from the phonetic norms of the language.* A great many of these departures may be phonemic; many others are not. Under certain circumstances, *any* abnormality of speech can contribute to unintelligibility.

The fact that any phonetic abnormality can contribute to unintelligibility does not mean that all departures from the norm should be treated as though they were of equal importance. We have adopted an order of arrangement based primarily on simple numerical frequency, considering first and at greatest length those difficulties most prevalent in our classes. It was necessary at times, of course, to modify this arrangement, in the interests of logic and good pedagogy, by grouping similar problems together. We also considered that an ''error'' that involved an entire sentence, such as a faulty intonation pattern, was obviously of more importance than one that affected only a single sound.

Problems such as improper voicing, aspiration, and vowel length, which recur in connection with a series of different consonants or vowels, we have treated as a whole rather than as matters to be taken up over and over again in connection with each individual sound. In other words, we felt that the substitution of /k/ for its voiced counterpart /g/ in a word like *big* /bɪg/ reflected not so much an imperfect control of these two sounds as it did a general inability to voice final consonants. We noted that students who substituted /bɪk/ for *big* /bɪg/ also almost invariably substituted /eytš/ for *age* /eydž/ and /ɪs/ for *is* /ɪz/. We consequently did not prepare a separate section and drills on /k/ and /g/, but included these sounds in a lesson on voicing. For the same reason we did not attempt to drill all difficult consonant clusters separately, but treated the problem they represent in a general lesson on consonant clusters and combinations. In a sense, then, our approach has been synthetic rather than analytical.

In its final form the manual has a cyclic arrangement. After an initial lesson that introduces the student to the phonetic symbols, it proceeds at once to the problem of the weakening of unstressed vowels, explaining only enough about vowel classification to make clear the significance of weakening and the identity of the vowel sounds. It then moves on to the closely related and crucially important subject of rhythm and stress in words and sentences. The elements of intonation and the connection between intonation patterns and stress are next treated in three lessons. Until some control of rhythm and intonation has been achieved, drills involving connected discourse may do more harm than good, and it is futile to hope to achieve mastery of the individual sounds that make up the larger patterns. If the pattern is wrong, the sounds cannot be entirely correct. If the pattern is right, correct sounds are much easier to produce.

In Lessons 8 and 9 the principles of consonant classification, voicing, and aspiration are explained and applied, with particular emphasis on the pronunciation of the endings -s and -ed. The effect of an initial or final position on articulation is underscored. Lesson 10 deals with the liquids /l/ and /r/ and their influence on preceding vowel sounds, and also with the group of syllabic consonants.

Attention is then shifted back to vowels. Detailed analyses of the formation of the individual sounds are given, and the problem of stressed vowel substitutions is attacked. Lessons 13 and 14 deal with prevalent consonant substitutions that are the effect, not of improper voicing or aspiration, but of a formation of the individual sounds that is abnormal in some other respect. Lesson 15 attacks the problems produced by clusters of consonants in both initial and final position as well as those produced medially in words and phrases. Mention has already been made of the new Lesson 16, which deals with the ways in which various linguistic environments lead to changes in the pronunciation of words during more or less informal oral communication.

The two final lessons of the manual concern the way English vowel sounds are represented in spelling. These lessons are intended to help students to internalize the systematic elements in English spelling as they relate to pronunciation, and to recognize cases in which vowels are irregularly spelled.

III. Use of the Manual

Since the students using the manual will presumably be familiar already with the normal spelling of common English words, we saw no advantage in writing all exercises in phonetic symbols in an attempt to protect users of the book from possible mispronunciations arising from the inconsistencies of English spelling. That problem needs to be attacked in other ways. A great deal of transcribed material has nevertheless been included, especially in the earlier lessons. The purpose of these transcriptions is to facilitate the breaking up of existing faulty speech habits by providing a new type of visual stimulus, thus

making it possible for the students' analytical faculties to intervene more effectively in the formation of sounds and patterns of sounds. This effect is best
achieved while they are first becoming familiar with the symbols, and the law
of diminishing returns appears to make itself felt soon thereafter. Toward the
end of the text special symbols and markings are used more and more spar-
ingly, and the transition is thus made back to normal orthography, to the language situation in which the student has been finding himself all along in his
other classes and in which he will continue to use English.

It was never intended that the manual should teach students to make phonetic transcriptions and to mark intonation themselves. All that is aimed at is
an ability to read symbols and to follow intonation lines. It is true that in
several cases the class is asked to transcribe and mark the intonation patterns
of a few carefully chosen sentences. The purpose of these exercises, however,
is merely to achieve passive recognition more rapidly by means of a little active
experience. The instructor is strongly warned against making the ability to
write in phonetic symbols an end in itself.

The phonetic symbols we finally decided upon as those best suited to our
purposes can most accurately be described as an *eclectic and pedagogical* system of transcription. It is eclectic because the symbols have been borrowed
from a number of different sources representing different analyses of the phonology of English. From George L. Trager and Henry L. Smith we got the
diphthongal symbols for the stressed vowels in *beat* /biyt/, *bait* /beyt/, *boat*
/bowt/, and *boot* /buwt/ as well as the diacritically marked symbols for the
consonants in *ship* /šɪp/, *vision* /vížən/, *child* /tšayld/, and *judge* /džədž/. From
Charles C. Fries and Kenneth L. Pike came the idea of using the single symbol
/ə/ to represent the four somewhat different vowel sounds in *but* /bət/
(stressed), *sofa* /sówfə/ (unstressed), *bird* /bərd/ (stressed before /r/), and *father*
/fáðər/ (unstressed before /r/). And the idea for transcribing front vowels before
/l/ or /r/ as centering diphthongs—*feel* /fiəl/, *here* /hɪər/, *sale* /seəl/, *there*
/ðɛər/, and *pal* /pæəl/—was suggested to us by the transcriptions used in some
of these environments by British phoneticians such as Daniel Jones.

Our system is pedagogical because, in every case, the final choice of symbols was based on the practical advantages and/or disadvantages of using those
symbols in the classroom to help nonnative speakers pronounce English better.
Thus we decided to use a single symbol for the four slightly different /ə/-like
sounds, as mentioned in the preceding paragraph, in order to spare students the
work of learning three extra symbols that seemed to have little practical effect
on their pronunciation. On the other hand, the extra combinations of symbols
for representing centering diphthongs seemed justified because of the success
we have had using them in the classroom as a graphic means of representing
the special quality a front vowel has when it stands before /l/ or /r/. Our ex-

perience has shown that the transcription of *will* as /wɪəl/ and *bell* as /bɛəl/ is a very definite aid in combatting the tendency of many students to pronounce such words with a pure vowel sound and with the tongue held unnaturally high.

There were also sound pedagogical reasons for our decision to use /ɪ/ to represent the pronunciation of an unstressed y in final position, as in *party* /pártɪ/. Actually, the pronunciation of this sound seems to vary, dialectally and idiosyncratically, between /ɪ/ and /iy/ in many parts of the United States. There may be an increasing tendency to pronounce it as /iy/, particularly in singing. In recent decades many American phoneticians have begun representing this sound as /iy/ or the equivalent. But the Kenyon and Knott dictionary represents it as /ɪ/, as do a number of other American dictionaries and—so far as we can discover—as do all non-American dictionaries of English. We have chosen to use /ɪ/ rather than trying to teach our students that a large group of unstressed vowels are pronounced with the diphthongal sound of /iy/, whose symbol strongly suggests a *stressed* vowel. You will remember that one of the greatest problems of our students is to learn how to *obscure* unstressed vowels. It is nearly impossible to get most of them to pronounce an /iy/ that really sounds unstressed.

Whenever possible, the exercises provided at the end of each lesson are made up of entire sentences and even connected paragraphs rather than individual words. In writing the exercises we have often referred to English frequency counts in order to make sure that we were using the most widely understood words that would fit the context. The subject matter of the exercises has been drawn largely from the everyday-life situations most familiar to students. There are no special review lessons, but every lesson contains review exercises; great care has been taken to ensure the recall of important principles at spaced intervals.

Even so, we recognize that any course in the pronunciation of English that asked of its students no more than the completion of the work prescribed in the pages of this manual would be woefully incomplete. Analytical explanations and controlled drills, interspersed with communicative activities as in this new edition, are certainly a useful part of learning to pronounce a new language; there seems to be no more effective way to break up deeply ingrained habits of faulty speech and initiate the formation of new habits. However, as has been pointed out, the fundamental way of acquiring a better pronunciation or improving any other skill is by practicing that skill, by pronouncing. There is no substitute for very extensive, well-motivated, and well-intentioned use of the language in a natural communicative situation. No textbook can completely supply that need, and a single course seldom lasts long enough to develop the skill of pronunciation as fully as one could hope for.

In learning a new language a speaker usually internalizes its relatively restricted phonological system at an earlier stage than its much more extensive grammatical and lexical systems. This means that the choices involved in pronouncing the language are made largely below our level of awareness, as part of firmly established habits. On the other hand, we are more often aware of the grammatical and lexical choices we make as we speak, and have a considerable degree of voluntary control over them. It thus requires a longer time for us to change our pronunciation than it does for us to correct our faulty grammar or improve our choice of words; the improvement of pronunciation generally requires first becoming aware of automatic habits so that they can be broken and new habits can be established.

Teachers should therefore not be discouraged if the practical effects of a phonetics course—or the results of working through a pronunciation manual—seem to be slow in coming. In fact much of the improvement may not become evident until some time after the course has ended. Teachers should make every effort to provide their students with ways to continue after the end of the course the process of becoming-aware-of-habit/ breaking-it/ establishing-new-habit. The principal immediate benefit of the course for some students may not go beyond learning what their problems are and how to go about solving them. But that is at least the first step in a process that can be pushed through to completion in due time if a student has the will to do so and knows how to go about it.

It is encouraging to remember that there are advantages as well as disadvantages in the fact that phonology is a quite restricted system. Just a few small changes in one's pronunication—for example, producing an authentic American retroflex r, or saying *of* in its normal reduced form /əv/—can result in a large improvement in the over-all impression made by a person's speech.

We therefore hope the instructor will supplement in various ways the exercises carried out in the class. Students should be encouraged to carry on, outside of class, the oral reading suggested at the end of most lessons, and they should be given additional suggestions that even more such reading be done. Better integration will be secured if the materials read are those used in other phases of the students' work in English, or in their classes in other subjects. During such reading, the students' attention should initially be focused on one type of difficulty: for example, final -ed, or the stress on nominal compounds. Reading aloud is clearly one of the most effective mechanisms for learning to monitor one's own pronunciation. It can also help students to progress from step two to step three as they become increasingly engrossed in the *meaning* of what they are reading.

With this end in view, we have done quite a bit of play-reading in our classes. Using such props as the classroom afforded, and with books in hand, the students read the lines and walk through the actions. In selecting plays, we give preference to those that are written in a simple modern conversational language free from dialectal peculiarities. A large cast and well-distributed lines are also advantages, as they make it possible for more individual students to participate. While the play is going on, coaching by the instructor is kept to a minimum so that the attention of the participants can be concentrated on the meaning of what they are saying.

Like other kinds of oral reading, play-reading can be continued by students independently even after the last meeting of the course. Reading all the roles of a play aloud, while trying to make each of the different characters sound convincing, can be real fun as well as an excellent way of internalizing new habits of pronunciation.

How much time would be required for completion of the manual within the framework of a course such as that described here? Ideally, three instructional hours per week for two semesters, a total of approximately ninety class hours, would not be excessive. The entire program—diagnosing students' needs, becoming familiar with the subject matter of the text, performing the exercises, carrying out communicative activities, and motivating supplementary reading aloud to be continued after the course has ended—could be effectively developed within a course of those dimensions. Unfortunately, that much time will often not be available, especially if pronunciation is merely one phase of a general course in English as a Second Language.

If faced with the necessity of eliminating items from the program, the authors would probably first omit Lessons 17 and 18, which deal with the relationship between spelling and pronunciation. Though the identification of student needs through the analysis of individually recorded diagnostic passages can be of undoubted value, it is also very time-consuming, and a great deal of it simply cannot be done in a short course. Lessons 1 through 10 constitute, in our opinion, the hard core of the book. With a small, well-prepared group of students, some changes in pronunciation habits might perhaps be initiated in as little as thirty hours of class time.

IV. Use of the "Accent Inventory"

The "Accent Inventory" of the manual should be of service to resourceful teachers in a wide variety of ways. Here we can only suggest some of the fundamental and particularly effective uses to which it may be put, as shown by actual classroom experience.

As its name suggests, the basic function of the "Inventory" is to make it possible to take stock of the types of difficulty each student is having with English speech at the beginning of the semester's or year's work. It provides a diagnosis of individual weaknesses and a prescription of corrective measures. It should also facilitate the teacher's task of deciding which sections of the manual are to be stressed in work with the entire class.

The "Diagnostic Passage" is recorded on tape by each student as early in the course as possible. This passage, on which the "Inventory" is based, is only eleven sentences long. Admittedly, somewhat more revealing results might be achieved if the analysis could be based on a large volume of spontaneous conversational material, rather than on a few sentences to be read. Students do get tense when they know they are being tested, and the intonations of oral reading may often vary from those of ordinary conversation. The conversation-based inventory, however, because of the tremendous amount of time and ingenuity it requires, can hardly be carried out effectively and systematically with an entire class. The reading of these sentences is a practical substitute, which will be valid to the extent that the teacher succeeds in putting students at ease when the recording is made, and getting them to read naturally and informally. The sentences should be treated, so far as possible, as a matter-of-fact conversation, involving no unusual emotion or stresses.

Based as it is on the reading of a very small amount of material, the inventory can probably be well carried out only if the "Diagnostic Passage" is recorded. No teacher's ear and hand would be quick enough to note all the elements of faulty diction while listening to a single reading of so brief a passage. And repeated readings always vary slightly. A recording, on the other hand, may be played any number of times as the diagnostician jots down what he or she hears.

The student is requested to make this initial recording with nothing more in the way of preparation than a casual preliminary reading of the "Diagnostic Passage" at home to become familiar with the thought of the sentences. If the teacher will record a "correct" version of each sentence immediately after the student's version, the subsequent usefulness of the recording will be increased.

The teacher then analyzes each student's version of the eleven sentences. The "Inventory" is printed on perforated pages both preceding this introduction and following Lesson 18. Either or both of these copies can thus be removed without damaging the book. We suggest that a copy be taken up from each student so that the teacher can keep it for whatever length of time is needed for preparing the analysis. The teacher plays each recording repeatedly and makes notes of "errors" heard until he or she feels the analysis is reasonably complete. The various classifications of the "Check List of Errors" should help the inexperienced diagnostician listen systematically and recognize some elements of the foreign "accent" which otherwise has gone unnoticed. For this analytical work, a tape recorder with an instantaneous-repeat mechanism is extremely useful. With such a mechanism, the machine may be stopped and started with a minimum of tone distortion, and may be made to repeat sentences and even words.

When adequate notes have been made, the teacher or a laboratory assistant corrects the "Diagnostic Passage" and marks the appropriate items in the "Check List of Errors" in each student's copy.

In phrases like *let me* (Sentence 10), if the t is merely pronounced with too much aspiration, the error is classified under Section IV-E of the "Check List"; on the other hand, if the student, in an effort to pronounce t clearly, goes so far as to insert an /ə/ between t and m, in addition to aspirating the t, and thus disturbs the rhythm of the sentence, the error is classified under I-F-1. Because of the arrangement of the manual and the fact that errors in the pronunication of -ed and -s may involve vowels as well as consonants, it seemed best to make separate headings to the "Check List" (V-A and B) to cover errors of choice between /d/-/t/-/ɪd/ and /z/-/s/-/ɪz/. If -ed or -s is omitted altogether, the error should be noted under IV-H-2 or 5. In the case of errors involving a front vowel before /l/ or /r/, as in *feel* (Sentence 9), the substitution of /fiyl/ or /fil/ for /fiəl/ should be noted under V-D.

The corrected and marked copies of the "Inventory" are not returned to the students until the latter have completed their study of at least the first four or five lessons of the manual, and can therefore be expected to recognize most of the symbols used and understand something of the principles involved. At the time the copies are returned, every effort should be made to impress on the class the significance of this diagnosis and prescription. It should be pointed out that each heading of the "Check List" contains a reference to the section of the manual in which that particular type of speech difficulty is treated. The list will serve as an individual guide to the text. All members of the class should study their own weaknesses carefully. They should mark in some way those sections of the manual that are of particular concern to them and on which they should concentrate their future attention.

When the students have had time to study their diagnosis, they are given an opportunity, individually with the instructor or in class, to listen as their recording is played. The purpose is to permit them to "hear their own mistakes," and the instructor should do everything possible to help them do so, using the repeat mechanism when needed. This is a very necessary step in accent correction. Clear realization of shortcomings must precede improvement. As they listen to themselves, the students should have before their eyes the marked "Diagnostic Passage" that has been returned to them.

The class will have many occasions for *extensive* pronunciation work of various kinds in the eighteen lessons that make up the body of the manual, and in the additional oral reading and conversation that may be suggested by the instructor. The "Inventory," on the other hand, can be used to motivate complementary *intensive* exercise—frequently repeated drills concentrated on a very small amount of material with absolute mastery as the aim in view. If students could succeed in learning to repeat just the eleven sentences of the "Diagnostic Passage" perfectly, without trace of "accent," it would probably mean that they had acquired sufficient control over their organs of speech to enable them eventually to eliminate all their faulty speech habits. Perfection in these eleven sentences may therefore be urged on the class as one of the specific objectives of the course.

Drills aimed at the achievement of such mastery may take various forms. If they have access to a language laboratory, students may play their recordings often and try to imitate the teacher's "correct" version of each sentence. A particularly effective type of intensive drill may be carried out if there is available a tape recorder with a repeat mechanism, as mentioned above. By means of this mechanism, the recorder can be made to play back each of the teacher's "correct" sentences many times at quick, regular intervals. The student first listens, then imitates again and again, concentrating on timing, intonation, and the grouping of words. When the teacher or assistant thinks the imitation is adequate, the machine is shut off, and the student repeats the sentence two or three times more in the same rhythm, without the accompaniment of the recorded voice.

New recordings of the "Diagnostic Passage" may, of course, be made at any time during the term. A last recording and quick analysis, carried out as part of the final examination, will help the teacher assign grades based on objective evidence of practical achievement. This chance to hear oneself again at the end of the course, and to compare one's speech at that time with earlier efforts, should send the conscientious student away from the class with a gratifying realization of the progress that has been made.

LESSON 1

The Phonetic Alphabet

I. Learning to Pronounce English

The fundamental method by which a student learns to pronounce English is by imitating the pronunciation of English-speaking persons under conditions that approach as nearly as possible those of normal communication. During this course you will have many opportunities to imitate the speech of your instructor and others; do so as accurately and as often as you can. The strange sounds and rhythms may seem a little funny at first, but you must try to forget that, and imitate without reservations. You have probably been amused at the peculiarities in the speech of an American pronouncing, or attempting to pronounce, your own language; now you must try to reproduce those same peculiarities in English. Your success will depend largely on the sharpness of your ear and your ability as an imitator.

Sometimes imitation does fail, however. The instructor may pronounce a word or sentence many times for you, and you still may be unable to say it exactly as he or she does. This may be because you are hearing and reproducing well only a few of the most important sounds that make up the word. It will be of benefit to you then if the instructor can *write out* the word for you, sound by sound, using symbols that are always pronounced in the same way. One of the most typical features of English is the manner in which its unimportant, unstressed vowels are pronounced. Your attention may not be called

1

to these at all when you *hear* a word spoken, but you can *see* them as clearly as the stressed vowels in a phonetic transcription. The eye is more analytical than the ear. We can see separately all the symbols that make up a written word, but we can hardly hear individually all the sounds that compose it as it is normally spoken.

Most people learn most things better through the eye than through the ear. Even in learning to pronounce, where you must depend primarily on hearing, there is every advantage in being able to have your eye aid your ear. Something learned in two different ways is probably four times as well learned. The ordinary spelling of an English word sometimes has so little apparent relation to its sound that the spelling is not useful as a guide to pronunciation.

There will be times when you may wish to write down the pronunciation of a new word, so as to be able to recall it later. Unfortunately, we cannot remember a mere sound clearly for very long; but a phonetic transcription will make recall easier. When no English-speaking person is present to pronounce a word for you, your only recourse may be to try to reconstruct the sound of the word from the symbols in a dictionary. Practice in reading symbols will help you learn to make accurate reconstructions.

There will be times too when, to succeed in making an English sound perfectly, you will need to know exactly what to do with your tongue, lips, and other organs of speech. For instance, in order to make the t-sound in English, the tip of the tongue touches the roof of the mouth somewhat farther back than is the case with many other languages. Merely hearing the t and trying to imitate it, you might never guess this fact.

In other words, though you must rely chiefly on your ear and imitation to acquire a good accent, a knowledge of the number and identity of English sounds, the symbols used to represent them in phonetic writing, the way in which they are produced, and a few of the laws that govern their behavior will be of great advantage to you and will increase your chances of success. This text is designed to give you such information and to aid you in learning to apply it. The text is not a course in English pronunciation, but merely a useful aid in such a course. The science of phonetics may be considered the grammar of pronunciation; a knowledge of phonetics can help you to pronounce no less, and no more, than a knowledge of grammar can help you to speak and write.

II. Why a Phonetic Alphabet?

The first step in your work with phonetics will be to familiarize yourself with a set of symbols by means of which the important sounds of English—all those that serve to distinguish one word from another word[1]—may be represented. There will be a symbol for every such sound, and no more than one symbol for any given sound.

The set of symbols used in this manual is an adaptation of the widely known Smith-Trager system. This adaptation is better suited to our purposes than are systems of diacritical markings such as those employed in most well-known English dictionaries. Use of the latter may involve learning up to thirty different vowel symbols, with each sound represented by several different symbols. You will find various versions of the Smith-Trager system used in much technical writing on English pronunciation as well as in many bilingual dictionaries intended for students of foreign languages.

III. Table of Symbols

In the table that follows are included *approximate* French, German, Japanese, and Spanish equivalents for most of the American English sounds. These equivalents are *not scientifically accurate* in most cases, and are given only because they may make it easier at first for you to identify the various sounds.

A written accent marks the stressed vowel of words of more than one syllable: *reason* /ríyzən/. When there are two or more stressed syllables, the most important is marked / ́/, and that with secondary stress / ̀/: *preposition* /prὲpəzíšən/.

---

[1]Recognition of the difference between *bed* and *bead,* when the words are spoken, depends on ability to distinguish between the vowel sounds in the two words. There must, therefore, be separate symbols to represent these two sounds. The r in the word *water* is pronounced in different ways in various parts of the United States and Great Britain, but variety of pronunciation does not mean variety of meaning. For our purposes, one symbol will suffice to represent the various r sounds. An alphabet based on this principle is properly called a phonemic alphabet, and phonemic symbolization has been used in this text except that deviations have sometimes been made for pedagogical purposes. As mentioned in the Introduction, we consistently refer to the transcription as phonetic because students are more accustomed to this term and because several pedagogical devices employed in the manual are phonetic in character. However, because the approach is basically phonemic, we have followed the practice of using slant lines (/) to enclose all transcriptions, even those which are obviously phonetic: for example, /:/ for vowel length and /ʰ/ for aspiration.

The Phonetic Alphabet

Symbol	English Examples		French	German	Japanese	Spanish
				Approximate Equivalent in		
CONSONANTS						
1. /b/	boat	/bowt/	bébé	baden	ban	también
2. /d/	dark	/dark/	doigt	dumm	dan	un dedo
3. /f/	far	/far/	fait	Feind	furui	fino
4. /g/	gold	/gowld/	garder	gut	gakkō	golpe
5. /h/	home	/howm/	(none)	haben	hachi	gente
6. /k/	cold	/kowld/	car	kaufen	kin	vaca
	kodak	/kówdæk/				
7. /l/	let	/lɛt/	laisser	lange	(none)	lado
8. /m/	man	/mæn/	même	morgen	uma	mano
9. /n/	next	/nɛkst/	non	nein	nani	nombre
10. /ŋ/	ring	/rɪŋ/	(none)	singen	ginkō	naranja
	sink	/sɪŋk/				
11. /p/	part	/part/	peu	Papier	pera	pelo
12. /r/	rest	/rɛst/	(none)	(none)	(none)	(none)
13. /s/	send	/sɛnd/	sou	Haus	suru	sino
	city	/sítɪ/				
14. /š/	ship	/šɪp/	chez	schön	shuppatsu	(none)
15. /t/	ten	/tɛn/	temps	Tür	to	tener
16. /θ/	think	/θɪŋk/	(none)	(none)	(none)	cita (as pronounced in Madrid)
17. /ð/	that	/ðæt/	(none)	(nonc)	(none)	dedo
18. /v/	very	/vɛrɪ/	vain	November	(none)	(none)
19. /w/	went	/wɛnt/	oui	(none)	waru	huevo
20. /y/	you	/yuw/	hier	jung	yuku	hierro
21. /z/	zoo	/zuw/	chose	dieser	zashiki	desde
	rose	/rowz/				
	knows	/nowz/				
22. /ž/	pleasure	/plézər/	je	(none)	(none)	(none)
	vision	/vížən/				
23. /hw/	when	/hwɛn/	(none)	(none)	(none)	(none)
24. /tš/	children	/tšíldrən/	Tchèque	Putsch	cha	mucho
25. /dž/	jury	/džúrɪ/	djinn	(none)	jama	yo (when pronounced with emphasis)
	edge	/ɛdž/				
	age	/eydž/				

The Phonetic Alphabet

Symbol	English Examples		French	German	Japanese	Spanish
				Approximate Equivalent in		

SIMPLE VOWELS

Symbol	English Examples		French	German	Japanese	Spanish
1. /a/	far	/far/	âme	V<u>a</u>ter	ā	m<u>a</u>lo
	hot	/hat/				
2. /æ/	am	/æm/	m<u>a</u>l	(none)	(none)	(none)
3. /ɛ/	get	/gɛt/	lève	Bett	empitsu	el
	bread	/brɛd/				
	said	/sɛd/				
4. /ɪ/	in	/ɪn/	(none)	sitzen	(none)	(none)
	become	/bɪkə́m/				
5. /ɔ/	for	/fɔr/	note	wollen	oru	orden
	all	/ɔl/				
	ought	/ɔt/				
6. /ʊ/	put	/pʊt/	(none)	dunkel	putto	(none)
	could	/kʊd/				
	good	/gʊd/				
7. /ə/[2]	but	/bət/	me	Knabe	(none)	(none)
	bird	/bərd/				
	other	/ə́ðər/				
	ago	/əgów/				
	reason	/ríyzən/				

---

[2]The student who has a good ear will probably note that the vowel of *but* /bət/ is not quite the same as that of *bird* /bərd/, where the /ə/ sound is given a special "coloring" by the /r/ that follows it. Some works on English pronunciation employ as many as four separate symbols to represent variants of the /ə/ sound: [bʌt] in a stressed syllable, [əgow] in an unstressed syllable, [bɝd] stressed and followed by r, and [faðɚ] unstressed and followed by r. In order to require the learning of as few symbols as possible and in following the phonemic principle, this manual uses only /ə/ and /ər/ in transcribing these four variants.

The Phonetic Alphabet

Symbol	English Examples		French	Approximate Equivalent in		
				German	Japanese	Spanish
DIPHTHONGS[3]						
1. /ey/	late	/leyt/	thé	Leben	eigo	peine
	raise	/reyz				
2. /iy/	see	/siy/	fini	sieht	ie	sí
	receive	/rɪsɪyv/				
3. /ow/	go	/gow/	dôme	Boot	hirou	bou
	coat	/kowt/				
4. /uw/	rule	/ruwl/	fou	Stube	kū	mula
	too	/tuw/				
5. /ay/	I	/ay/	aïe	mein	ai	hay
	cry	/kray/				
6. /aw/	now	/naw/	(none)	Haupt	au	pausa
	house	/haws/				
7. /ɔy/	boy	/bɔy/	(none)	heute	oi	sois
	noise	/nɔyz/				
DIPHTHONGS BEFORE /l/ OR /r/[4]						
1. /iə/	feel	/fiəl/	vie (as pronounced in the Midi)	(none)	(none)	(none)
	we're	/wiər/				
2. /ɪə/	hill	/hɪəl/	(none)	(none)	(none)	(none)
	hear	/hɪər/				
3. /eə/	sale	/seəl/	née (as pronounced in the Midi)	(none)	(none)	(none)
4. /ɛə/	well	/wɛəl/	plaie (as pronounced in the Midi)	(none)	(none)	(none)
	there	/ðɛər/				
5. /æə/	shall	/šæəl/	(none)	(none)	(none)	(none)

---

[3]The diphthongization of /ey/, /iy/, /ow/, and /uw/ is not as noticeable as that of /ay/, /aw/, and /ɔy/, but for the sake of simplicity in description and practicality in teaching they are so symbolized.

[4]We have found that a diphthongal symbolization of the front vowels before /l/ and /r/ is a definite aid in combatting the tendency of students to pronounce such sounds with a pure vowel and with the tongue held unnaturally high. We have not used the glide /y/ in the transcription of the /iə/ and /eə/ diphthongs because it would give the appearance of two syllables in a word such as *feel*: /fiyəl/.

VARIOUS PHONETIC MARKINGS[5]

1. ʔ Indicates a glottal stop: *oh, oh* /oʔo/, as in "Oh, oh! Look what I did."
    (See Lesson 4, final paragraph of Section IV.)
2. ʰ Means that the preceding consonant sound is aspirated: *time* /tʰaym/.
    (See Lesson 9, Section I.)
3. : Means that the preceding sound is lengthened: the /iy/ of *bead* /biy:d/
    is longer than the /iy/ of *beat* /biyt/. (See Lesson 9, Section II.)
4. ˌ Means that the consonant under which it is placed is pronounced as a
    syllabic: *didn't* / dɪdn̩t/, *little* /lɪtl̩/. (See Lesson 10, Section III.)

IV. How Words Are Transcribed

Note that the phonetic symbols should be printed rather than written cursively, so that they may more easily be read. In order that words spelled out in the traditional manner may not be confused with these transcriptions, the latter should always be printed between slant lines: *fish* is pronounced as /fɪš/.

In transcribing a word in phonetic symbols, the guiding principle to be kept in mind is that the transcription must represent *all* the distinctive sounds heard when the word is pronounced, and *only* those sounds. Do not be misled by the traditional spelling. Silent letters—those not heard in the pronunciation of the word—are not transcribed: for example, the e in *bone* /bown/, and the gh in *eight* /eyt/. Doubled consonants usually do not mean that the consonant is pronounced twice, so they are replaced in transcriptions by single consonants: *matter* /mætər/. Two words may be spelled differently, as are *sun* and *son*, but pronounced and transcribed alike: /sən/. On the other hand, if a word has two or more different pronunciations when used in different ways, as has *bow*, these must be represented by different transcriptions: /baw/, "to bend one's head"; and /bow/, "instrument used for shooting arrows."

As has been pointed out, the transcription used in this book provides a symbol for each distinctive English sound. A great many of these symbols— /b/, /d/, /f/, /k/, /l/, /m/, /n/, /p/, /r/, /t/, /v/, /w/, and /z/—are exactly like the normal printed letters of the alphabet; as symbols they *always* represent the same basic sound that they *usually* represent as letters. These are, of course, very easy to remember. Certain other symbols are also just like normal letters;

---

[5]These phonetic markings appear as pedagogical devices in certain sections of the manual but are not a part of the basic system of symbolization.

but the symbol always has the same basic sound, whereas the corresponding letter is commonly pronounced in more than one way:

/g/   always like the g in *good* /gʊd/,
       never like the g in *George* /džɔrdž/;

/s/   always like the s in *said* /sɛd/,
       never like the s in *rise* /rayz/;

/h/   always pronounced as in *home* /howm/,
       never silent as in *hour* /awr/;

For some other sounds, the traditional letters cannot serve as symbols, and it is necessary to provide new symbols. Since these may be strange to you, to learn them well will require some effort. Most vowel symbols fall in this class. The eleven vowel sounds of English cannot be represented accurately and simply by the five letters normally used in spelling vowels. Lesson 2 will help you to associate the vowel symbols with the sounds they represent. The new consonant symbol /ŋ/ is necessary because the spelling ng is confusing. In words spelled with ng the g is usually silent, as in *ring* /rɪŋ/; we could not represent *ring* in symbols as /rɪng/ since no phonetic symbol is silent and the /n/ symbol must always have the same sound. In the same way we need /š/, which usually represents the letters sh, because the sh sound cannot be made by simply pronouncing /s/ and then /h/. The symbol /ž/, as in *vision* /vížən/, is a rather rare English sound, spelled with letters that are ordinarily pronounced in quite a different way in other words. The /θ/ and /ð/ symbols are needed because the two distinctive sounds they represent are normally both written in the same way, with the letters th: *thigh* /θay/, *thy* /ðay/.

Not all the letters that represent consonants in English spelling are needed as phonetic symbols. Thus, the letter c is usually pronounced like an s or a k: *city* /sítɪ/, *cool* /kuwl/. Therefore c is not used as a symbol in transcriptions. For similar reasons, the letters j, q, and x are not used as symbols. To represent j we have /dž/, which is also used in transcribing the "soft" sound of g: *just* /džəst/, *age* /eydž/. The combination qu is transcribed as /kw/: *quick* /kwɪk/. Usually x is transcribed as /ks/ or /gz/: *fix* /fɪks/, *exact* /ɪgzǽkt/.

V. Exercises

A.   Go through the phonetic-alphabet table (Section III) several times, pronouncing the sound represented by each symbol.

B.   Pronounce these sounds and cite an English word in which each of them is heard.

1. m	7. hw	13. y	19. ey	25. θ	31. ər
2. æ	8. ʊ	14. a	20. tš	26. v	32. b
3. ɛ	9. dž	15. ž	21. s	27. f	33. w
4. iy	10. g	16. ow	22. z	28. ay	34. t
5. š	11. uw	17. ɔ	23. ɛə	29. aw	35. n
6. ɪ	12. ə	18. ŋ	24. ɔy	30. ð	36. l

C.   Pronounce these combinations of sounds.

1. pa	6. tšow	11. iys	16. wɔ	21. ðuw	26. awž
2. hwiy	7. raw	12. uk	17. ɛn	22. θɔy	27. ɪd
3. gæ	8. džæ	13. šɛ	18. aym	23. iər	28. æəl
4. av	9. ɪŋ	14. ðey	19. yə	24. ərk	29. θæ
5. low	10. əb	15. fɛ	20. eyz	25. hɔ	30. ʊt

D.   Pronounce these very common words and write them as they are usually spelled in English.

1. tərn	6. sɪŋ	11. tray	16. huw	21. mǽtər
2. sɪks	7. džəst	12. kɔz	17. hwɪtš	22. réyzɪz
3. læst	8. θriy	13. tap	18. smɔl	23. ríyzən
4. kud	9. tawn	14. ðɛm	19. ðow	24. plɛ́žər
5. bɔyz	10. gad	15. hɪər	20. yəŋ	25. mə́nɪ

E.   Your teacher will pronounce for you the English examples listed in the phonetic-alphabet table. Transcribe each example phonetically without looking at the table.

F.   Can you read these phrases?

1. ɪnðəmɔ́rnɪŋ	6. ɪnəmínɪt	11. təðəmúwvɪ
2. ənínglɪšklæs	7. wiykənǽsk	12. ɪnðɪæftərnúwn
3. wiərglǽd	8. ætðədrǽgstɔr	13. frəmðəθíyətər
4. təðətíytšər	9. təðəkánsərt	14. ɪnðəwíntər
5. hiyzəstyúwdənt	10. wiərhǽpɪ	15. nɛkstwíyk

LESSON 2

Classification of Vowels

I. The Five Fundamental Vowels

The fundamental vowel sounds, those that occur in many languages, are /iy/, /ey/, /a/, /ow/, and /uw/. It is worth noting that in symbolizing these sounds the five vowel letters of the ordinary roman alphabet are used—sometimes alone, as in /a/, or in combination with y and w, as in /iy/, /ey/, /ow/, and /uw/. We have used the symbols /y/ and /w/ to represent diphthongization, an upward movement of the tongue in the production of the vowel sound. The /y/ glide indicates that the tongue moves upward toward the front of the mouth; the /w/ glide indicates that the tongue moves upward toward the back of the mouth. This upward movement in the making of these vowel sounds is a characteristic that distinguishes English vowels from the so-called pure vowels of many other languages.

The relationship of these five vowel sounds to one another may be shown by means of a vowel chart (Figure 1).

The vowel pronounced farthest to the front of the mouth is /iy/. Pronounce that sound; then pronounce /ey/. In moving from /iy/ to /ey/, note that there are two important changes in the position of the organs of speech: the jaw is lowered, and the spot where the tongue approaches the roof of the mouth most closely is shifted away from the front teeth toward the throat. If you pronounce /ey/, then /a/, you will feel the same two types of change occur again. From /a/ to /ow/, the movement from front to back continues, but the jaw begins to

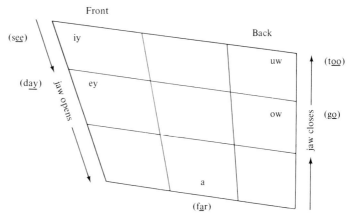

Figure 1. The five fundamental vowels[1]

rise, or close, again; and these two movements also mark the shift from /ow/ to /uw/.

Now pronounce several times the entire series /iy-ey-a-ow-uw/, and try to feel the regular progression in the organs of speech: from front to back as you move from left to right on the chart; and with jaw lower, then higher again, as you move from top to bottom, then back to the top, of the chart. Note also that the lips are widely spread for /iy/, that the amount of spreading decreases with /ey/ and /a/, and that the lips are rounded for /ow/ and /uw/.

Figure 2 may help you to understand how different positions of the tongue correspond to different parts of the vowel chart.[2]

II. The Eleven Vowels of American English

Students of English are usually well acquainted with the five fundamental vowel sounds and find them quite easy to pronounce and identify. Familiarity with them may help you to master the six other vowels in the language, those that are represented by symbols unlike those of the ordinary roman alphabet: /ɪ/, /ɛ/, /æ/, /ɔ/, /ʊ/, and /ə/.

The symbol /ɪ/ represents a sound intermediate between /iy/ and /ey/. In other words, /ɪ/ is pronounced farther back than /iy/, but farther forward than

---

[1]The vowel charts that appear here have been adapted, with permission of the publisher, from John S. Kenyon, *American Pronunciation,* 10th ed. (Ann Arbor: George Wahr Publishing Company, 1958).

[2]The face diagrams in this text, which are based on x-ray films, have been adapted, with his permission, from those done by Peter Ladefoged. See, for example, Peter Ladefoged, ''Some Possibilities in Speech Synthesis,'' *Language and Speech,* Vol. 7, Part 4 (October–December, 1964), 205–214.

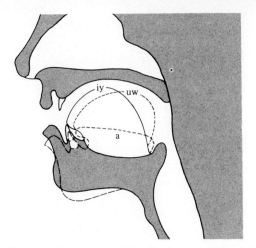

Figure 2. Tongue position for /iy/, /a/, and /uw/

/ey/; it is pronounced with the jaw and tongue lower than for /iy/, but higher than for /ey/. This relationship should be obvious to you if you will repeat three or four times the series /iy-ɪ-ey/.

Between /ey/ and /a/ there are two intermediate vowels: first /ɛ/, then, farther back and lower, /æ/.

Between /a/ and /ow/ is /ɔ/, and between /ow/ and /uw/ is /ʊ/.

This leaves only the position of /ə/ (and its variant /ər/; see note on p. 5) to be determined. The vowel /ə/ is the sound English-speaking persons produce when their speech organs are relaxed and in a neutral position. It is the sound they make when they do not quite know what they are going to say and are looking for the right words: "It's not that. Uh-h-h . . . How shall I say it? Uh-h-h . . ." For reasons that will be explained in the next lesson, /ə/ is also the most frequently heard of all the English vowels; you will need to recognize and make it about as often as all the other vowels except /ɪ/ combined. It is the typical vowel that, more than any other sound, distinguishes English from many other languages.

Since it is neither a front nor a back vowel, neither as close as /iy/ nor as open as /a/, it is placed in a central position on the vowel chart.

In the combination /ər/, as in *bird* /bərd/, /ə/ begins in the usual position, but then immediately moves toward the back of the mouth as it blends into the complex /r/ sound that follows. Lesson 10 describes the formation of /r/ in detail.

The chart, with each of the eleven vowels of American English in its place, would appear as in Figure 3.

When a student of English mispronounces the vowel in a word, what he

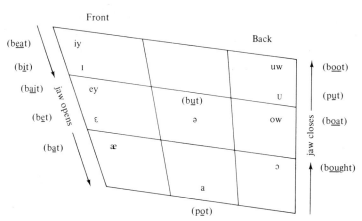

Figure 3. The vowels of American English

or she usually does is to substitute for the correct sound another sound very close to it. In other words, if you mispronounce the /ɪ/ of *bit,* you will probably say *beat* /biyt/. Usually /ɔ/ is confused with either /a/ or /ow/, the sounds that appear on either side of it in the diagram; /æ/ is confused with /ɛ/ and /a/; /ɛ/ with /ey/ and /æ/, and so on and so on. Because of the position of the speech organs when it is made, /ə/ may easily be mistaken for any of the other ten vowel sounds.

Notice that a word containing the sound appears in parentheses beside each symbol on the diagram. The only difference between the pronunciation of *boot* and *but* is the difference between /uw/ and /ə/. That is to say, the very meaning of the word depends on the quality of the vowel. If you wish to understand and be understood in English, you must be able to distinguish and make the distinction among the vowel sounds with great accuracy.

There are three vowel sounds in English that are not included in the vowel chart in Figure 3, since their high degree of diphthongization puts them in a separate class from other vowel sounds. These are the diphthongs /ay/, /aw/, and /ɔy/, that appear in the words *buy, bough,* and *boy.* Most students seem to have little or no difficulty in learning to pronounce them. Pronounce the diphthong /ay/, noticing how much the jaw moves. Pronounce /aw/ and /ɔy/. Notice how the jaw moves from an open position to a more closed position during the pronunciation of these diphthongs.

III. Exercises

A. Pronounce the ten vowel sounds around the edge of the vowel chart (Figure 3) several times in order, beginning first with /iy/, then with /uw/, and note carefully how the speech organs move in regular progression as you pass from one symbol to another.

B.   Learn to draw the vowel chart and to locate the eleven symbols on it.

C.   1. Phoneticians speak of "front vowels," "central vowels," and "back vowels." Judging by the arrangement of the vowels on the chart, which vowels would fall into each of the three groups?

2. We sometimes call /ɔ/ "open o" and /ow/ "close o." Can you explain why? Which is more open, /ow/ or /a/? /ɛ/ or /æ/?

3. Suppose that a fellow student pronounces *it* as /iyt/ instead of /ɪt/. In order to help him produce the correct sound, what would you tell him to do with his jaw, his tongue, and his lips? What would you tell him to do in order to change /guwd/ to /gʊd/? /gɔt/ to / gat/?

D.   Make a vowel chart and number the symbols on it around the edge of the chart from 1 to 10: /iy/ 1, /ɪ/ 2, /ey/ 3, and so on. Number the symbol /ə/ 11. Your teacher will pronounce several different vowel sounds; see if you can identify each by giving the number of the symbol that represents it. If you fail to identify a vowel correctly, note on the diagram the location of the sound you thought you heard with relation to the sound the teacher actually pronounced.

E.   Pronounce these very common words, and write them as they are usually spelled in English.

1. læf	9. tšeyndž	17. hwɛər	25. kəm
2. haws	10. ðɪs	18. θɪŋ	26. plíyz
3. yɪər	11. šowz	19. džɔy	27. kə́lər
4. sɔ	12. wəns	20. lardž	28. ə́rlɪ
5. rak	13. lɛŋθ	21. pʊt	29. wímɪn
6. seym	14. lʊk	22. eyt	30. byúwtɪfʊl
7. wiyk	15. lək	23. θrow	31. kə́mpənɪ
8. layk	16. muwv	24. klak	32. ə́ðər

F.   Can you read these phrases?

1. hiyəzfínɪšt	5. ðeykə́məngów	9. šiyəzhə́rdɪt
2. ayəvdə́nɪt	6. hiykənǽnsər	10. wiyšʊdtráyɪt
3. wiykənswím	7. hárdtəgɛ́t	11. ðeyíytənrə́n
4. íyzɪtəsíy	8. ənə́ftʊɪyt	12. íygərtəplíyz

G. 1. Listen while your teacher pronounces the following groups of words. They are all among the five hundred most frequently used in the English language, so you are probably already familiar with their pronunciation. In each group, four words have the same vowel sound, and one has a different vowel sound. Draw a line under the word that does not belong with the group, and write the symbol that represents the sound the other four have in common.

    a.   piece, sleep, each, bread, she

    b.   sit, if, first, him, quick

    c.   plain, death, they, great, name

    d.   learn, friend, left, head, next

    e.   add, back, have, warm, laugh

    f.   rock, got, stop, cod, law

    g.   talk, thought, draw, off, both

    h.   close, though, lost, road, most

    i.   book, full, put, food, should

    j.   wood, blue, two, move, do

    k.   does, foot, up, son, run

    l.   serve, bird, work, north, burn

2. Pronounce the groups of words above, making a clear distinction between the one word that has a different vowel sound and the other four words.

H. Divide a sheet of paper into 15 columns, and write one of the following symbols at the top of each column: iy, ɪ, ey, ɛ, æ, a, ɔ, ow, ʊ, uw, ə, ər, ay, aw, ɔy. Classify the following words under the symbol that represents their vowel sound. If necessary, your instructor will pronounce the words for you. Or ask a friend who is a native speaker of English to pronounce them for you. Exercises H and I could well be carried out with the students divided into small groups for discussion and drill among themselves.

1. with	26. wish	51. friend	76. front
2. ten	27. say	52. warm	77. crowd
3. strong	28. so	53. done	78. laugh
4. watch	29. those	54. great	79. God
5. south	30. high	55. bone	80. boy
6. late	31. rain	56. win	81. who
7. bring	32. month	57. book	82. they
8. good	33. mean	58. law	83. miss
9. gold	34. school	59. act	84. move
10. up	35. best	60. five	85. full
11. box	36. would	61. heart	86. wild
12. seem	37. voice	62. seize	87. kept
13. wide	38. since	63. mouth	88. this
14. off	39. glad	64. raise	89. her
15. arm	40. said	65. cost	90. car
16. fall	41. out	66. fence	91. corn
17. stand	42. love	67. some	92. stop
18. bridge	43. put	68. foot	93. please
19. through	44. point	69. lip	94. talk
20. down	45. were	70. soon	95. cap
21. light	46. come	71. have	96. church
22. street	47. not	72. touch	97. most
23. dead	48. true	73. could	98. girl
24. work	49. pass	74. she	99. bread
25. look	50. war	75. wing	100. give

I. Pronounce each of the columns of words you made in doing Exercise H, in order to be sure that all the words you classified together have the same vowel sound.

J. The following represent short conversations between two people. Practice reading them with another student, making them sound as natural as you can.

1. a. hawárүə

    b. fáyn, θǽŋks

2. a. ərүərédɪ

    b. yɛ́s, lɛtsgów

3. a. hwɛ́ərərүəgówɪŋ

    b. tυəmúwvɪ, dυүəwánəkə́m

    a. yɛ́s, aydláyktυ

4.   a.   həlów

     b.   həlów, ɪzmɛ́rɪðɛ́ər

     a.   nów, šiyznáthówmnáw

         meyaytéykəmɛ́sɪdž

     b.   nów, θǽŋks

         aylkɔlbǽkléytər

LESSON 3

Unstressed Vowels

I. The Importance of Stress

We put stress on a syllable when we pronounce it with such emphasis as to give it more importance than the surrounding syllables and make it stand out among them: for example, the *com-* of *comfortable* /kə́mfərtəbəl/, or the *-ter-* of *determine* /dɪtə́rmɪn/. Stress is sometimes called accent.

A long word frequently has two stressed syllables, one of which is usually more prominent than the other. An example is *economical*. We say that the most important syllable bears the primary accent, and the next most important bears the secondary accent.[1] In the case of *economical,* the primary accent falls on *-nom-* and the secondary on *e-*. These two syllables would be marked /′/ and /ˋ/ respectively: /ìykənámɪkəl/.

Strong stresses are one of the distinguishing features of the English lan-

---

[1] The authors of this manual accept the analysis, supported by Smith-Trager and other phoneticians, that there are actually four distinctive degrees of stress in English. For the sake of simplicity and pedagogical practicality, however, we use only the two symbols, /′/ and /ˋ/, rather than Smith-Trager's four symbols: /′/ for primary stress, /ˆ/ for secondary, /ˋ/ for tertiary, and /ˇ/ for weak. Our /′/, when it coincides with the peak of an intonation pattern (usually the last high note of the pattern), corresponds to Smith-Trager's /′/. Elsewhere our /′/ corresponds to their /ˆ/. Our /ˋ/ is the equivalent of their /ˋ/. We leave weak stresses unmarked. (See Lesson 5, Sections I and II.)

guage; the important syllables in English are more prominent, the unimportant syllables less prominent than in most other languages. Stress, then, is the key to the pronunciation of an English word, and the location of the accent should always be learned with the word. If you stress the wrong syllable, it may be quite impossible for anyone listening to understand what you are trying to say.

Stress does even more than give character and rhythm to a word; it also determines to some extent the value of all its vowels—whether an a is to be pronounced as /ey/ or /ə/, for example.

II. The Pronunciation of Unstressed Vowels

The vowel in a *stressed* syllable may be pronounced as any of the vowels or diphthongs we have listed in the Phonetic Alphabet (see Lesson 1, pp. 5–6): for example, /iy/, /ɪ/, /æ/, /ə/, /iə/, and so on. The vowel of an *unstressed* syllable almost always has one of three sounds: either /ə/, /ɪ/, or, less frequently, /ʊ/. No feature of English is simpler or more fundamental than this:

UNSTRESSED VOWELS ARE USUALLY PRONOUNCED /ə/, /ɪ/, OR (FOR SOME SPEAKERS) /ʊ/.[2]

This principle may be illustrated graphically on the vowel chart (Figure 4).

As was noted in Lesson 2, /ə/ is the most neutral vowel, the one English speakers produce automatically when their speech organs are relaxed, and,

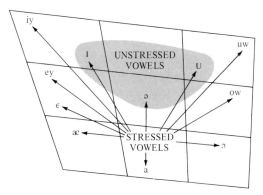

Figure 4. Pronunciation of unstressed vowels

---

[2]/ʊ/ is more or less equivalent to the Smith-Trager "barred i" sound, symbolized as /ɨ/.

therefore, the one that is easiest for them to make. Native speakers of English are apparently willing, in a stressed syllable, to make the effort necessary to produce any of the vowel or diphthong sounds, but they do not feel that an unstressed syllable is important enough to justify rounding the lips, or raising or lowering the jaw. So, however they may spell the vowel sound in an unaccented syllable when they write it, when they pronounce it they give it the "lazy" sound of /ə/, or of nearby /ɪ/ or /ʊ/. As there are more unstressed than stressed syllables in English, /ə/, /ɪ/, and /ʊ/ are among the most frequently heard vowel sounds.

Notice the way in which the unaccented vowels in the following polysyllables—words of more than one syllable—are pronounced:

apparently	/əpǽrəntlɪ/
apportionment	/əpɔ́ršənmənt/
congregation	/kàŋgrɪgéyšən/
Episcopalian	/ɪpìskəpéylyən/ or /-lyʊn/
insuperable	/ɪnsúwpərəbəl/

If a syllable bears a primary or secondary accent, its vowel may be pronounced in many different ways; but only three different vowels are found in the unstressed syllables above.

Persons who learn English as a second language often make the mistake of pronouncing unstressed vowels the way they are spelled. In your anxiety to make yourself understood, you will probably be tempted to say /æpǽrɛntlɪ/ and /iypìskowpéylyan/. Actually there will be less danger of your being misunderstood, and your English will sound much more natural if you will obscure the unstressed vowels, pronounce them /ə/, /ɪ/, or /ʊ/, and make no attempt to identify them as <u>a</u>, <u>e</u>, or <u>o</u>.

Unless you consult a pronouncing dictionary or a competent English-speaking person, there is no sure way of knowing whether the unaccented vowels of an unfamiliar word should be /ə/, /ɪ/, or /ʊ/. Frequently it makes no difference; /əpìskəpéylyən/ is just as natural as /ɪpìskəpéylyʊn/.

III. Where the Stress Falls

Unfortunately, there are no infallible rules for determining which syllable of a word should be stressed.[3] Many times you will need to turn to a dictionary

---

[3]In recent years the "generative phonologists" influenced by Noam Chomsky and Morris Halle have succeeded in demonstrating that English stress is much more predictable than it has

unless you hear the word spoken by someone familiar with it. Certain observations, however, should be of help.

1. The great majority (at least three out of four) of two-syllable words are accented on the *first* syllable: *never* /névər/, *breakfast* /brékfəst/, *Monday* /mə́ndɪ/. The largest group of exceptions to this generalization is made up of words that begin with a prefix. Most of these are accented on the *second* syllable: *display* /dɪspléy/, *exceed* /ɪksíyd/, *device* /dɪváys/, *belief* /bəlíyf/, *intent* /ɪntɛ́nt/.

2. Compound expressions:

   a. Compound *nouns* ordinarily have a primary accent on the first component and a secondary accent on the second: *bird's-nest* /bə́rdznɛ̀st/, *drugstore* /drə́gstɔ̀r/, *thoroughfare* /θə́rəfɛ̀ər/, *weatherman* /wɛ́ðərmæ̀n/.

   b. In compound *verbs* the reverse is true: there is usually a secondary accent on the first component and a primary on the second: *understand* /ə̀ndərstǽnd/, *overlook* /òwvərlúk/, *outrun* /àwtrə́n/.

   c. In the intensive-reflexive pronouns the stronger accent also falls on the *last* syllable: *myself* /màysɛ́lf/, *yourself* /yùrsɛ́lf/.

   d. Numbers ending in *-teen* may receive primary stress on either syllable, but it is best for a student learning English as a second language to put it on the *last* syllable, so as to distinguish clearly between *thirty* /θə́rtɪ/ and *thirteen* /θə̀rtíyn/, *forty* /fɔ́rtɪ/ and *fourteen* /fɔ̀rtíyn/.

3. A large group of words, which may be used either as nouns or verbs without change in their spelling, have a difference in stress to indicate the difference in usage. In such cases, the noun has primary accent on the first syllable, the verb on the last (compare 2-a and 2-b above). The nouns in this group of words sometimes have secondary accent on the last syllable: *increase* /ínkrìys/, *overflow* /ówvərflòw/. Sometimes—as in the case of *concert* and *object*—the meaning of the noun has little if any relationship to the meaning of the corresponding verb.

	Noun		Verb
/kánsərt/	concert	/kənsə́rt
/kándəkt/	conduct	/kəndə́kt/

traditionally been thought to be. Few if any of the rules they have formulated, however, are without numerous exceptions. Most of them seem too abstract and complex to be of much practical use, and many of these rules apply only to words of Greek and Latin origin.

/kánflɪkt/	conflict	/kənflíkt/
/kántɛ̀st/	contest	/kəntɛ́st/
/kántræ̀kt/	contract	/kəntrǽkt/
/kántræ̀st/	contrast	/kəntrǽst/
/kánvərt/	convert	/kənvə́rt/
/dɛ́zərt/	desert	/dɪzə́rt/
/ínklàyn/	incline	/ɪnkláyn/
/ínkrìys/	increase	/ɪnkríys/
/ínsərt/	insert	/ɪnsə́rt/
/ínsəlt/	insult	/ɪnsə́lt/
/ábdžɪkt/	object	/əbdžɛ́kt/
/ówvərflòw/	overflow	/òwvərflów/
/pə́rmɪt/	permit	/pərmít/
/prɛ́zənt/	present	/prɪzɛ́nt/
/prágrɪs/	progress	/prəgrɛ́s/
/prádžɛ̀kt/	project	/prədžɛ́kt/
/prówtɛ̀st/	protest	/prətɛ́st/
/rɛ́bəl/	rebel	/rəbɛ́əl/
/rɛ́kərd/	record	/rɪkɔ́rd/
/sə́rvèy/	survey	/sərvéy/
/sə́spɛ̀kt/	suspect	/səspɛ́kt/

4. Helpful generalizations can also be made about the large number of poly-
    syllabic English words that end in -ate. Some of these—such as *duplicate*
    and *associate*—may be used as adjectives, nouns, or verbs; others—such
    as *consulate* (noun), *educate* (verb), and *appropriate* (adjective or verb)—
    are used in only one or two of these three ways. In the case of all words
    of this group, however, use as an adjective or a noun is indicated by leav-
    ing the vowel of the ending unstressed and pronouncing it as /ɪ/ or/ə/. *I
    must go to the consulate* /kánsəlɪt/. Use as a verb is indicated by giving
    the ending secondary stress and pronouncing its vowel as /ey/. *He'll du-
    plicate* /dyúwpləkèyt/ *the letter.* Further examples are:

Adjective or Noun		Verb
/ǽdvəkɪt/	advocate	/ǽdvəkèyt/
/ǽgrəgɪt/	aggregate	/ǽgrəgèyt/
/ɔ́ltərnɪt/	alternate	/ɔ́ltərnèyt/
/ǽnɪmɪt/	animate	/ǽnɪmèyt/
/əprówprɪɪt/	appropriate	/əprówprɪèyt/

/əprǽksɪmɪt/	approximate	/əprǽksɪmèyt/
/dɪlíbərɪt/	deliberate	/dɪlíbərèyt/
/désəlɪt/	desolate	/désəlèyt/
/ɪlǽbərɪt/	elaborate	/ɪlǽbərèyt/
/éstɪmɪt/	estimate	/éstɪmèyt/
/grǽdžuɪt/	graduate	/grǽdžuèyt/
/íntɪmɪt/	intimate	/íntɪmèyt/
/mádərɪt/	moderate	/mádərèyt/
/prɪsípɪtɪt/	precipitate	/prɪsípɪtèyt/
/sépərɪt/ or	separate	/sépərèyt/
/séprɪt/		

5. In general, when a suffix is added to a word, the new form is stressed on the same syllable as was the basic word: *abandon* /əbǽndən/, *abandonment* /əbǽndənmənt/; *happy* /hǽpɪ/, *happiness* /hǽpɪnɪs/; *reason* /ríyzən/, *reasonable* /ríyzənəbəl/. Words ending *-tion, -sion, -ic, -ical, -ity,* and *-graphy,* however, almost always have primary stress *on the syllable preceding the ending.* The addition of one of these "troublesome endings" may, therefore, result in a shift of accent: *contribute* /kəntríbyut/, *contribution* /kàntrɪbyúwšən/; *biology* /bayálədžɪ/, *biological* /bàyəladžɪkəl/; *public* /pə́blɪk/, *publicity* /pəblísɪtɪ/; *photograph* /fówtəgræf/, *photography* /fətágrəfɪ/.

IV. Exercises

A. Your instructor will pronounce for you the following polysyllables. First decide which syllable is stressed in each case; then write down the symbols that represent all the vowel sounds in each word, and mark each stressed vowel. Example: the instructor will pronounce *about* as /əbáwt/; the student writes: 1.   ə—áw.

1.	about	8.	even	15.	measure	22.	something
2.	after	9.	exit	16.	mistake	23.	sometime
3.	another	10.	family	17.	mother	24.	story
4.	between	11.	general	18.	often	25.	thousand
5.	body	12.	hundred	19.	receive	26.	together
6.	color	13.	letter	20.	remember	27.	visit
7.	correct	14.	many	21.	service	28.	without

B. Arrange in separate lists the vowels that you heard in stressed syllables and those that you found in unstressed syllables. Are your results in agreement with Section

II of this lesson? Can you explain the apparent violation of the rule found in *sometime?*

C.   In order to increase your ability to recognize and place stresses, read this drill after your instructor, and then alone. Watch carefully the pronunciattion of unstressed vowels. Note that words with a similar pattern of stresses are grouped together; each group should be repeated rhythmically.

	a. í–2		b. 1–2́		c. í–2–3		d. 1–2́–3
1.	bury	1.	around	1.	vigilance	1.	distinguish
2.	judgment	2.	occur	2.	readiness	2.	abandon
3.	dollar	3.	submit	3.	mineral	3.	eraser
4.	minus	4.	disease	4.	emphasis	4.	delicious
5.	nation	5.	deceive	5.	similar	5.	paternal

	e. ì–2–3́		f. í–2–3–4		g. 1–2́–3–4
1.	overlook	1.	memorable	1.	mechanical
2.	evermore	2.	personally	2.	immediate
3.	premature	3.	accuracy	3.	absurdity
4.	magazine	4.	amicably	4.	catastrophe
5.	guarantee	5.	delicacy	5.	additional

	h. ì–2–3́–4		i. ì–2–3́–4–5		j. 1–2̀–3–4́–5
1.	corporation	1.	mathematical	1.	communication
2.	education	2.	zoological	2.	eradication
3.	sentimental	3.	nationality	3.	pronunciation
4.	scientific	4.	anniversary	4.	deliberation
5.	economic	5.	indeterminate	5.	appropriation

D.   Pronounce these very common words, and write them as they are usually spelled in English.

1.	šɪp	7.	pleys	13.	vɔys	19.	sépərɪt
2.	θæŋk	8.	sɛz	14.	naw	20.	læŋgwidž
3.	own	9.	brɔt	15.	fiəld	21.	néyšən
4.	drap	10.	tšɒrtš	16.	lərnd	22.	píktšər
5.	suwn	11.	hway	17.	krɔ́st	23.	ənə́f
6.	iyst	12.	gʊd	18.	wántɪd	24.	sɛ́vrəl

E.   Can you read these phrases?

1.	təðəlɛ́ft	3.	gívɪtəmíy	5.	mǽnənwʊ́mən
2.	anətrɪ́p	4.	ɪfwiyədnówn	6.	fərðəpówstmən

7. ɪnəkár
8. ætðəkɔ́rnər
9. ráytəlέtər
10. ǽskəkwέstšən
11. ɪnðəkə́ntrɪ
12. blǽkənblúw

F. Pronounce these families of words, paying particular attention to the location of the stresses and to the vowels in unstressed syllables. (See Section III–5 of this lesson.)

1. abominate /əbámɪnèyt/, abominable, abominableness, abomination
2. contribute /kəntríbyʊt/, contributor, contribution, contributive
3. abolish /əbálɪš/, abolition, abolishable, abolitionist
4. electric /əlέktrɪk/, electrical, electricity, electrify
5. apology /əpálədžɪ/, apologetic, apologize
6. attain /ətéyn/, attainable, attainability, attainment
7. material /mətírɪəl/, materialist, materialistic, materialize
8. philosophy /fɪlásəfɪ/, philosopher, philosophical, philosophize
9. method /mέθəd/, methodical, Methodist
10. negotiate /nɪgówšɪèyt/, negotiable, negotiation, negotiator, negotiability
11. telegraph /tέləgræ̀f/, telegraphic, telegraphy
12. liquid /líkwɪd/, liquidity, liquidate, liquidation

G. Mark the primary accent on all words of more than one syllable (see Section III-1, 2, and 3 of this lesson); then pronounce the following sentences several times.

1. Would you object if I gave her the present myself?
2. I don't understand why the class should protest or rebel.
3. No one suspected that the airplane had set a new record.
4. They will need a permit to make a bedroom of this storehouse.
5. He has progressed sixty miles in sixteen hours.
6. The conflict is over, and the crewmen have a new contract.
7. What progress have they made with their survey?
8. There's no contenting rebels.
9. The newspaper is conducting a contest to increase its circulation.
10. How was his conduct at the concert?
11. They protested an increase of only fifteen dollars an hour.
12. So far no suspects have been found.
13. You will convert no one by insults.
14. Will you yourself conduct the project?
15. The crowd overflowed into the hallway.
16. I'm inclined to insert a protest here.
17. The desert is full of contrasts.
18. The overflow rushed down the incline.

H. Pronounce the word in parentheses so as to give it the meaning indicated by the context of each sentence. (See Section III-4 of this lesson.)

1. (alternate)   I was elected an _____ representative to the college assembly. I _____ with another professor in my department when he cannot attend.

2. (estimate)   The garage gave me an _____ of the cost of repairing my car. They _____ it will cost at least $300.

3. (graduate)   They _____ next month. Most of them will continue their education as _____ students.

4. (separate)   We need to _____ the good apples from the bad ones. Let's put them in _____ baskets.

5. (precipitate)   Let's have no _____ actions. We don't want to _____ a crisis.

6. (intimate)   I am not really an _____ friend of hers. I wish she wouldn't _____ that I am.

7. (deliberate)   This pressure is _____. They don't want to give us time to _____.

8. (appropriate)   The Congress should not _____ so much money. It's not _____ at this time.

9. (delegate)   She makes a good _____. She knows how to _____ authority.

10. (elaborate)   I won't _____ the plan further. It's already _____ enough.

11. We are *(fortunate)* to have a Mexican *(consulate)* here.

12. Schools should *(educate)* students rather than *(indoctrinate)* them.

I. Read aloud several pages of English that are of particular interest to you, concentrating your attention on the pronunciation of the unstressed vowels of words of more than one syllable.

LESSON 4

Sentence-Stress and Rhythm

I. Stress in Groups of Words

In Lesson 3 we were concerned with word-stress, the stressing of syllables in words of more than one syllable. Our knowledge of stress must, however, go beyond words if we are to have the complete picture. We do not really talk in words, most of the time, but in sentences, or at least in phrases.

In the sentence *I am glad to see you,* there are normally two stresses: on *glad* and *see.* Because these are words of only one syllable, they have no word-stress, but the emphasis that is put on them is in many ways the same as that put on the first syllable of *history* /hístərɪ/. It is sometimes convenient, however, to distinguish between word-stress (hístory) and sentence-stress (I am gláad to sée you).

When sentence-stress falls on a word of more than one syllable, it usually falls on the syllable that normally receives word-stress: "I'll méet you to-mórrow."

In Lesson 3 it was pointed out that there is a great deal more difference between stressed and unstressed syllables in English than in most other languages; this is as true of sentence-stress as of word-stress. To an English-speaking person the rhythm of many other tongues (for example, Japanese, Spanish, Italian, Pilipino) seems to be mechanically regular—a series of little bursts of sound all of about the same size and force, like machine-gun fire.

English pronounced with such a rhythm would probably not be understood. If asked to draw a picture representing the rhythm of the syllables in Spanish, the speaker of English might produce a line of soldiers of very much the same size and following one another at rather regular intervals, as in Figure 5.

Figure 5. The seeming rhythm of some other languages

He might picture his own language as a series of family groups, each composed of an adult accompanied by several small children of varying sizes. A few of the adults might be childless, and some would be larger than others. (See Figure 6.)

Figure 6. The rhythm of English

In a language like French or Spanish, a line of poetry is usually determined by counting the total number of syllables, stressed and unstressed alike. Lines containing the same number of syllables are felt to be of the same length. In a line of English poetry the number of sentence-stresses is more important than the number of syllables. Here are two lines from Tennyson that are considered to be perfectly matched in rhythm and of the same length when read.

"Bréak, bréak, bréak,
On thy cóld gray stónes, O Séa!"

The unstressed syllables are so unimportant, rhythmically speaking, that it is not even necessary to count them. When a person recites those lines, it may take as long to say the first as the second, even though the first contains only three syllables and the second is made up of seven.

This leads to a significant observation regarding English pronunciation:

ACCENTS TEND TO RECUR AT REGULAR INTERVALS.

The more unstressed syllables there are between accents, the more rapidly (and indistinctly) those syllables are pronounced. This is true to a large extent even of prose.

Have your teacher or a native speaker of English pronounce these two sentences for you at normal speed:

The bóy is ínterested in enlárging his vocábulary.
Gréat prógress is máde dáily.

Note how he or she unconsciously crushes together the unstressed syllables of the first sentence in order to get them said in time, and how the stressed syllables of the second sentence are somewhat lengthened so as to compensate for the lack of intervening unstressed syllables. If we were to illustrate these two sentences as suggested above, they might look something like this (Figure 7):

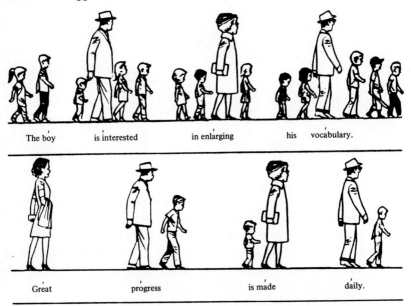

Figure 7. Examples of English sentence rhythm

The problem of acquiring a good English speech rhythm may be divided into five parts:

1. Giving proper emphasis to stressed syllables, and making them recur rather regularly within a thought group.
2. Weakening unstressed words and syllables, and obscuring the vowels in most of them.
3. Organizing words properly into thought groups by means of pauses.
4. Blending the final sound of each word and syllable with the initial sound of the one following within the same thought group.
5. Fitting the entire sentence into a normal intonation pattern.

Intonation patterns will be studied in Lessons 5, 6, and 7, and the rest of this lesson will treat the other four phases of the problem.

II. Which Words Should Be Stressed?

Grammarians sometimes divide all words into two classes: (1) *content words*, which have meaning in themselves, like *mother, forget,* and *tomorrow;* and (2) *function words,* which have little or no meaning other than the grammatical idea they express, such as *the, of,* and *will.* In general *content words* are *stressed,* but *function words* are left *unstressed,* unless the speaker wishes to call special attention to them.

Content words, usually *stressed,* include

1. Nouns.
2. Verbs (with the few exceptions listed under function words).
3. Adjectives.
4. Adverbs (including *not* and verbs contracted with *not,* such as *don't*).
5. Demonstratives: *this, that, these, those.*
6. Interrogatives: *who, when, why,* and so on.

Function words, usually *unstressed,* include

1. Articles: *a, an, the.*
2. Simple prepositions: *to, of, in,* and so on.[1]
3. Personal pronouns: *I, me, he, him, it,* and so on.

---

[1]Compound prepositions, those that include a noun, are stressed on the noun: *in spíte of, instéad of,* and so on.

4. Possessive adjectives: *my, his, your,* and so on.
5. Relative pronouns: *who, that, which,* and so on.
6. Common conjunctions: *and, but, that, as, if,* and so on.
7. *One* used as a noun-substitute, as in *the réd dréss and the blúe one.*
8. The verbs *be, have, do, will, would, shall, should, can, could, may, might,* and *must.* These are easy to remember, as they are the verbs that may be used as auxiliaries: *He is resígning. Do you sée it? We must wáit.* Even when they are the principal verb in the sentence, they are usually unstressed: *Hárry is my bést friénd. Bárbara has a lóvely smíle.* On the other hand, they are stressed when they come at the end of a sentence *(I thóught he was smárter than he ís),* and when they are used in tag questions such as *dídn't we* and *are théy (Áll móvies áren't máde in Hóllywood, áre they?).*

We have already seen (in Lesson 3, Section III, 2-a) that compound nouns ordinarily have a primary accent on their first component. This is true whether such nouns are written with a hyphen (like *bírd's-nest*) or without a hyphen (like *drúgstore*). These nominal compounds may, of course, also be written as two separate words, in which case the first of the two words ordinarily receives sentence-stress while the second does not: *an apártment house, búsiness affairs, a sócial worker.* In fact, native speakers of English use this sentence-stress pattern as a signal to listeners that they are to interpret the two words as a nominal compound, with a special meaning, rather than as a sequence of independent words. Thus *She's a sócial worker* means that she makes her living by helping people solve social problems, whereas *She's a sócial wórker* presumably means that she is a worker who enjoys social relationships with other people. In the first of the above two examples, then, though *worker* is certainly a noun, therefore a *content* word, it is not given sentence-stress, so that it will be recognized as part of a nominal compound.[2]

Though most verbs are also *content* words, in two-word verbs made up of a verb and adverb it is normally the *adverb* that receives sentence-stress, not

---

[2]Not all two-word sequences that look as though they might be nominal compounds are stressed on the first component. An important group of apparent exceptions is made up of sequences in which the first component announces the material of which the second component is máde. In these sequences both components receive sentence-stress: *It's a góld wátch* (the watch is made of gold), *It's an ápple píe* (the pie is made of apple). Compare the last example with *It's an ápple tree* (the tree is *not* made of apple). There are in English minimal pairs of two-word sequences that differ in sentence-stress and therefore differ in meaning: *It's a métal cutter* (it cuts metal), *It's a métal cútter* (the cutter is made of metal). The best explanation of the difference seems to be that the *métal cutter* is felt as a nominal compound, with a special meaning of its own, while the *métal cútter* is felt as a sequence of two independent words, modifier plus noun.

the verb: *to split úp, to put ón.* (Compare Lesson 3, Section III, 2-b.) Do not confuse these genuine two-word verbs with other verbs, such as *look* and *listen,* that may be followed by a prepositional phrase: *to lóok at him, to lísten to him.* A good way to tell the difference between, for example, *to put on* and *to look at* is to put both expressions into a question beginning with *what: Whát are you putting ón? Whát are you lóoking at?* Note that *at* may be placed before *what* and thus separated from the verb: *At what are you looking?* But the two-word verb cannot be divided in this way: *On what are you putting?* does not make sense.

In the great majority of cases, then, it is a simple matter to determine where the stresses are placed in a sentence. One has only to apply the principles outlined above.

1. I dón't imágine you can succéed in a búsiness venture.
2. In an hóur it will be réady to turn óver to you.
3. Thís réd róse is to be plánted hére.
4. He éats thrée fúll méals éach dáy.
5. I shall delíver it to you.
6. She sáys that she líkes the apártment, dóesn't she?

Which are the content words? Which are the function words? Why is there no sentence-stress on *venture* in Sentence 1? Why no stress on *turn* in Sentence 2? Why no stress on *be* in the same sentence? Why is *doesn't* stressed in Sentence 6? Why stress *don't* in Sentence 1? Why stress *this* in Sentence 3?

If a native speaker of English violates these principles and distributes the sentence-stresses in some other way, he or she usually does so for one of two reasons:

1. He may wish to call special attention to a word by placing *contrastive stress* on it. If the speaker of Sentence 1 above wishes to suggest that *you* cannot succeed in a business venture though perhaps someone else could, he will stress the function word *you* as well as the content words *imagine, succeed,* and *business.* Such contrastive stress on a word adds a meaning that the sentence would not otherwise have.
2. He may wish, unconsciously, to give the sentence *a more regular rhythm.* In English speech one stressed syllable is usually separated from the next by one, two, or three unstressed syllables. But Sentence 4, if stressed according to the "rules," contains six successive stressed syllables without any intervening unstressed ones. A native speaker of English might feel this to be an unnatural rhythm and instinctively suppress some of the stresses: *He eats thrée full méals each dáy.* Sentence 5, if stressed

according to the "rules," ends in a series of four unstressed syllables. The native speaker might therefore find it natural to stress the function word *to* as well as the content word *deliver: I shall delíver it tó you.*

Students of English should not, however, allow these unusual stresses they may occasionally notice to confuse them and lead them to distribute stresses randomly. The basic principles—content words stressed, function words unstressed—are easy to follow. Particular care should be taken to resist the tendency, widespread among those learning English as a foreign language, to stress auxiliary verbs *(can, may,* and so on), personal pronouns *(I, you, he,* and so on), and possessive adjectives *(my, your, his,* and so on). All of these are *function words.* The main verb is ordinarily more significant than the auxiliary, and *I* and *my* are not as important as we sometimes think.

III. The Pronunciation of Unstressed Words of One Syllable

The group of unstressed words of one syllable includes most of the commonest words in the language: the ten words most frequently used all belong in that class: *the, of, and, to, a, in, that, it, is,* and *I.* These ten make up 25 percent of all that is written and spoken in English. Or, putting it another way, one out of every four words we use will be *the,* or *of,* or *and,* and so on. Unfortunately, several of the ten are precisely the words that learners of English most often mispronounce. *It is probable that in no other way can you improve your English so much and so easily as by learning to pronounce them naturally.*

The rhythm pattern made up of the alternation of stressed and unstressed syllables is powerfully reinforced in English by the phenomenon known as the weakening or obscuring of vowels. By pronouncing the vowel of an unstressed syllable as /ə/, /ɪ/, or /ʊ/, a speaker weakens that syllable and increases the contrast between it and stressed syllables. We have already seen, in Lesson 3, how the weakening of vowels works in polysyllables. As might be expected, it occurs also in quite a few words of only one syllable when these latter words do not receive sentence-stress. This leads us to another observation regarding English pronunciation:

THERE IS A STRONG TENDENCY TO WEAKEN THE VOWELS OF THE MOST COMMON UNSTRESSED WORDS OF ONE SYLLABLE JUST AS THE UNACCENTED VOWELS OF POLYSYLLABLES ARE WEAKENED; THAT IS, TO PRONOUNCE THEM /ə/, /ɪ/, OR /ʊ/.

Thus, contrary to what is taught in many beginning English classes, the indefinite article *a* is ordinarily /ə/, not /ey/: *in a minute* /ɪn ə mínɪt/. Only in a few rare cases is *a* stressed, and given the sound /ey/: *the article "a"* /ðɪ ártɪkəl éy/.

There are, then, two separate pronunciations of this and other similar words: the weak form and the stressed form. A partial list of such words is given below.

Words Most Frequently Weakened

Word	Stressed Form	Weak Form	Example
*a	/ey/	/ə/	in *a* car /ɪn ə kar/
*an	/æn/	/ən/	get *an* egg /gɛt ən ɛg/
*and	/ænd/	/ən/	high *and* low /hay ən low/
are	/ar/	/ər/	two *are* ready /tuw ər rédɪ/
can	/kæn/	/kən/	you *can* come /yuw kən kəm/
had	/hæd/	/əd/	I *had* been /ay əd bɪn/
has	/hæz/	/əz/	it *has* gone /ɪt əz gɔn/
have	/hæv/	/əv/	we *have* seen /wiy əv siyn/
*of	/av/	/əv/	three *of* us /θriy əv əs/
*or	/ɔr/	/ər/	one *or* two /wən ər tuw/
that	/ðæt/	/ðət/	those *that* went /ðowz ðət wɛnt/
*the	/ðiy/	/ðə/ or /ðɪ/	on *the* right /an ðə rayt/
*to	/tuw/	/tə/ or /tʊ/	five *to* two /fayv tə tuw/
was	/waz/	/wəz/	it *was* late /ɪt wəz leyt/

The words in the list that are marked with an asterisk (*) are almost always weakened: *a, an, and, of, or, the,* and *to.*

That is weakened when used as a relative pronoun or a conjunction: *the word that you want* /ðə wə́rd ðət yuw wánt/, *I know that he will* /ay nów ðət hiy wíəl/. It is stressed and pronounced /ðæt/ as a demonstrative: *the reason for that* /ðə ríyzən fɔr ðǽt/.

The verbs *are, can, had, has, have,* and *was* are usually obscured or weakened, but are given their clear pronunciation whenever they receive sentence-stress: that is, at the end of a sentence or in a tag question. (See item 8 under "Function Words," Section II of this lesson.)

Whó *can* /kən/ gó? Jóhn *can* /kæn/.

The flágs are /ər/ an éxcellent idéa, áren't /arnt/ they?

Can has the added feature of being pronounced with /æ/, rather than /ə/, in the contraction *can't: I can't tell you* /ay kǽnt tɛ́əl yuw/. Since the final /t/, as normally pronounced in a combination like *can't tell,* is nearly impossible to hear, a person listening to the sentence would understand it as negative or affirmative depending on whether he heard /æ/ *(can't)* or /ə/ *(can).* The weakening of vowels can indeed affect meaning! If you fail to obscure the a of *can* in *I can tell you,* you may be understood to say precisely the opposite of what you intended.

The vowels of many other unstressed words of one syllable *may* be weakened; the weak forms listed here are those most important to use in order to avoid a "foreign accent."

IV. Thought Groups and Blending

By means of pauses we normally divide all but the shortest sentences into two or more parts, or thought groups. A thought group, then, is a portion of a sentence set off from the rest by a pause or pauses. In this manual we shall indicate pauses by a single diagonal line: *There may be time for a swim / if you come at once.*

When we make a pause in a sentence, it is usually for one of three reasons:

1. To make the meaning clear: *When the wind blows / the waves run high.*
2. For emphasis: *Frankly, / I'm disappointed in you.*
3. Or, in a long sentence, simply to enable the speaker to catch a breath.

It is obviously impossible to draw up a neat set of "rules" for the division of sentences into thought groups. Different persons will wish to emphasize different ideas, and individuals vary a great deal in their ability to keep on talking without stopping for breath. A speaker is ordinarily free to group words in several different ways, according to personal preference.

This does not mean, however, that a pause may be made anywhere in a sentence. It would certainly be unnatural to pause between *the* and *meaning* in *Phrasing depends upon the meaning of what you say.* In general, no pause is made within closely related word groups such as adjectives or articles and the nouns they modify, auxiliary verbs and the accompanying main verbs, prepositions and the nouns dependent on them, adverbs modifying adjectives, subject pronouns and verbs, verbs and their object pronouns, and so on. But between any of the large grammatical divisions of a sentence pauses may occur.

Analyze carefully the following passage, in which have been marked all the places where a native speaker of English would be at all likely to pause.

It is not strange / that chlorophyll / has been called / green blood. This substance / is carried about / in little green disks / which, / like the corpuscles of our blood, / can move about / just as if they had / a life of their own. If the sun / is too strong, / they can turn / their edges / toward it, / or sink / to the bottom / of the cells. When there is little sun, / they may rise / to the top of the cells / to make the most / of the light.

Of course, no one speaker would pause so often. If pauses are made too frequently, the effect is unpleasant; if they are made too infrequently, the speaker may run out of breath. If the material is written out, the author's punctuation will be a good guide, though more pauses will often be necessary than there are commas, semicolons, and other such marks.

To distribute pauses intelligently, it is first of all necessary that speakers understand the full meaning of what they are saying. And meaning can never be made clear to the hearer unless one groups words in a clear-cut fashion. The foreign student's most frequent error with regard to pauses is a failure to organize sentences into thought groups that can be recognized as such. The pauses are too timid, or bear no relation to the intended meaning.

Within thought groups, words and syllables are not pronounced as separate units; they flow along smoothly, without jerkiness, and one seems to blend into the next. A person who did not know any English would find it hard to tell where one word ended and another began. The blending between the two words of *read it* is as close as that between the two syllables of *reading*. Within a thought group a speaker does not audibly interrupt, even briefly, the outward flow of breath. The blending is accomplished by this constant flow of breath, and by the fact that even while one sound is being formed the speech organs are already moving on to the position in which the next is to be formed.

Those who are learning English as a second language often spoil the blending within thought groups by inserting little puffs of air or /ə/ sounds in order to divide combinations of consonants that seem difficult to them: *I don't think so* /ay downtə θɪŋkə sow/. (This phenomenon is treated in some detail in Lesson 9, Section III.) Blending may also be spoiled by making glottal stops, that is, by cutting off completely the outflow of breath for an instant by holding the vocal cords tightly together, thus closing the glottis. Glottal stops, indicated by the symbol /ʔ/, are comparatively rare in standard English, occurring necessarily in only a few special combinations like *oh, oh!* /oʔo/ (to express dismay). In some other languages (Hindi, Arabic, German, Hawaiian) they are more common, and may even serve to distinguish between one word and another (Danish, Pilipino). The student of English should not use glottal stops to separate vowel from vowel or consonant from vowel; for example, the /iy/ and /ow/ of *be over* /biy owvər/ should be blended.

A fuller treatment of the phonetic modifications that take place in word groups will be found in Lesson 16, "The Sandhi of Spoken English."

V. Exercises

A. Do you understand the meaning of the following expressions? Each is a phrase of the sort that makes up most of our speech. Each is written as one word, and in actual conversation, with blending well done, would be pronounced as one word. Pronounce the phrases several times, making the contrast between stressed and unstressed syllables very strong. The ten most common English words are all used here, those which make up 25 percent of all that is said and written in English. As a foundation for future progress, can you learn to pronounce these ten words naturally?

1.	əvðəlésən	8.	ɪzðətrúwθ	15.	aykənméykɪt
2.	əvðədéy	9.	ðətwiynów	16.	ɪtwəzméyd
3.	əvəwərd	10.	təbiyhǽpɪ	17.	wiərgówɪŋ
4.	ɪnəbəs	11.	tuəvmétyuw	18.	ðowzðətkéym
5.	ɪzəfrénd	12.	šiyəztówldmiy	19.	fáyvərsíks
6.	ɪzəkwéstšən	13.	hiyəzsíynɪt	20.	bǽkənfɔ́rθ
7.	ɪzənǽnsər	14.	ayədθɔ́t	21.	sɔ́ltənpépər

B. Pronounce each of the following expressions as a blended unit, as you did the transcribed phrases of the preceding exercise. Be very careful to weaken and obscure unstressed syllables naturally. Sentence-stress is marked in each case.

1. a. supplánt
    b. the plánt
    c. the tónes
    d. the cárs

    e. the begínning
    f. that you gó
    g. in the máil

    h. on the róad
    i. with the óthers
    j. for the
        perfórmance

2. a. unáble
    b. a náme
    c. a níght
    d. an órange

    e. a stúdy
    f. in a húrry
    g. in a móment

    h. for a náp
    i. for an ápple
    j. at a garáge

3. a. of the wár
    b. of the péace
    c. of his stóry
    d. of a réstaurant

    e. of a proféssor
    f. is of úse
    g. will be of sérvice

    h. is míschievous
    i. the rést of us
    j. the sóund of it

4. a. today
    b. to town
    c. to try
    d. to enter

    e. to belong
    f. to be found
    g. to the board

    h. to an end
    i. I came to him
    j. he said to me

5. a. performed
    b. are formed
    c. are broken
    d. are allowed

    e. are a family
    f. we are thankful
    g. I was right

    h. she was afraid
    i. was the speaker
    j. was a beauty

6. a. submit
    b. had missed
    c. had left
    d. has brought

    e. has developed
    f. it has opened
    g. have become

    h. have been decided
    i. would have liked
    j. may have caught it

7. a. consent
    b. can send
    c. can tell you
    d. can defend

    e. can have happened
    f. he can dance
    g. I can see it

    h. I can't see it
    i. you can trust him
    j. you can't trust him

8. a. arrest
    b. or the rest
    c. or a bus
    d. understand

    e. one or two
    f. uncertain
    g. and certainly

    h. and he did it
    i. black and blue
    j. James and I

C. Unstressed words are often hard to distinguish in the stream of speech. This exercise is to give you practice in hearing and comprehending such unstressed words. First, your teacher may want to dictate the exercise to you, supplying in each sentence one of the words in parentheses for you to identify and write down. Then, you could practice pronouncing the sentences several times at normal conversational speed with stresses as marked, inserting in turn each of the words in parentheses.

   1. Where did (he, she, they) go?
   2. Please give (them, him, her) the tickets.
   3. She brought (his, him, us) food.
   4. They haven't offered (as, us) much money.
   5. Were you asked (your, her) name?
   6. Is Bob (on, in) this bus?
   7. Would you play it (as, if) they requested it?
   8. When are you going to tell me (the, a, her) story?

9. The bóok cáme (from, for) the líbrary.
10. It's bétter (that, than) you thínk it ís.
11. The stóre (could, can, would) bríng you the páckage.
12. I'd líke thís (and, or, for) thát.
13. We néed óne (of, and, or) twó.

D. Here are four series of sentences, with sentence-stresses marked. In each series except the last, sentence *b* contains more syllables than sentence *a,* sentence *c* more than sentence *b,* and so on, but the number of stresses is always the same; the addition of the extra syllables does not mean any appreciable lengthening of the time it takes to say the entire sentence. (See Section I of this lesson.) Tap on a table with your pencil, slowly and regularly, in groups of three beats. Then pronounce each series of sentences several times, making a stressed syllable fall on each beat, and bringing in all unstressed syllables between beats. Each time you read, tap a little faster.

1. a. Dógs éat bónes.
    b. The dógs éat bónes.
    c. The dógs will éat bónes.
    d. The dógs will éat the bónes.
    e. The dógs will have éaten the bónes.
2. a. The cár is hére nów.
    b. The cár is out frónt nów.
    c. The cár will be out frónt sóon.
    d. The cár will be out frónt in a móment.
3. a. Bóys néed móney.
    b. The bóys will néed móney.
    c. The bóys will néed some móney.
    d. The bóys will be néeding some móney.
    e. The bóys will be néeding some of their móney.
4. a. A drúgstore's the pláce to have lúnch.
    b. We shall sóon finish úp for the seméster.
    c. Júne is a níce mónth.
    d. We were enchánted by her intélligent conversátion.
    e. Gréat dáy in the mórning!

E. The passage below, in ordinary conversational style, is to be prepared for rhythmic reading by

1. Marking all normal sentence-stresses. (See Section II of this lesson.)

    a. *Forget-Me-Not* (in Sentence 2 in the ''Passage for Reading'' below) is a compound noun, and the indefinite pronoun *anything* (3 and 5) is like a compound noun; where should they be stressed (Lesson 3, Section III, 2-a)?

b. Where should the intensive pronoun *themselves* (7) be stressed (Lesson 3, Section III, 2-c)?

c. *Card game* (6) is an example of a nominal compound; where is it stressed (Section II of this lesson)?

d. *Call out* (3 and 6), and *put down* (3 and 6) are two-word verbs; position of stress (Section II of this lesson)? Are *comes to* (3) and *think of* (5) two-word verbs?

e. Would you stress *because* (7), *you* (8), *is* (8)? Why, or why not?

2. Marking also any contrastive stresses you think should be made (see last two paragraphs of Section II of this lesson).

a. Do you see any function words—which, of course, would normally be left unstressed—to which special attention should be called? Sentence 5? Sentence 6?

b. Do you find any places where it might be well to violate the normal principles of sentence-stress in order to secure a more regular rhythm? Sentence 3?

3. Setting off thought groups by inserting (/) wherever you feel a pause should be made (Section IV of this lesson).

a. Would you pause after *that* (1), *first* (3), *green* (5)? Why, or why not?

b. Sentence 1 is almost too long to read without a pause; would it be better to break it after *game* or the first *play?* Why? Would you break Sentence 7 after *people* or *things?*

PASSAGE FOR READING

1. There's a little game I want us to play that I used to play at school.

2. It's called Forget-Me-Not. 3. I'm going to call out some words—just anything at all—and as I say each word, you're all to put down the first thing that comes to your mind. 4. Is that clear? 5. For instance, if I should say "grass," you might write "it's green," or anything else you think of. 6. Or

if I call out "bridge," you might put down "a card game." 7. It's an inter-

esting game because it shows the reactions of people to different things and

tells you a lot about the people themselves. 8. You see how simple and easy

it is?[3]

Naturally it is not expected or desired that all students should mark this
passage alike. After you have marked it, read it several times, making sentence-stresses recur rhythmically and blending the words in each thought group.
If the teacher finds that you tend to break up thought groups with glottal stops
or otherwise, it may help you prevent this if you will draw a line linking words
or syllables between which you are likely to interrupt the flow of breath:
say each (3), different things (7).

F. Mark the stresses in the sentences that appear below, and transcribe each sentence
in phonetic symbols. Write each word separately, rather than running words together in phrases as in Exercise A. After you have made your transcription, your
instructor will pronounce the exercise, so that you may check your transcription
with his or her pronunciation. Pay particular attention to the obscured and clear
sounds of verbs that may be used as auxiliaries, such as *can* and *have*. Finally,
practice reading the material from your corrected transcription.

1. What can I give as an answer?
2. I'm afraid it will be hard to get back.
3. He says that he will come if he can.
4. I thought she would be pretty, and she was.
5. She has worked with children since she finished school, hasn't she?
6. Men have shown no patience with it, but women have.
7. The car had been brought, and was ready to use.
8. If I had seen you sooner, we could have gone together.

G. There follow three stanzas of a well-known poem. It has a strong rhythm that may
help you learn to make stressed syllables recur regularly and to obscure unstressed
syllables. It also provides some excellent examples of stress-timed, as opposed to

---

[3]Adapted from *You Can't Take It with You* by Moss Hart and George S. Kaufman, copyright,
1937, by Moss Hart and George S. Kaufman, and reprinted by permission of the publishers,
Rinehart & Company, Inc.

syllable-timed, rhythm. Mark the sentence-stresses, with your instructor's help if necessary; note what types of words are stressed and unstressed, and check your findings with Section II of this lesson. Why do you suppose *must* is stressed in the first line? Why is it necessary to lengthen *tall* in order to maintain the rhythm of the second line? Read the poem several times, being particularly careful of the way in which you pronounce function words such as *to* and *and;* or, better still, memorize the selection.

SEA FEVER

I must go down to the seas again, to the lonely sea and the sky,
And all I ask is a tall ship and a star to steer her by;
And the wheel's kick and the wind's song and the white sail's shaking,
And a gray mist on the sea's face, and a gray dawn breaking.

I must go down to the seas again, for the call of the running tide
Is a wild call and a clear call that may not be denied;
And all I ask is a windy day with the white clouds flying,
And the flung spray and the blown spume, and the sea-gulls crying.

I must go down to the seas again, to the vagrant gypsy life,
To the gull's way and the whale's way where the wind's like a whetted
    knife;
And all I ask is a merry yarn from a laughing fellow-rover,
And quiet sleep and a sweet dream when the long trick's over.

JOHN MASEFIELD (1874–1967)

H. The class might like to record "Sea Fever" on tape. If so, the selection should first be rehearsed a number of times, as a choral reading. This careful preparation, motivated by the recording, is the chief value of the exercise. The first two lines of each stanza might be assigned to three different individuals with distinctive voices. The last two lines of each stanza could be said by the entire class in chorus. Other good poems to work with would be Robert Frost's "Stopping by Woods on a Snowy Evening" and Alfred Noyes' "The Highwayman."

I. While working on this lesson, each student should read aloud, with attention concentrated on sentence-stress and rhythm, as many passages as possible from books in which he or she is interested.

LESSON 5

Rising-Falling Intonation

I. What Intonation Is

Intonation is the tune of what we say. More specifically, it is the combination of musical tones on which we pronounce the syllables that make up our speech. It is closely related to sentence-stress. Often, but by no means always, a syllable with sentence-stress is spoken on a higher musical note than the unstressed syllables. In such cases, intonation is one of the elements of stress, the others being loudness and length. (Lesson 7 deals in some detail with cases in which sentence-stress does *not* coincide with a higher musical note.)

It is possible to identify on a piano or other musical instrument the note or notes on which any given syllable is pronounced. Expressive speakers sometimes use as many as twenty-five different notes to give variety and meaning to what they say. Others may use a much smaller range. We could, then, mark the intonation of sentences by writing them on something resembling a musical staff.

	morn-
Good	
	ing.

Have you ever listened to the tune of your own voice? What tune do you use when you say "What time is it?" and "Good morning"? Can you identify any of the notes on a piano? Which word did you pronounce on the highest note? Which word or syllable on the lowest note? Can you draw a line that will show the tune of *What time is it?* by rising and falling at the proper places?

Each speaker has his or her own range of notes, and it is not necessary, in order to pronounce English well, for you to imitate someone else's intonation, note for note. What is important is not that a given syllable be pronounced on the note *do* and another on *re,* but the direction of the shift between syllables, the general movement of the voice up or down. Most native speakers of English, pronouncing the same words under similar circumstances, would make their voices rise or fall at approximately the same places. But it is hardly ever possible to say that a given intonation pattern is absolutely obligatory in a particular case. There are almost always alternate patterns that are also natural, and that you can sometimes hear if you listen closely to native speakers of English.

In marking intonation, we shall use a simplified system[1] that divides the tones into four types: normal, high, low, and extra-high. We can then show the movements of the voice up or down by drawing lines at four different levels over or under the passage we are explaining. A line drawn *at the base of the letters* of a word indicates that that word is pronounced on a *normal* tone, a line *above the word* marks a *high* tone, a line *some distance below the word* marks a *low* tone, and a line *some distance above the word* marks an *extra-high* tone. Can you make your voice follow the lines?

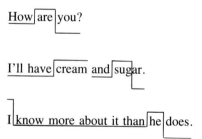

---

[1]Much of the material of Lessons 5, 6, and 7, as well as the system for marking intonation, is derived from Kenneth L. Pike's *The Intonation of American English* (Ann Arbor: University of Michigan Press, 1946). The chief weakness of this marking system (or of any marking system) appears to be that, unless it is well explained, it may give students the impression that English intonation is much less flexible than is really the case. One should always keep in mind that, in practice, the voice often does not rise and fall exactly at the place indicated by the markings; the change from one tone to another may be gradual and extended over several syllables. In spite of this weakness, it seems to us that the Pike system of markings is the most teachable yet devised because of its clarity, simplicity, and graphic quality.

Usually the movement from one tone to another takes place *between syllables,* and is called a *shift*. A shift is indicated by a *straight vertical line,* as that between *how* and *are* in the first example above, or that between *are* and *you*. Sometimes, however, the voice slides from one tone to another while it is pronouncing a syllable; such movement *within a syllable* is marked by a *line curving up or down,* and we shall call it a *slide*.

all day long

In this last example, we begin to pronounce *long* on a note higher than normal,[2] and then the voice slides down to a note lower than normal before the end of the syllable.

II. Rising-Falling Intonation

It is at the end of a sentence that native speakers of English use intonation most uniformly. In this position in certain types of sentences the voice often rises above normal, then falls below normal. This means that the rising-falling intonation pattern looks like this:

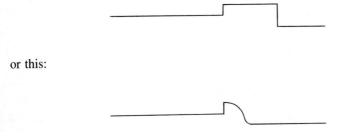

or this:

The key to such a pattern is the location of the high note: what comes immediately *before* this high note is spoken on a *normal* tone, and what comes *after* is spoken on a *low* tone. In a short sentence, if you know where to put the high note, the rest of the pattern falls mechanically into place.

---

[2]Care should be taken to avoid exaggeration: making the high tones too high and sliding up or down too slowly. Normally the slides are made quite rapidly and unobtrusively.

THE HIGH NOTE NORMALLY COINCIDES WITH THE LAST SENTENCE-STRESS.

Note these examples.

The situátion is difficult.

I sáid I cóuldn't héar you.

In both sentences above there are, after the last sentence-stress and its high note, one or more unstressed syllables left to receive the low note. The downward movement of the voice is then a *shift,* shown by a vertical line between the syllable with the high note and the following syllable. In some cases, on the other hand, the last sentence-stress and its high note may come on the very last syllable, leaving no room for the low note that must follow, as in *The cóffee is hót.* It is then that the voice makes a *slide,* shown by a curved line. Both the high and the low notes are heard as the last syllable is pronounced, and the voice descends from the high to the low note within the syllable (the phenomenon referred to at the end of Section I of this lesson).

The cóffee is hót.

Whát tíme did you cáll?

This sliding from one note to another *within* a single stressed syllable means that the vowel of the syllable will be so lengthened that it may break into two slightly different vowels—a diphthong. If we were trying to represent the sounds as closely as possible, the above examples might be transcribed as

ðə kɔ́fɪ ɪz háət   (rather than /hat/)

hwát táym dɪd yuw kɔ́ul   (rather than /kɔl/)

These two-toned syllables and the resultant diphthongization constitute one of the important differences between English and many other languages. Here intonation and vowel formation meet. The proper use of slides will make it much easier to give normal diphthongal quality to the right vowels and thus to make English sound like English.

The fact that the high note usually coincides with the last sentence-stress in speaking, helps us to distinguish between such grammatically different sequences as the following:

1. Nominal compounds and sequences of independent words

    bláckbird   I sáw a bláckbird.
       (a certain species of bird)

    bláck bírd   I sáw a bláck bírd.
       (any bird black in color)

2. Nominal compounds and sequences in which the first component tells the material of which the second component is made. (See Lesson 4, Footnote 2.)

    stéak knife   I'd líke a stéak knife.

    stéak dínner   I'd líke a stéak dínner.

3. Nominal compounds and verbs followed by objects

    chécking accounts   They're chécking accounts.

    chécking accóunts   They're chécking accóunts.

4. Two-word verbs and verbs followed by prepositions

    look úp   Whát are you looking úp?

m. I'd like to speak to you.   t. I'd like to know.

n. I'd like to look at it.   u. I'd like a cigarette.

o. I'd like a balcony seat.   v. I'd like to find out.

p. I'd like a ring.   w. I'd like to finish up.

q. I'd like an "A."   x. I'd like a new car.

r. I'd like to see.   y. I'd like a bowl of soup.

s. I'd like to leave.   z. I'd like a piece of cake.

2. Your instructor will ask you or one of the other students the question

What would you like?

Answer by using one of the sentences above. You, in turn, ask someone else this same question, and he or she also will answer, using one of the sentences above. Continue the exercise until everyone has had an opportunity to ask the question and receive an answer.

B. 1. Repeat these *wh*-questions after your instructor. Be sure to use the rising-falling intonation.

a. What did you bring?   d. What did you find?

b. What did you want?   e. What did you ask?

c. What did you forget?   f. What did you think up?

g.   What did you think of?   q.   What did you run over?

h.   What did you tell her?   r.   What did you speak about?

i.   What's he carrying?   s.   What's he giving you?

j.   What's he waiting for?   t.   What's he studying it for?

k.   What's he talking about?   u.   How did you come?

l.   How are you feeling?   v.   Who wrote it?

m.   Which is the library?   w.   Why did you take it?

n.   When do we eat?   x.   Which ones are the best?

o.   When can I study?   y.   How did he do it?

p.   Where's the Art Building?   z.   Whom did you want to speak with?

2.   Your instructor will ask you a question from the list above. You will answer
     the question and then ask another student one of the questions from the list.
     The drill will continue until every student has participated. (Caution to the
     teacher: do not allow students to take a long time to answer the questions.
     Keep the exercise moving rapidly by being willing to supply a cue for the
     answer when a student hesitates.)

C.   First, read over the following exercise silently to make sure you understand the
     meaning of each sentence. Then pronounce the entire series several times, concen-
     trating on rhythm and intonation. These sentences should be of practical use to you
     the next time you visit an unfamiliar city.

1. ðÍs ɪz nyuw yɔ́rk

11. tɛ́əl ɪm tə kəm ɪ́n

2. ay níyd ə rúwm

12. aym rɛ́dɪ tə gów

3. hwɛ́ərz ðə howtɛ́l

13. aym hə́ŋgrɪ

4. ɪts níər ðə láybrɛrɪ

14. hwɛ́ərz ðe dáynɪŋ ruwm

5. wɪəl téyk ə tǽksɪ

15. wɪəl íyt ɔ́ðər

6. ráyt yʊr néym híər

16. haw mə́tš dɪd ɪt kɔ́st

7. rɪ́ŋ fɔr ðə bɔ́y

17. ɪts bín ə gʊ́d trɪ́p

8. húw brɔ́t ðə bǽgz

18. péy fɔr ɪt náw

9. gív ɪm ə tɪ́p

19. ðǽt wɪəl biy fáyn

10. húwz æt ðə dɔ́r

20. wɪəl biy síyɪŋ yuw

D. Be very careful in placing the high note as you pronounce the following pairs of sentences.

1. a. In Pasadena, there's a playhouse.
    b. Most children like to play house.

2. a. I know nothing about that and couldn't care less.
    b. He's always a little careless.

3. a. Try to keep the street cleaner.
    b. Try to keep the street-cleaner.

4. a.   In India, the British no longer have a strong hold.
    b.   Gibraltar is a stronghold.

5. a.   That boy has found a bird's-nest.
    b.   I've never seen those birds nest.

E. With the help of other members of your class and of your instructor, try to divide
    the following representative list of nominal expressions into these four categories:

    1. typical nominal compounds, with sentence-stress and the high note on the first
        component (see Lesson 4, p. 32);
    2. expressions in which the first component tells the material of which the second
        component is made, with sentence-stress on both components but the high note
        on the second component (see Lesson 4, Footnote 2);
    3. expressions that according to the above ''rules'' should belong in Category 1
        but that are really pronounced as though they belong in Category 2, or vice
        versa;
    4. expressions that can be pronounced either like those in Category 1 or like those
        in Category 2, but that may have a consequent difference in meaning.

    When you have assigned all the expressions to the proper categories, pronounce
    the items in each category separately, and try to accustom yourself to the stress-
    and-intonation patterns. Native speakers of American English would agree on the
    pattern for most of the expressions, but there would probably be an occasional
    disagreement.
        This exercise might well be carried out as a small-group activity, provided
    that the instructor checks the work that is done.

1. amusement park	15. coffee cup	29. geography book
2. atomic bomb	16. computer program	30. gold watch
3. baseball game	17. cotton skirt	31. grocery bill
4. beach boy	18. cream cheese	32. ham sandwich
5. beef stew	19. credit card	33. high school
6. birthday party	20. dancing girl	34. kitchen sink
7. brick wall	21. dollar bill	35. laundry soap
8. candy maker	22. Easter parade	36. legal system
9. canned goods	23. English teacher	37. library book
10. chemistry text	24. filling station	38. loving cup
11. cherry pie	25. fish eater	39. master's degree
12. chicken salad	26. flying machine	40. orange marmalade
13. chocolate cake	27. French class	41. orange tree
14. city hall	28. gas station	42. paper weight

43.	police car	46.	school year	49.	ten-cent stamp
44.	reform school	47.	social security	50.	wax paper
45.	repair department	48.	sorority girl		

F. Outside of class your instructor will mark the intonation patterns of the passage below and record the material, following his or her own markings. The recording will then be played several times, sentence by sentence, for the class. Listen to his or her intonation and try to mark the passage so as to show what the patterns were. Some patterns with which you are not yet familiar will probably be used, but don't try to analyze these. The exercise is intended merely to help you develop your ability to hear intonation.

PASSAGE TO BE MARKED

1. I usually get up early. 2. It takes me about half an hour to brush my teeth,

dress, and get ready to leave the house. 3. On Tuesdays and Thursdays I some-

times take a swim before breakfast. 4. Do you like to swim? 5. There's noth-

ing else like it to start the day off right. 6. What else would give you such an

appetite?

G. The material below is to be prepared for reading and then is to be read.

1. There are fifteen sentences of various kinds in the exercise. Do you recall the types of sentence in which rising-falling intonation is normally used? All but four of these sentences would normally be pronounced with rising-falling intonation. Try to find the four exceptions, and eliminate them.

2. Mark the sentence-stresses of the eleven sentences that remain.

   a. *Coffee machine* (in Sentence 5) and *napkin holder* (9) are nominal compounds. Position of stress?

b.   Are *cleaned up* (4), *pick out* (8), and *look at* (1) two-word verbs? Position of stress?
c.   Where would it be best to stress *fifteen* (13)?
d.   Would *can* be stressed (10)? *Have* (12)?

3.   Mark the intonation of each sentence. First, put the high note on the last sentence stress; then fill in the rest of the rising-falling pattern. Everything that precedes the high note may be marked as normal. Which sentences end in slides? How do you recognize them?

SENTENCES TO BE MARKED

1.   Let's look at the people.

2.   What shall we order?

3.   Where is the waiter?

4.   He hasn't cleaned up the table.

5.   He's there by the coffee machine.

6.   Do you know what you want?

7.   May I see the menu?

8.   What shall I pick out?

9.   Pass me the napkin holder.

10.   We'd better order as soon as we can.

11. Will you have an appetizer?

12. We have time enough to finish.

13. We have fifteen minutes.

14. I'll take the regular dinner.

15. Will you bring us our coffee later?

H. Transcribe in phonetic symbols Sentences 1, 3, 6, 9, 10, 13, and 15 of the preceding exercise. After you have made your transcription, your instructor will read the sentences and perhaps transcribe the exercise in class, so that you can check your work. Practice reading your corrected version.

I. Outside of class, do as much reading aloud as you can, concentrating your attention on weakening the vowels in unstressed words of one syllable. Selections from a play are particularly appropriate to read, especially if you can find someone to alternate with you in reading the parts.

LESSON 6

Rising Intonation

I. The Use of Rising Intonation

At the end of a sentence, two types of intonation are most common: rising-falling and rising. In the preceding lesson we studied rising-falling intonation and learned that it is used for statements, commands, and *wh*-questions. In the present lesson we shall deal with rising intonation, the second common end-of-sentence type.

IN ENGLISH, RISING INTONATION IS NORMALLY USED AT THE END OF QUESTIONS WHICH DO NOT BEGIN WITH AN INTERROGATIVE WORD (that is to say, general questions that may be answered merely by *yes* or *no*).

Are you ready?   Will you read it for me?

These yes-no questions are easy to identify grammatically because they begin with words such as the following:
1.   *will, would, shall, should, can, could, may, might,* and *must*

Shall I answer the telephone?

Can you help me?

2. *have, has, had*

Has he written to you?

Have they finished?

3. *am, is, are, was, were*

Is she at home?

Were they asleep?

4. *do, does, did*

Does he like it?

Did they see it?

The voice normally goes up to a high note *on the last sentence-stress,* just as in the rising-falling pattern. The difference between the two lies in the fact that, in the rising intonation, the syllables that follow the rise are pronounced on the high note too.

Does she expect to take a dictionary with her?

When we leave the voice high at the end of a sentence, we arouse in the listener a feeling of incompleteness, in contrast to the sense of completeness aroused by a lowered voice. Rising intonation suggests that something further must be said, either by the speaker or by the hearer.

Any statement may be made into a yes-no question by the use of rising intonation alone, without changing the words otherwise.

It's time for the class to end.   (statement)

It's time for the class to end?   (question)

We noted in Lesson 5 that questions beginning with an interrogative word, *wh*-questions, are normally given rising-falling intonation. What would be the effect of pronouncing such a question with rising intonation?

What's the day of the month?

It becomes an *echo question,* a question about what was previously said. A native speaker of English would normally interpret it as meaning something like "Is that really what you just said?" or "Will you please repeat what you said?" Thus the single word *what,* pronounced with rising intonation,

What?

means "I don't understand; please repeat".

Note that the meanings of the intonation patterns we have considered up to now may thought of as *grammatical meanings;* these patterns help convey such concepts as affirmation, negation, special interrogation, general interrogation, imperative forms, compounding, contrasting, and so on. The most basic use of intonation is to signal these grammatical meanings. Students will therefore need to make every effort to master the use of these intonation patterns. They are an integral part of the grammatical system of English, as essential to the structure of the language as are other grammatical signals such as word order, inflectional endings, and function words. In Lesson 7, Section II, we will look briefly at other—less basic—intonation patterns, which may be said to have *lexical meanings:* surprise, incredulity, irony, and so on. These are similar to the meanings of content words such as nouns, adjectives, and adverbs.

II. Nonfinal Intonation

What has been said up to this point applies to the raising or lowering of the voice *at the end of a sentence,* where suitable intonation is most necessary and easiest to predict. There is less that is definite to be said about the intonation of that part of the sentence that precedes the last important word. *Nonfinal intonation* may vary widely from speaker to speaker, with little corresponding variation in meaning.

Nevertheless, you should know that in any sentence we may pronounce on a note higher than normal the stressed syllable of any word or words to which we want to call the special attention of the listener. These may be specially stressed function words (see Lesson 4, Section II, paragraph beginning ''If a native speaker of English . . .'') or content words.

What do you know about politics?   (Note *you.*)

There are lots of cigarettes in the box.   (Note *lots.*)

He has an unusual number of friends.   (Note *unusual.*)

With particular frequency special attention is thus called to *demonstrative* and *interrogative* words.

I think that is a good idea.

What do you want with a car?

In *contrasts* and *comparisons,* special attention is called to *both* ideas being contrasted or compared. This means that, if both ideas are included in a single thought group, one of them will be nonfinal. However, the two stressed elements are not pronounced on the same high note but on different notes, one high and one extra-high. This difference in level between the two notes serves to emphasize the idea of contrast. It is one of the few cases in which an extra-high note seems to be obligatory in an intonation pattern that has a grammatical meaning. (Most often patterns with extra-high notes have an emotional, lexical meaning.)

Curiously, it appears to make no difference which element is given the extra-high note. Either sentence in each of the following pairs is equally natural.

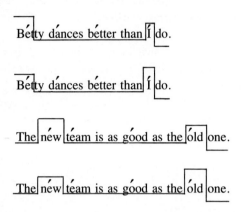

If a sentence is divided by pauses into *two or more thought groups,* each thought group has its own separate intonation pattern. When the speaker comes to the end of the first thought group, he or she may do one of three things:

1. *End the group with the rising-falling pattern—up to a high note on the final stress, then down to a low note.* This is done before a long pause such as might be marked by a colon (:) or semicolon (;).

     I'll tell you the truth: / it can't be done.

     I don't want to go; / it's dangerous.

     I say he can; / he says he can't.

2. *End the group by a high note on its final stress, then a return to normal.* This is done when the speaker wishes to suggest that what follows is connected with what was just said.

You say it's easy, / but you won't try it.

If you want me to, / I'll call her.

3. *End the group with the rising pattern.* This occurs, in general, whenever the speaker wishes to create suspense.

When I come back, / I'll give you a present.

If you want to learn chemistry, / you've got to work.

It should be clearly understood that the choice between these three nonfinal patterns usually depends more on *the attitude of the speaker* than on the grammatical structure and meaning of the sentence. Patterns 1, 2, and 3 above indicate progressively closer degrees of connection: the higher the note at the end of the first thought group, the closer the connection to the second group. A speaker using Pattern 1 is treating the two groups almost as though they were separate sentences. Pattern 2 indicates a normally close relationship. Pattern 3 emphasizes the closeness of the relationship. It is therefore usually impossible to say that, before a nonfinal pause, one type of intonation is "right" and all others "wrong." As far as grammar and logic are concerned, the last example above might just as well be

If you want to learn chemistry, / you've got to work.

On the other hand, there are some *special constructions* of whose intonation we can be more certain.

1. SERIES WITH *and. Rising intonation on all members of the series except the last; rising-falling intonation on the last member.*

I went to the bank / and the post office.

He speaks English, / Italian, / and French.

2. ALTERNATIVES WITH *or*. *Like a series—rising intonation followed by ris-ing-falling intonation—if the speaker wishes the utterance to be heard merely as a sequence of items.*

We eat at a drugstore, / a cafeteria, / or a restaurant.

However, *or* often carries a meaning of contrast or comparison. *If the speaker wishes to emphasize this meaning of contrast, he or she will give an extra-high note to one of the alternatives* (see pp. 61–62 of this lesson).

You can do it in writing / or orally.

You can do it in writing / or orally.

This contrastive extra-high note seems to be obligatory in *questions with or* where the speaker wishes the hearer to make a choice between two or more alternatives.

Do you prefer Los Ángeles / or San Francisco?

Do you prefer Los Ángeles / or San Francisco?

On the other hand, if *or* merely means that the utterance is to be inter-preted as a *double question,* to be answered by *yes* or *no,* it is spoken with the intonation pattern of one, or two, yes-no questions.

Have you ever visited Los Ángeles or San Francisco?

Have you éver vísited Los Ángeles / or San Francisco?

Serious confusions can result if a listener does not understand the difference between these two types of questions with *or*. (See Exercise F of this lesson.)

3. DIRECT ADDRESS. *The safest pattern for a learner of English to use in pronouncing names (or words substituted for names) and titles addressed directly to the person to whom he or she is speaking is rising intonation. Normal politeness requires that the direct address begin on a low note and then rise to normal.* Direct address may come at the end of the sentence or elsewhere, and it does not affect the intonation of the rest of the sentence.

I'm glád to sée you, / my fríend.

Míster Róberts, / hów are you feeling?

If your voice does not rise at all, your hearer may think you are irritated with him.

Cóme hére thís mínute, / Jóhnny.

In the following sentence, if your voice begins to rise on a *normal* note and then goes up to *high,* rather then beginning *low* and rising to *normal,* you may sound like a cannibal

Whát will we éat for bréakfast, / Móther?

instead of like a loving daughter.

Whát will we éat for bréakfast, / Móther?

4. TAG QUESTIONS, SUCH AS *aren't you, will he*. These show clearly the essential difference between rising-falling and rising intonation. *If the tag question is pronounced with the* rising-falling *pattern* (high to low in this case),

You're|hún|gry, / áren't|you?

the whole sentence is to be interpreted as a statement of fact, *and indicates that the speaker is confident that the hearer will agree. When the tag is pronounced with the* rising *pattern (normal to high),*

You're|hún|gry, / áren't|you?

the sentence is a genuine question, *which means that the speaker is not sure whether or not the hearer is hungry, and that the latter is asked to confirm or deny the idea, to answer* yes *or* no. Note that the intonation of the part of the sentence that precedes the tag is not affected by the addition of the latter; though, in the examples above, *you're hungry* is nonfinal, it has the same intonation that it would be given if it came at the end of the sentence.

Tag questions are introduced by the same kinds of words that are used in yes-no questions. (See Section I of this lesson.)

1. *will, would, shall, should, can, could, may, might,* and *must*

He wón't|hélp|me, / wíll|he?

I can|gó, / cán't|I?

2. *have, has, had*

He hásn't|fín|ished, / hás|he?

You've eaten, / haven't you?

3. *am, is, are, was, were*

I was right, / wasn't I?

He isn't here, / is he?

4. *do, does, did*

They don't agree, / do they?

He finally arrived, / didn't he?

III. Exercises

A. Pronounce each group of sentences in the following exercise several times so as to accustom yourself to the various intonation patterns. Your instructor will try to see that you do not fail to blend the words together smoothly.

1. Yes-no questions

a. Do you remember me?

b. Is there a room for me?

c. Do you have anything cheaper?

d. Will you keep it long?

e.   Are you going to stay with us?

f.   Are you living here?

g.   Is that Phil over there?

h.   Is this where we eat?

i.   Will you meet us this evening?

j.   Is the second floor too low for you?

2.   Contrasts and comparisons

a.   You know it as well as I do.

b.   Sandra is older than Don.

c.   This room is more expensive than that one.

d.   The breakfasts are better than the dinners.

e.   Yesterday's picture was as interesting as today's.

3.   Alternative and double questions

a.   Shall we wait here, / or outside?

b. Which do you like better, / Toyotas / or Fords?

c. Have you ever seen ice / or snow?

d. Does that store sell fish / or meat?

4. Series

a. I saw Charles, / Bernard, / and Robert.

b. It's open today, / tomorrow, / and the day after.

c. We could go at ten, / eleven, / or twelve.

5. Degrees of connection

a. Children often eat hamburgers; / adults usually prefer steaks.

b. I say we do; / he says we don't.

c. This one is five; / that one is six.

d. If you want me to, / I'll serve you now.

e. As you said, / it's a very nice place.

f. In a minute, / I'll have a surprise for you.

g.   I looked down, / and there was my key.

B.   In order to improve your ability to control the ups and downs of your voice, to hear and produce an intonation pattern, it is suggested that a recording of Exercise A be made in class. As many students as possible should record groups of sentences, and these should be played back to the class immediately. The students will try to detect any failure to reproduce a natural pattern.

C.   Read each of these sentences, first as a statement, then as a question, using only intonation to show the difference. (See Section I of this lesson.)

1.   The story begins long ago.
2.   They were riding in an old car.
3.   The car began to cross the river.
4.   The bridge had been washed away.
5.   The children were in the back seat.
6.   They were talking at the tops of their voices.
7.   No one could hear anything.
8.   One of the children fell out.

D.   Your instructor will call on individual students to ask each of the following questions. Each student selected may choose to ask the question as a regular *wh*-question or as an echo question. When the question has been asked, the student will then call on another student to answer it in the way suggested by its intonation. The expected answer to a regular *wh*-question is, of course, to provide the information requested. On the other hand, the expected answer to an echo question is to indicate in some way whether or not the original question has been correctly understood: for example, "Yes, that's what I said." (See the next-to-last paragraph of Section I of this lesson.)

1.   What's the first day of the week?
2.   Who's the best skater?
3.   Where's the bus stop?
4.   When's the next class?
5.   Which way is north?
6.   How is "athlete" spelled?
7.   Why is the cat hungry?
8.   How long have they lived in this country?

E.   Each of these sentences involves a contrast or comparison. Therefore, in each sentence special attention is called to two ideas, one given a high note and the other an extra-high note. In order to familiarize yourself with the intonation pattern, repeat each sentence twice, once with the extra-high note first and once with it last. (See pp. 61–62, Section II of this lesson.)

1. Peace is always preferable to war.
2. Oleo is as tasty as butter.
3. I'd rather travel by ship than by plane.
4. She can play the piano or the guitar.
5. It's not Thursday, it's Friday.

F. 1. The story is told of a new immigrant who arrived in San Francisco. As required by law, the U.S. Immigration Inspector questioned him. Looking sternly at the immigrant, the Inspector asked:

  Do you advocate the overthrow of the U.S. Government by force / or by violence?

Terrified but trying hard to be cooperative, the immigrant thought a long time, then timidly answered:

  By violence.

He was not admitted to the United States.
    Can you explain the story? How did the Inspector intend his question to be answered? Why did the immigrant answer as he did? Could he have profited by a lesson on intonation?

2. Demonstrate the intonation pattern with which you think each of these questions should be asked. In some cases it may be possible to use either of two different patterns, depending on the meaning you want to convey. (See pp. 64–65, Item 2 of this lesson.)

    a. Do you prefer popular or classical music?
    b. In winter do you like to skate or ski?
    c. Will you have coffee or tea?
    d. Have you ever played roulette or blackjack?
    e. Is the traffic light red or green?
    f. Which comes first, the chicken or the egg?

G. Pronounce each of the following questions in two ways: first, as if you were really
asking for information; then, as if you knew the hearer would agree with you and
you were merely making polite conversation. After each reading of each sentence,
another student should try to make the response that your intonation shows you
expect. (See the end of Section II in this lesson.)

1. It's getting hotter, isn't it?

2. You don't think it will rain, do you?

3. It doesn't rain here in December, does it?

4. The nights are always warm, aren't they?

5. You can count on good weather in October, can't you?

6. The rainy season doesn't ever begin until winter, does it?

7. There's a lot of fog here, isn't there?

8. The mornings are warmer than the afternoons, aren't they?

9. The days are getting longer, aren't they?

10. Dinner is served at six o'clock, isn't it?

11. Concerts usually begin at eight o'clock, don't they?

12. They usually finish before eleven, don't they?

13. The library isn't open after midnight, is it?

14. The busses don't run on Sunday, do they?

15. The museum is open on Mondays, isn't it?

H. 1. The sentences below are to be marked for rhythm and intonation, and then
read. A systematic way of analyzing material for this purpose is to

a. Mark all sentence-stresses. In this exercise, all words may be stressed
normally; there are no specially stressed function words. (See Item 1 toward the end of Lesson 4, Section II).

b. Divide into thought groups by placing a diagonal bar (/) at pauses. Be sure to mark as separate thought groups all (1) parts of a series, (2) alternatives, (3) words used in direct address, and (4) tag questions.

c. Mark the intonation of each group. First, locate the final high note or rise. In this exercise, this may in all cases coincide with the last sentence-stress. Second, determine whether the pattern should be rising-falling or rising, by deciding whether the group is a statement, command, *wh*-question, yes-no question, echo question, nonfinal group, or one of the special constructions listed in *b* above. Third, mark the intonation line from the final high note to the end of the group, distinguishing between shifts and slides. Fourth, decide whether or not you wish to give a high note to any nonfinal sentence-stresses, and mark such notes. Lastly, draw a line under the rest of the group, indicating normal pitch.

This exercise could well be carried out as a small-group activity.

SENTENCES TO ANALYZE

1. Good morning, Ms. (/mɪz/) Peterson. How are you feeling?

2. If it rains, we'll call off the whole thing.

3. You'll agree that it's the truth, won't you?

4. We are studying composition, pronunciation, and grammar.

5. There are two ways of accomplishing it: by kindness, or by threats.

6. He translates from English to French, and from French to English.

7. Which syllable is accented?

8. Ms. Kim, will you open the door?

9. Do you speak better than you read, or read better than you speak?

10. Is the test on Monday or Tuesday?

I. Practice reading or repeating these short conversations with another student, making them sound as natural as you can. (See Lesson 4, Section II, p. 32.)

1. a. may fréndz ə sówšəl wərkər.

   b. šiyz ə sówšəl wərkər?

   a. yέs, / ɪts ə vέrɪ yúwsfʊl prəfέšən.

2. a. hiyz ə vέrɪ sówšəl wərkər.

   b. yέs, hiyz vέrɪ sówšəl.

     hiy láyks tə tók tʊ έvrɪbadɪ.

   a. ay θíŋk hiyd rǽðər biy sówšəl ðæn biy ə wərkər.

3. a. ðíyz ər may lívɪŋ kwɔ́rtərz.

   b. háw kən ə kwɔ́rtər biy lívɪŋ?

   a. ay míyn ðíyz ər may lívɪŋ kwɔrtərz.

   b. ɔ́w, yuw míyn ðís ɪz hwέər yuw lív.

LESSON 7

More About Intonation

I. Intonation and Focus

The meaning of a sentence that contains a number of different elements—subject, verb, object, pronouns, adjectives, time expressions, expressions of place, and so on—may be unclear because of the very number of those elements. This is especially true of yes-no questions, such as "Will you drive to the office tomorrow?" In written form and out of context, such a question may be ambiguous. Does it mean, "Will *you* drive, rather than *your wife?*" Does it mean, "Will you *drive,* rather than *walk?*" Does it mean, "Will you drive *to the office,* rather than *to the beach?*" Or does it mean, "Will you drive *tomorrow,* rather than *today?*" In other words, what is the *focus* of the question? What kind of information does the speaker expect as an answer?

Different languages may use different grammatical devices to signal focus. French, for example, most often uses word order: the equivalent of "Is it *you* that will drive to the office tomorrow?", "Is it *to the office* that you will drive tomorrow?", "Is it *tomorrow* that you will drive to the office?" and so on. Chinese also uses word order. Malayo-Polynesian languages add certain affixes to verbs to indicate focus. In English, the favorite device for indicating focus seems to be intonation. This is possible because of the great freedom that exists in English to give the high note of the intonation pattern to any element in a sentence.

We can say each of the following sentences, and the meaning of each sentence is quite clear:

Will you drive to the office tomorrow?   (rather than someone else)

Will you drive to the office tomorrow?   (rather than going some other way)

Will you drive to the office tomorrow?   (rather than from the office)

Will you drive to the office tomorrow?   (rather than somewhere else)

Will you drive to the office tomorrow?   (rather than some other day)

IN ENGLISH, ATTENTION IS FOCUSED ON ONE OF THE ELEMENTS IN A THOUGHT GROUP BY USING ONLY ONE HIGH NOTE, AND BY MAKING THE VOICE RISE ON THE STRESSED SYLLABLE OF THE WORD THE SPEAKER WISHES TO SINGLE OUT.

Up to now in this text, we have assumed that the high note will coincide with the last sentence stress. (See the "rule" in Lesson 5, at the beginning of Section II.) A look at the above examples will show, however, that this is not necessarily true when focus is needed to make the meaning of the sentence clear.

Unless students of English learn to use this freedom to place the high note wherever it is needed, they may fall back on the grammatical devices their own language uses to indicate focus, and thus produce such unnatural sentences as "Is it to the office you will drive tomorrow?" This freedom in the placement of the high note in English extends to rising-falling intonation as well as to rising intonation:

Why do you insist on going home so soon?

The need for focusing attention on one element in a thought group arises regularly in

1. *Making a question specific.*

Was it you who did that?

When do you hope to come back?

2. *Answering a specific question.*

(Who took the new car?)

I took the new car.

(Did you take the new car, or leave it?)

I took the new car.

(Did you take the new car, or the old one?)

I took the new car.

3. *Contradicting an idea expressed elsewhere or merely implied.*

(He's not working hard.)

Yes, he is working hard.

(Johnny will bring it to you.)

I wánt you to bríng it to me.

(Will you please bring it here?)

Jóhnny will bríng it to you.

I líke this tápe bést.

But we dó belíeve you.

II. Lexical (Emotional) Intonation

There are many intonation patterns, other than those so far described in this manual, that are at times used by native speakers of English. Most of them would be classified, however, as having lexical rather than grammatical meanings. (See Lesson 6, end of Section I.) That is to say, they add to the basic meaning of a sentence emotional overtones such as surprise, disbelief, shock, fear, respect, determination, sarcasm, irony, friendliness, suspicion, and many more. These lexical patterns thus have meanings that are similar to those of content words rather than to those of function words.

An extra-high note is often part of a lexical intonation pattern. Such a note seems to *intensify the force* of any emotional adjective or adverb to which it is attached:

That's térrible!   (shock)

How amázing!   (surprise)

She pláys extrémely wéll.   (approval)

Frequent use of such an intensifying extra-high note may, in fact, be one of the distinctive characteristics of feminine speech.

Another tendency in feminine speech may be relatively frequent use of an intonation pattern associated with *coaxing* or *persuading*. This emotional pattern begins on a high note, comes down to a low note, and finally rises to normal on the last sentence stress:

Don't behave like that.

Won't you have dinner with us?

You don't really need candy.

A more masculine pattern may be to indicate *determination* by giving a separate stress and a downward slide or shift to every word in a thought group:

Don't you behave like that.

We will not be deterred by criticism.

All three of the preceding patterns, however, are certainly used at times by both female and male speakers.

Many would agree that a yes-no question that begins on a normal note, rises to high on the last sentence-stress, then returns to normal has overtones of *irony:*

Do I know him?   (He's my brother!)

Are you certain?   (I don't think you are at all.)

An authoritative work on intonation[1] describes thirty different "primary

---

[1] Kenneth L. Pike, *The Intonation of American English* (see p. 45, Footnote 1).

intonation contours.'' However, beyond the point we have reached, the principles become too vague to be of much practical value to a student of English. The patterns are less predictable, and there is less agreement as to their meaning. The choice of patterns depends on intangible personal factors such as speakers' attitudes, rather than on grammatical constructions and logic.

The common types we have already studied are entirely sufficient for normal conversational purposes. With them you can say almost anything in a clear and natural way. Become as familiar with them as possible, and for a while try to use them for everything you say in English. Then, little by little, you can add new patterns—you will probably do so instinctively—by imitation.

Above all, do not make the mistake of thinking that all the various types of intonation you have been accustomed to using in your own language will have the same meaning if you transfer them to English. Some of the intonation patterns of your mother tongue may not exist in English, and others will have entirely different meanings.[2]

III. Inventory of Intonation Patterns

Lessons 4, 5, 6, and 7 have been focused on the rhythm and intonation of English. The most essential intonation patterns have been described and their meanings identified. Before we move on in subsequent lessons to a detailed examination of the individual sounds of the language, it may be useful to bring all these intonation patterns together in the form of an inventory, so as to help you see the over-all picture.

In the inventory the patterns are identified in the first column by a phrase describing their type, then in the second column by a formula made up of a series of numbers, and finally in the third column by one or more examples. Lines are drawn over and under the words in the examples to indicate pitch levels, according to the system with which you are already familiar. The numbers in the second column correspond to the lines as follows: 1 indicates a low pitch, 2 a normal pitch, 3 a high pitch, and 4 an extra-high pitch. Thus the 2-3-1 pattern is what we have been calling rising-falling intonation, and 2-3 represents rising intonation.

These numerical formulas are included here because they are a concise and easy way to identify intonation patterns in writing. Numbers are not as

---

[2]For example, English is the only language the authors know of in which tag questions with rising-falling intonation are used to indicate expected agreement. (See Lesson 6, Section II-4.) Such tag-question formulas as the French *n'est-ce pas,* the German *nicht wahr,* and the Spanish *no* or *verdad* always have rising intonation.

graphic as are lines for indicating intonation, so numbers are less helpful when students are practicing patterns. But numbers are useful in identifying patterns quickly and clearly. Also, if you ever want to read more about the intonation of American English, you will find these numbers used in most of the material written on the subject.

Inventory of Intonation Patterns Having Grammatical Meanings

Type	*Formula*	*Examples*
1. Statements, requests, commands, *wh*-questions	2-3-1	It's raining. Let's go. What time is it?
2. Yes-no questions	2-3	Did she answer? She's not here?
3. Echo questions	2-3	What time is it?
4. Contrasts, comparisons	3-2-4-1 or 4-2-3-1	His Arabic is better than mine. She sounds like her mother.
5. Implicit contrasts	4-2-3-1 or 2-4, and so on	I wouldn't do that. Can you believe that?

(continued)

Inventory of Intonation Patterns (continued)

6. Nonfinal distantly connected   2-3-1   Let's not go; / it's too late.

    Nonfinal closely connected   2-3-2   If you say so, / I believe you.

    Nonfinal suspense   2-3   You know what, / I'm going to kiss you.

7. Series with *and*   2-3 / 2-3 / 2-3-1   We read plays, / novels,[3] / and poetry.

8. Alternatives with *or*   2-3 / 2-3 / 2-3-1   Come at eleven, / twelve,[3] / or two.

9. Alternative questions requiring a choice   2-3 / 2-4-1 or 2-4 / 2-3-1   Will you speak first, / or last?
                                             Will you tell them, / or say nothing?

10. Double yes-no questions   2-3 / 2-3   Do they sell chicken, / or turkey?

11. Direct address   1-2   Jim,[3] / can you help me?

12. Tag questions (real questions)   2-3   His name isn't Jones, / is it?[3]

(continued)

---

[3]Notice that in series, alternatives, direct address, and tag questions *the number of syllables is sometimes insufficient to permit developing the intonation pattern normally:* that is to say, with the high note of the pattern on the last sentence-stress. Thus, in the example given for Pattern 7 above, the thought group *novels* has only two syllables. While saying those two syllables, the

Inventory of Intonation Patterns (continued)

13. Tag questions   2-3-1   It's a nice day, / isn't it.
    (agreement
    expected)

14. Focus   (Depends on where the voice rises. Applicable to any
                         pattern.)

Did they buy the house at the end of the street?

Did they buy the house at the end of the street?

Did they buy the house at the end of the street?

Did they buy the house at the end of the street?

Did they buy the house at the end of the street?

Yes,/ they bought that house.

Yes,/ they bought that house.

Yes,/ they bought that house.

---

voice will typically rise. So that the upward movement may be clear, the stressed syllable *nóv-* is needed for the lower note, and the unstressed syllable *-els* for the higher note. As a result the high note of the pattern is given to an *unstressed* syllable. The same is true of *is it* in the example for Pattern 12. In the examples for Patterns 8 and 11, we need to use a rising pattern on just one syllable, so we get upward slides on *twelve* and *Jim*.

IV. Exercises

A. Pronounce each group of sentences several times, until the intonation patterns seem entirely natural to you.

1. Series of alternatives with *or*

    a. You can have white wine, / sherry, / or vodka.

    b. That dress must be cerise, / carmine, / or scarlet.

    c. A home run, / a triple, / or even a double will do.

    d. I can't twist it, / bend it, / or break it.

    e. Any season is suitable: / summer, / fall, / winter, / or spring.

2. Direct address

    a. Hello, / Diane.

    b. Where are you, / dear?

    c. I'd like a word with you, / George.

    d. What are you doing here, / young fellow?

    e. I think I've seen you before, / Ms. Jackson.

    f.   Sandy, / this is Robert Jones.

    g.   If you're interested, / Dad, / we could go out to eat.

3.   Tag questions (real questions)

    a.   You want a second helping, / don't you?

    b.   The election comes in September, / doesn't it?

    c.   It will be cooler in the mountains, / won't it?

    d.   This is the way to the Administration Building, / isn't it?

    e.   You knew it all the time, / right?

4.   Tag questions (agreement expected)

    a.   There's a pleasant breeze, / isn't there?

    b.   You have a beautiful view, / haven't you?

    c.   There's never enough money, / is there?

    d.   Summer's almost over, / isn't it?

    e.   He talks too much, / doesn't he?

5. Intensification

    a. This is great!

    b. She's a beautiful girl!

    c. That's very wrong!

    d. What a strange sensation!

    e. I never saw such an idiot!

B. 1. By using suitable intonation, make this sentence, *I put my red shirt away,* serve as an answer to each of the following questions. (See Section I of this lesson.)

    a. What did you put away?

    b. Where did you put your red shirt?

    c. Did your wife put your shirt away for you?

    d. Which shirt did you put away?

    e. Whose shirt did you put away?

  2. Formulate a question that might result in each of the following answers.

    a. She lost her credit card.

    b. She lost her credit card.

    c. She lost her credit card.

    d.   <u>She lost her credit card.</u>

C.   Authors do not normally know anything about the theory of intonation, yet they frequently indicate by putting a word in italics that their sentences should be read with a certain intonation pattern. The lines below are taken from well-known plays. How do you think the authors intended them to be spoken?

    1.   They don't want *me*.
    2.   *That's* a train trip for you.
    3.   I don't know *what* I'm going to do.
    4.   *Everybody* graduated this year.
    5.   We *don't* have to show you.

D.   The following exercise is to be done as you did Exercise H in Lesson 6: mark all sentence-stresses, then divide into thought groups by diagonal bars, finally mark the intonation of each group. In deciding what the intonation pattern should be, you may wish to consult the Inventory of Intonation Patterns in Section III of this lesson. In this exercise watch out for a few examples of function words with contrastive stress (see Lesson 4, end of Section II), of high pitches occurring on *unstressed* syllables (Section III, Footnote 2 in this lesson), and of upward slides.

    1.   This town has garages, stores, and a high school.
    2.   Is the school on the left-hand side of the street?
    3.   It's on the right-hand side, near the grocery store.
    4.   This is where your brother lives, isn't it?
    5.   He doesn't live here; my sister does.
    6.   Come on, Joe, it's time to head back to the big city.

E.   Transcribe the following series of connected sentences in phonetic symbols; then mark sentence-stresses, pauses, and intonation. After you have completed your analysis, your instructor will read the sentences, so that you can check your work with his or her pronunciation. It is not expected that each member of the class will mark the sentences in exactly the same way. Finally, practice reading your corrected transcription.

    1.   Yes, dear, I know what I'm to bring home: bread, sugar, and cheese.

    2.   It's written down here in my notebook, so I won't forget it.

3. Shall I get a pound of cheese, or half a pound?

4. What kind of cheese do you want?

5. As for me, I like any cheese.

6. But I'm sure you want Wisconsin cheese, don't you?

F. Practice reading or repeating these short conversations with another student, making them sound as natural as you can. Notice that in each conversation the intonation pattern gives to the single word *what* an entirely different meaning. After the class has practiced these conversations, pairs of students can perhaps make up similar conversations of their own. One way of doing this might be as follows. Student ''a'' makes a statement. Student ''b'' responds with the word *what,* using one of the three intonation patterns. Student ''a'' then needs to find a reply appropriate to the meaning given to *what* by the intonation with which it was pronounced.

1. a. ay džəst réd ən íntrıstıŋ bʊ́k.

    b. hwát?

    a. ay sέd ay džəst réd ən íntrıstıŋ bʊ́k.

2. a. ay džəst réd ən íntrıstıŋ bʊ́k.

    b. hwát?

    a. ''hɔ́ŋgər əv mέmərı,'' bay ə mέksıkən-əmέrıkən ɔ́θər.

3. a.   ay džə́st rɛ́d ən íntrıstıŋ bʊ́k.

    b.   hwát? duw yuw|ríəlı rı́yd|bʊ́ks?

G. We end the four lessons on rhythm and intonation with the special Diagnostic Passage below. It should help you find out how well you have learned the basic features of the intonation of English, and at the same time should enable your instructor to discover if there are features to which the class should devote further attention.

Your instructor may ask you to make an individual recording of the Diagnostic Passage for evaluation. If so, you will do a better job if you do not practice the material in advance. Read it once or twice so as to make sure you understand the meaning of the sentences. Then, while you are recording, forget about pronunciation and concentrate on the meaning of what you are saying.

In analyzing your recording, your instructor may find it helpful to use the numbers of the intonation patterns, as listed in the Inventory of Intonation Patterns in this lesson, to call your attention to any unnatural patterns that he or she may notice in the recording.

DIAGNOSTIC PASSAGE FOR ANALYZING INTONATION

1. Have you ever visited New York or Washington?   2. They are certainly interesting cities, aren't they?   3. Did you go there by plane or some other way?   4. In Washington you can see the White House, the Capitol, and the Supreme Court Building. 5. You don't like Washington better than New York, do you?   6. I must say, John, that New York is livelier.   7. Which one is livelier?   8. New York, because of its nightclubs and sporting events.   9. Did you pick out your hotel there, or did a travel agent do it?   10. Do you expect to fly East on your next vacation?   11. No, my friend; the West is the place for me.

H. Outside of class, read aloud several pages of simple conversational material (a modern play, if possible), concentrating your attention on the intonation of questions.

Classification of Consonants; the Endings -ed and -s

I. Voiced and Voiceless Sounds

An important way in which one speech sound may differ from another is in voicing or the lack of it. We say that a sound is *voiced* if *our vocal cords vibrate* as we pronounce it; a sound is *voiceless* if it is pronounced *without such vibration*. Press your thumb and forefinger lightly against the sides of your larynx (the central part of your throat, where sounds are made); then pronounce /z/ and /s/ alternately in imitation of your teacher. You should be able to feel the vibration of the vocal cords as you say /z/, and notice no vibration as you say /s/. In other words, /z/ is a voiced sound and /s/ is voiceless.

Now try pronouncing /š/ and /ž/. Which of the two sounds is voiced?

Another means of distinguishing the two types is to stop your ears as you pronounce the sounds aloud. In the case of voiced sounds, you should then be able to hear clearly the vibration of the vocal cords. You will hear nothing, except perhaps the rushing of the air, as you say the voiceless sounds.

THE VOICED CONSONANTS ARE

b	l	ŋ	v	z
d	m	r	w	ž
g	n	ð	y	dž

THE VOICELESS CONSONANTS ARE

f	k	s	t	hw
h	p	š	θ	tš

ALL VOWEL SOUNDS ARE VOICED

Do not try to memorize the above lists. It is much better to pronounce all the sounds to yourself, with fingers on throat or in ears, until you can tell instantly whether each one is voiced or voiceless.

You may have noticed that there are a number of pairs of consonants—such as /s/ and /z/, /š/ and /ž/—which seem to be very much alike except that one is voiced and the other voiceless. The consonants /b/ and /p/ form another such pair: both sounds are made in the same place (between the lips) and in the same manner (by closing the lips, then opening them to let the air escape explosively); but /b/ is pronounced with vibration of the vocal cords, and /p/ without vibration. We may say that /b/ is the voiced counterpart of /p/. How many more such pairs can you discover?

Pronounce a prolonged /v/. In the middle of the sound, without interrupting the flow of air through your mouth, make your vocal cords stop vibrating. What sound is left? What is the voiceless counterpart of /v/?

What happens if you stop the vibration of the vocal cords while pronouncing /m/? We may say, then, that /m/ has no voiceless counterpart in English. The same is true of /l/, /n/, /ŋ/, /r/, /w/, and /y/. On the other hand, there are no voiced sounds corresponding to /h/ and /hw/.

This leaves the following pairs:

/b, p/	/g, k/	/v, f/	/ž, š/
/d, t/	/ð, θ/	/z, s/	/dž, tš/

The first pair, /b/ and /p/, may be regarded as two parts of the same sound; so may /d/ and /t/, /g/ and /k/, and so on. In each case, the first symbol represents the voiced half of the sound, the second symbol the voiceless half.

Because there is so little difference between /z/ and /s/, for example, it is extremely easy to make the error of pronouncing one in place of the other. In some languages, such as German, there are very few final voiced consonants. When speaking English, a person whose first language is German will therefore have a strong tendency to unvoice final consonants whenever possible. If he sees the word *bed,* he may think he pronounces it as /bɛd̲/, but to an American it will probably seem that he says /bɛt̲/. We shall speak of this problem again in later lessons.

II. Stops and Continuants, Sibilants

It is sometimes useful to classify consonants in a second way, as *stops* or *continuants*. A continuant is a sound—like /m/—that may be prolonged as long as the speaker has breath to pronounce it. A stop must be pronounced instantaneously and cannot be held—like /t/.

Is /n/ a stop or a continuant? What is /s/? /k/? /b/? /f/?

Among the continuants, four consonants are known as sibilants, because of the hissing sound with which they are pronounced. These are /z/, /s/, /ž/, and /š/. Note that these four make up two voiced-voiceless pairs: /z, s/ and /ž, š/. The classification of sibilant is significant, as we shall see shortly, in determining the pronunciation of the ending -s, which is so frequently used in English.

III. Point of Articulation

We shall also need to be able to classify consonants in one other way, as to their *point of articulation,* or the place in the mouth where they are pronounced. Six of these points are shown in Figure 8.

If we begin at the front of the mouth and work back, we shall find first a group of three sounds made with *the lips:* /b/, /p/, and /m/. Try making them. (In technical language they are called *bilabials*.)

Between *the upper teeth and the lower lip,* we make two English sounds: /v/ and /f/. *(Labiodentals.)*

By establishing light contact between the tongue tip and the back of *the upper and lower front teeth,* we make /ð/ and /θ/. *(Interdentals.)*

By touching the tip of the tongue to *the tooth ridge* (just behind the upper teeth), we make four sounds: /d/, /t/, /n/, and /l/. In some other languages (French, Greek, Hebrew, Russian, and so on) these same sounds are pronounced with the tongue tip touching the upper teeth themselves. *(Alveolars.)*

By allowing the air to escape through *a narrow passage between the tongue and the hard palate,* we form /z/, /s/, /ž/, and /š/. *(Palato-alveolars.)*

Pressing the back of the tongue against *the soft palate,* we form /g/, /k/, and /ŋ/. *(Velars.)*

The points of articulation of the other consonants—/h/, /y/, /r/, /w/, /hw/, /tš/, and /dž/—will be described in sections of later lessons devoted specially to those sounds.

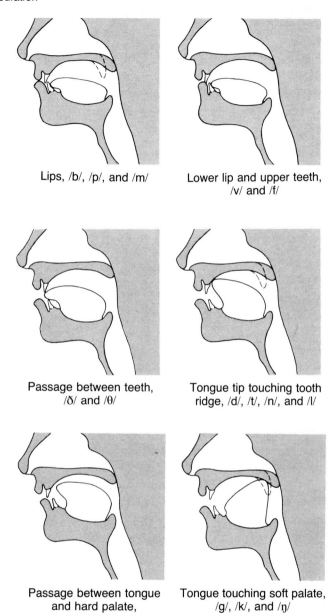

Lips, /b/, /p/, and /m/

Lower lip and upper teeth, /v/ and /f/

Passage between teeth, /ð/ and /θ/

Tongue tip touching tooth ridge, /d/, /t/, /n/, and /l/

Passage between tongue and hard palate, /z/, /s/, /ž/, and /š/

Tongue touching soft palate, /g/, /k/, and /ŋ/

Figure 8. Points of articulation of consonants

IV. Pronunciation of -ed

The ending -ed, added to regular English verbs to form the past tense and past participle, has three different pronunciations: /t/ as in *wished* /wišt/, /d/ as in *failed* /feəld/, and /ɪd/ as in *needed* /níydɪd/.

The sound the ending will have in any given word is determined by a very simple phonetic principle: when two consonants are pronounced together, as /r/ and /d/ in *cared* /kɛərd/, *it is easier to voice both consonants or leave both voiceless than it is to voice one and leave the other voiceless.* Therefore, the ending -ed is pronounced /d/ after a voiced sound, and /t/ after a voiceless sound. You will remember that /d/ and /t/ are the two halves of a voiced-voiceless pair; in phonetic terms, this pair /d, t/ is the sign of the past tense and past participle.

How would the ending -ed be pronounced after a vowel? Remember that all vowels are voiced.

Suppose one wishes to add the sound /d/ or /t/ to a word that already ends in one of those two sounds, in other words, to add /d, t/ to /d, t/. It is almost impossible to do so without inserting some sort of a vowel sound between the two consonants. Because vowels are voiced, the insertion of a vowel here means that the final d will be pronounced as /d/ rather than /t/. In other words, after t or d the ending -ed is pronounced as a separate syllable, /ɪd/.

THE ENDING -ED IS PRONOUNCED

1. /d/ AFTER ALL VOICED CONSONANTS EXCEPT /d/, AND AFTER ALL VOWEL SOUNDS:
   planned /plænd/, *judged* /džədžd/, *played* /pleyd/
2. /t/ AFTER ALL VOICELESS CONSONANTS EXCEPT /t/:
   rocked /rakt/, *kissed* /kɪst/, *ripped* /rɪpt/
3. AS A SEPARATE SYLLABLE, /ɪd/ (or /ʊd/), AFTER /d, t/:
   protected /prətéktɪd/, *intended* /ɪnténdɪd/

The most common errors that result from failure to observe the above principles are

1. The pronunciation of -ed as a separate syllable after consonants other than /d/ or /t/:

   robbed as /rábɪd/, instead of /rabd/
   thanked as /θǽŋkɪd/, instead of /θæŋkt/

2. The pronunciation of -ed as /t/ after /l/, /r/, or a vowel:

dared as /dɛərt/, instead of /dɛərd/
killed as /kɪəlt/, instead of /kɪəld/

3. Apparent omission of the entire ending:
    answered as /ǽnsər/, instead of /ǽnsərd/

There are only two types of exception to these rules. One is a group of *adjectives* that end in -ed and therefore look like verbs: *ragged, wretched,* and so on. Contrary to the principles outlined above, the ending of these words is pronounced as a separate syllable, /ɪd/: /rǽgɪd/, /rɛ́tšɪd/.

A *naked* /néykɪd/ child   A *two-legged* /túwlɛ̀gɪd/ animal

A *ragged* /rǽgɪd/ coat   A *wicked* /wíkɪd/ idea

The *rugged* /rə́gɪd/ rock   A *wretched* /rɛ́tšɪd/ day

An *aged* /éydžɪd/ minister (Compare: He has *aged* /eydžd/ a lot.)

The *blessed* /blɛ́sɪd/ Virgin (Compare: The Pope *blessed* /blɛst/ the crowd.)

A *dogged* /dɔ́gɪd/ determination (Compare: The little boy *dogged* /dɔgd/ his brother's steps.)

The other type of exception is found in the case of *adverbs* such as *deservedly, supposedly,* and *markedly.* These can be analyzed as:

verb ending in a consonant sound + -ed- + -ly.

In *all* such adverbs the -ed- is pronounced as a separate syllable, /ɪd/.

The patient has improved *markedly* /márkɪdlɪ/.
We made the decision *advisedly* /ədváyzɪdlɪ/.
I will support you *unreservedly* /ənrɪzə́rvɪdlɪ/.

V. Pronunciation of -s

In English, to make a noun plural or possessive, or to put a verb in the third person singular form of the present tense, we add /z, s/ to the end of the word. This ending is spelled in several different ways: -s (two hours, he says), -es (several churches, she kisses), -'s (a moment's time), or -s' (the grocers' prices). However it may be spelled, the ending is pronounced, according to strict phonetic principles, in one of three ways: /z/, /s/, or /ɪz/. The principles

are the same as those which determine the pronunciation of -ed. Can you formulate them for yourself?

THE ENDING -s (-ES, -'s, OR -s') IS PRONOUNCED

1. /z/ AFTER ALL VOICED CONSONANTS EXCEPT /z/ AND /ž/, AND AFTER ALL
   VOWEL SOUNDS:
   games /geymz/, *calls* /kɔlz/, *laws* /lɔz/
2. /s/ AFTER ALL VOICELESS CONSONANTS EXCEPT /s/ AND /š/:
   grants /grænts/, *wraps* /ræps/, *Jack's* /džæks/
3. AS A SEPARATE SYLLABLE, /ɪz/ (or /ʊz/), AFTER A SIBILANT (/z, s/ or
   /ž, š/):
   dishes /díšɪz/, *George's* /džɔ́rdžɪz/, *foxes* /fáksɪz/

   The above rules apply only when *s* is added to a word as an ending. If the
final *s* is a part of the basic word itself, as in *as, yes,* and so on, there is no
logical way to decide whether it will be pronounced /s/ or /z/. We must familiarize ourselves with the pronunciation of each word individually. Here is a list
of the most common such words.

/z/		/s/	
as	/æz/	*this*	/ðɪs/
has	/hæz/	*thus*	/ðəs/
his	/hɪz/	*us*	/əs/
is	/ɪz/	*yes*	/yɛs/
was	/waz/ or /wəz/		

VI. Exercises

A. Are the following sounds voiced or voiceless? Divide them into two lists, and
compare your results with the lists in Section I of this lesson.

1.	f	8.	w	15.	k	22.	tš
2.	l	9.	š	16.	iy	23.	p
3.	t	10.	r	17.	ž	24.	ð
4.	b	11.	dž	18.	a	25.	m
5.	s	12.	θ	19.	d	26.	h
6.	n	13.	v	20.	y	27.	ey
7.	æ	14.	ŋ	21.	z	28.	g

B. 1. What is the voiced counterpart of: š, f, k, tš, θ, p, s, t?
    2. How would a person with a German accent probably pronounce the under-
        scored letters in this sentence (see Section I): "Hi<u>s</u> language show<u>s</u> that he i<u>s</u>
        gla<u>d</u> to ha<u>v</u>e the jo<u>b</u> and the bi<u>g</u> salary that goe<u>s</u> with it"?

C. Classify the following sounds as *voiced* or *voiceless, stop* or *continuant,* and give
    the *point of articulation* of each. For example, /d/ is a voiced stop, made with the
    tongue tip touching the tooth ridge.

1.	v	4.	b	7.	n	10.	š	13.	ð
2.	p	5.	θ	8.	m	11.	d	14.	ž
3.	f	6.	s	9.	k	12.	z	15.	g

D. Suppose a student from Latin America pronounces the word *very* incorrectly, /b<u>é</u>rɪ/
    instead of /v<u>é</u>rɪ/. Keeping in mind what you know about points of articulation,
    what would you tell him to do with his lips, teeth, and so on, in order to change
    /b/ to /v/? How would you help a French student to say *think* as /θɪŋk/ instead of
    /sɪŋk/? *those* as /ðowz/ instead of /zowz/? A Chinese student to pronounce *man* as
    /mæn/ instead of /mæŋ/? A German student to pronounce *that* as /ðæt/ instead of
    /dæt/? A Scandinavian to say *thanks* as /θæŋks/ instead of /tæŋks/?

E. Pronounce each of these words, and write the phonetic symbol that represents the
    sound you gave to the ending. Then, in each case, explain why the ending is
    pronounced as it is.

1.	added	7.	longed	13.	believed	19.	kicked
2.	wished	8.	armed	14.	answered	20.	boxed
3.	caused	9.	aired	15.	showed	21.	lasted
4.	dropped	10.	asked	16.	lighted	22.	reached
5.	crossed	11.	changed	17.	laughed	23.	turned
6.	robbed	12.	minded	18.	followed	24.	watched

25.	belongs	31.	bees	37.	ages	43.	acts
26.	bottoms	32.	bags	38.	blesses	44.	branches
27.	breaks	33.	attends	39.	articles	45.	caps
28.	bridges	34.	arrives	40.	chances	46.	confuses
29.	appears	35.	fixes	41.	cars	47.	armies
30.	allows	36.	chiefs	42.	America's	48.	animals

F. 1. Read these words aloud. In which of them is -<u>ed</u> pronounced as a separate
        syllable? You may want to look some of them up in your dictionary.

a.	naked	d.	rugged	g.	wicked	j.	ragged
b.	baked	e.	stretched	h.	picked	k.	flagged
c.	hugged	f.	wretched	i.	tricked	l.	tagged

2. Can you make up an appropriate sentence using each of these adverbs?

a.	deservedly	c.	supposedly	e.	resignedly	g.	allegedly
b.	markedly	d.	assuredly	f.	advisedly	h.	unreservedly

G. On page 94 of this lesson, you will find listed the three most common types of error made in pronouncing -ed. The errors made in pronouncing the ending -s, -es, and so on, are fundamentally the same as items 2 and 3 on that list. Can you restate those two items in terms of -s, and give examples?

H. Practice reading the following sentences at normal conversational speed. Be sure to pronounce the -s and -ed endings accurately.

While Ruth was washing the dishes one night, she cut her finger on a knife.

She washed and bandaged it while her sister finished the dishes.

"I have two assignments to hand in tomorrow. I won't be able to type them very well now," Ruth complained.

Her sister stated emphatically, "Don't expect me to type your papers for you. I've got things of my own to do tonight."

"I'll give you the earrings I bought yesterday if you'll do it."

Ruth's sister laughed, but she refused to say anything.

"I'll make your bed for the rest of the week, too," promised Ruth.

Her sister smiled.

"You'll do it?" asked Ruth.

"Yes. You talked me into it," answered her sister, "but maybe I agreed too soon.

Who knows what you might have promised if I had waited a little longer."

I. Where would the high or extra-high note or notes of the intonation pattern fall in the sentences below? In each of them the special attention of the hearer should be focused on one or two ideas, because of a comparison, contrast, contradiction, or a desire to make a question or an answer specific. (See Lesson 7, Section I.) The sentences make up a connected passage, and should be considered in the light of what precedes and follows. Underline the syllables on which attention is to be focused, and then read the exercise with the proper intonation.

1. Her composition is better than mine.

2. Isn't his still better?

3. No, I have a higher grade than he has.

4. What grade did Bob get?

5. He got an "A."

6. No, he didn't get an "A."

7. He got "C" on his paper.

8. On the one he handed in this afternoon, or the one he handed in yesterday afternoon?

9. The one he handed in this afternoon.

10. What was the subject of the paper?

J. Practice reading or repeating these short conversations with another student, making them sound as natural as you can.

1. a. hwát ə wə́ndərfʊl táym tə biy əwéyk!

   ay ləv ðə kúwl əv ðə mɔ́rnɪŋ.

   b. əspéšəlɪ wɛn nówbadɪ ɛ́əls ɪz əráwnd.

   a. ɪts sów kwáyət;/ ðɛərz sə́tš ə dɪláytfʊl brɪ́yz.

2.   a.   <u>ɪts ə wíkɪd séym híy wəz ɪléktɪd.</u>

     b.   yɛ́s,/ ðɪ əðər kǽndɪdɪt wəz mə́tš bétər.

     a.   <u>ay kǽnt mǽdžɪn / way sów mɛ́nɪ píypəl vówtɪd fər hɪ́m.</u>

3.   a.   dównt wɛ́ər ðǽt ówld rǽgɪd šə́rt tə <u>klǽs.</u>

     b.   hwáy?/ <u>duw yuw θíŋk ɛ́nɪbadɪ kɛ́ərz wat ay wɛ́ər?</u>

     a.   ðə klǽs džə́st də́zənt siým tə biy ən əprówprɪɪt pléys fər ðǽt šə́rt.

K.   Read aloud several pages from a book you are studying, concentrating your attention on the pronunciation of the -<u>s</u> and -<u>ed</u> endings.

LESSON 9

Initial and Final Consonants

I. Aspiration at the Beginning of Words

In Lesson 8 we considered the eight pairs of consonants: /b, p/, /d, t/, /g, k/, /ð, θ/, /v, f/, /z, s/, /ž, š/, and /dž, tš/. It was pointed out that, in each of these pairs, the first sound is similar to the second, except that the first is voiced and the second voiceless. This information is accurate as far as it goes, but it does not go far enough. It is true that the difference which is most often mentioned between two words such as *big* /b<u>ı</u>g/ and *pig* /p<u>ı</u>g/ is that the initial consonant of *big* is pronounced with vibration of the vocal cords, and the initial consonant of *pig* without vibration. But that is not the only difference.

Both /b/ and /p/ are stops, which means that they cannot be prolonged for more than a very short time. They are normally pronounced so rapidly that it would be difficult for the hearer to tell whether the vocal cords have vibrated or not. This may be one of the reasons why the English language has developed an additional type of difference between initial voiced and voiceless consonants: *aspiration or the lack of it*. For our practical purposes, we shall define aspiration as *the pronunciation of a consonant with an <u>h</u>-sound or, putting it another way, with the sound of escaping air*. The /p/ of *pig*, then, is pronounced with the sound of escaping air. When we say the /b/ of *big*, no such sound of air is heard.

When they come at the beginning of a word, all other voiceless consonants are aspirated, as /p/ is. This principle may be stated as follows:

ALL VOICELESS CONSONANTS ARE ASPIRATED AT THE BEGINNING OF A WORD.[1]

It may help you to remember the principle if you think of it this way: at the beginning of a word, a consonant is pronounced either with the sound of escaping air (aspirated) or with vibration of the vocal cords (voiced).

In many other languages, initial voiceless consonants are not regularly aspirated, and people who learned one of these languages first find it hard to aspirate properly in English. For example, a Spanish-speaking student may intend to say "I don't have the time," but be heard as saying "I don't have the dime." Or a German student may intend to say "I am so tired," but seem to mispronounce the so as /zow/. Such mispronunciations may, then, lead to misunderstandings, or at least are likely to be noticed as elements of "foreign accent." Both students would improve their pronunciation by forming the initial consonant of the word in question with more sound of escaping air and without vibration of the vocal cords.

When we are writing phonetic symbols and think that it is important to show that a consonant is aspirated, we can write a small *h* above the line and after the symbol. Note the difference in aspiration between *tear* /t^{h}ɛər/ and *dare* /dɛər/, *thigh* /θ^{h}ay/ and *thy* /ðay/, *choke* /tš^{h}owk/ and *joke* /džowk/. We use the small *h* in the phonetic transcriptions in this manual, however, only when attention is being directed specifically to aspiration.

Medial consonants are those that occur within a word, after the first vowel sound and before the last. They are aspirated much like initial consonants *when the medial consonants stand at the beginning of a stressed syllable: apartment*

---

[1]The assumptions of the current group of generative phonologists give them good theoretical reasons for defining aspiration differently, as "a period of voicelessness after the release of an articulation" (Peter Ladefoged, *A Course in Phonetics,* 1975, p. 277). It is not helpful, however, to advise students of English as a Second Language to pronounce an initial or final voiceless consonant with a "period of voicelessness" after it. Some phoneticians speak of aspiration only in relation to stops, and describe the sound of escaping air that also clearly accompanies the pronunciation of voiceless continuants as the result of a "fortis" or "forceful" feature of such sounds. We have found, however, that it is not helpful, either, to advise ESL students to pronounce, for example, the final /s/ in *guess* /gɛs/ "with great force"; indeed, the practical results of such advice can be startling. These problems have led the authors of this manual to our broad definition of aspiration and to our use of the word in reference to all consonants, continuants, as well as stops. Like many other decisions made in the preparation of this textbook, which is aimed at improving the pronunciation of nonnative speakers of English, the decisions regarding the treatment of aspiration were based on the need for practicality in giving advice and for simplicity in stating generalizations.

/ə-pʰárt-mənt/, *contain* /kən-tʰéyn/, *refer* /rɪ-fʰə́r/. Elsewhere they have much less aspiration: *paper* /pʰéy-pər/, *taking* /tʰéy-kɪŋ/, *ceasing* /sʰíy-sɪŋ/.

A special case among medial consonants is a variant of /t/—one that occurs between voiced sounds, usually vowels, and that does *not* stand at the beginning of a stressed syllable. Examples are the *t*'s in *átom* and *húrting* (but not the *t* in *áfter,* which stands between a voiceless and a voiced sound; nor that of *retéll,* which stands at the beginning of a stressed syllable). This special *t* is made by a quick flap of the tongue against the tooth ridge with vocal cords vibrating. Many educated Americans seem to make no difference of any sort between this type of /t/ and a /d/. *Atom* and *Adam* sound alike in their speech, and the hearer must rely on the meaning of the sentence in order to know which is intended. It seems true, however, that many speakers do make a slight difference between the two sounds. Perhaps the best advice to an ESL student is to pronounce this special medial /t/ "somewhat like a /d/," without aspiration and very rapidly: *butter* /bə́tər)/, *pretty* /prítɪ/, *forty* /fɔ́rtɪ/.

II. The Lengthening of Vowels before Final Consonants

Even more often than at the beginning of words, voiced consonants are confused with their voiceless counterparts at the end of words: *I live* (/lɪf/ instead of /lɪv/) *in California,* or *Who was* (/was/ instead of /waz/) *it?* In the speech of students of English, this type of error is probably more frequent than any other type, with the exception of the failure to give unstressed vowels their normal sound of /ə/, /ɪ/, or /ʊ/.

In doing the exercises of Lesson 8, you may have had great difficulty making a word like *years* sound like /yɪərz/ instead of /yɪərs/, even though you knew the final sound should be voiced, and tried hard to make your vocal cords vibrate as you pronounced it. The fact is that voicing of the lack of it is not the only difference between the /s/ and /z/ sounds at the end of a word. Just as in the case of the initial consonants, we do not rely on vibration of the vocal cords alone to distinguish a final voiced consonant from its voiceless counterpart.

There are at least three differences between the sound of *bus* /bəs/ and that of *buzz* /bəz/. The first is, of course, that /z/ is voiced, /s/ is voiceless. The second is that the vowel before /z/ is lengthened; it usually takes almost twice as long to say *buzz* as to say *bus*. The third difference—the aspiration of the final /s/—will be discussed in Section III of this lesson.

When we feel it is important to show that a vowel is lengthened, we place a colon (:) after it: *buzz* /bə:z/.

The second difference mentioned above between final /s/ and /z/ serves to

distinguish all voiced consonants at the end of words from their voiceless counterparts; *bed* /bɛ:d/ takes longer to say than *bet* /bɛt/, *rib* /rɪ:b/ longer than *rip*
/rɪp/, *bag* /bæ:g/ longer than *back* /bæk/.

BEFORE A FINAL VOICED CONSONANT, STRESSED VOWELS ARE LENGTHENED.

If you will deliberately try to lengthen the vowel, it may be easier for you
to make *years* sound like /yɪərz/ rather than /yɪərs/. This lengthening will also
increase the tendency toward diphthongization that is noticeable in many
stressed English vowels.

III. Aspiration at the End of Words

The third difference between final /s/ and /z/, as in *bus* and *buzz* (or in /yɪərs/
and /yɪərz/) is that the /s/ is pronounced with a great deal of aspiration, the /z/
with very little. As the /s/ is being aspirated, it is also often lengthened. In
other words, at the end of /bəs/ a listener can hear very clearly the sound of
air escaping through the teeth; at the end of /bəz/ there is much less sound of
escaping air.

To sum up: if you find it hard to make a word like *years* sound like /yɪərz/
instead of /yɪərs/, the difficulty with /z/ may be overcome by trying consciously to

1. Make your vocal cords vibrate to the end of the word;
2. Lengthen the final vowel sound;
3. Allow very little sound of escaping air.

On the other hand, to change a word like /bəz/ to /bəs/ would require the
opposite procedures of

1. Making sure your vocal cords do *not* vibrate for the final consonant;
2. *Shortening* the final vowel sound;
3. Producing the final consonant with *more* sound of escaping air and thus
    lengthening it.

Note that in /bəz/ it is the *vowel* that is lengthened; in /bəs/ it is the final
consonant.

The aspiration that helps distinguish /s/ at the end of a word, however, is
not typical of all other voiceless consonants in the same position. Usually it is
heard only with final voiceless *continuants* (/f/, /s/, /š/, /θ/), and with /tš/, but

not with final voiceless *stops* (/k/, /p/, /t/). Note the difference between the two sets of examples below:

safe /seyf̱ʰ/,	*save* /sey:v̱/
place /pleys̱ʰ/,	*plays* /pley:ẕ/
teeth /tiyθʰ/,	*teethe* /tiy:ð̱/
rich /rɪṯš̱ʰ/,	*ridge* /rɪ:ḏẕ̌/

but

lack /læḵ/,	*lag* /læ:g̱/
rip /rɪp̱/,	*rib* /rɪ:ḇ/
debt /dɛṯ/,	*dead* /dɛ:ḏ/

AT THE END OF A WORD VOICELESS CONTINUANTS ARE ASPIRATED BUT VOICELESS STOPS ARE NOT.

Many ESL students do, however, try to aspirate final consonants other than voiceless continuants. An Italian may pronounce *I don't think so* as /ay downtʰ θɪŋkʰ sow/. The little puffs of air after /t/ and /k/ sound like extra syllables. In extreme cases, the student may even add an /ə/ at the end of *don't* and *think* in order to pronounce the /t/ and /k/ more clearly: /ay downtʰə θɪŋkʰə sow/. This, of course, completely destroys the natural rhythm of the sentence.

Normally, two movements are necessary for the production of a stop such as /t/, /k/, or /p/. There is first a *closure,* or stopping of the outflow of air: for /t/, the tongue tip presses against the tooth ridge; for /k/, the back of the tongue rises and presses against the soft palate; for /p/, the lips are closed. As soon as a little pressure has been built up, comes the second movement, the *release* of the air: for /t/ the tongue tip leaves the tooth ridge; for /k/, the back of the tongue falls away from the soft palate; for /p/, the lips open. It is during this second movement that aspiration, the sound of escaping air, may be heard to a greater or lesser degree.

In conversational American English, there is such a powerful tendency to avoid the strong aspiration of final consonants (other than voiceless continuants) that at the end of a word we regularly pronounce only the first half of a stop. *We make the closure, but do not pronounce the release.* If we say "A ship!" the sound ends when our lips come together for the /p/, and the lips may not open again for some time. If we say "You're right," we similarly avoid any "finishing sound" after /t/. It may seem to you that this would mean that the final /p/ or /t/ would simply not be heard. A native speaker of English, however, learns by long practice to distinguish between final stops by the sound of their closure alone.

IV. Exercises

A.   Summarize this lesson by writing *yes* or *no* after the questions in the following
     table, and by supplying additional examples.

Table of Differences between Voiceless and Voiced Consonants in Various Positions

Between an initial voiceless consonant (like the /k/ in <u>k</u>ʊd/) and its voiced counterpart (/<u>g</u>ʊd/):

	/<u>k</u>ʊd/	/<u>g</u>ʊd/
1. Is it voiced?	_____	_____
2. Is it aspirated?	_____	_____
Additional examples:	/_____/ and /_____/	
	/_____/ and /_____/	

Between a final voiceless stop and its voiced counterpart:

	/sæ<u>t</u>/	/sæ<u>d</u>/
1. Is it voiced?	_____	_____
2. Preceding vowel lengthened?	_____	_____
Additional examples:	/_____/ and /_____/	
	/_____/ and /_____/	

Between a final voiceless continuant and its voiced counterpart:

	/rey<u>s</u>/	/rey<u>z</u>/
1. Is it voiced?	_____	_____
2. Is it aspirated?	_____	_____
3. Preceding vowel lengthened?	_____	_____

Additional examples: /_____/ and /_____/

/_____/ and /_____/

B. What advice (regarding aspiration, vowel length, and voicing) would you give a fellow student who made the following errors in pronunciation?

1. *had* as /hæ<u>t</u>/ instead of /hæ<u>d</u>/
2. *than* as /<u>θ</u>æn/ instead of /<u>ð</u>æn/
3. *five* as /fay<u>f</u>/ instead of /fay<u>v</u>/
4. *dog* as /dɔ<u>k</u>/ instead of /dɔg/
5. *bus* as /bə<u>z</u>/ instead of /bə<u>s</u>/
6. *sing* as /<u>z</u>ɪŋ/ instead of /<u>s</u>ɪŋ/
7. *languages* as /lǽŋgwɪt<u>š</u>ɪz/ instead of /lǽŋgwɪd<u>ž</u>ɪz/

C. The following pairs of words differ in that the first word of each pair contains a voiceless consonant, and the second contains the voiced counterpart of that consonant. Transcribe the words in phonetic symbols. Then, using the signs [ʰ] and [:], mark the additional difference or differences in each case. Finally, pronounce each series of words horizontally and vertically, taking great care to aspirate consonants and lengthen vowels as marked. Repeat this drill several times. It is best to use the same intonation for all words.

1. Initial (and Medial) Consonants

a.	chest	/		/	jest	/		/
b.	thigh	/		/	thy	/		/

    c.   fine   /   /   vine   /   /

    d.   sink   /   /   zinc   /   /

    e.   tie   /   /   die   /   /

    f.   pour   /   /   bore   /   /

    g.   infest   /   /   invest   /   /

    h.   stacker   /   /   stagger   /   /

2.   Final Stops

    a.   rack   /   /   rag   /   /

    b.   rip   /   /   rib   /   /

    c.   hit   /   /   hid   /   /

    d.   peck   /   /   peg   /   /

    e.   heart   /   /   hard   /   /

    f.   ape   /   /   Abe   /   /

3.   Final Continuants

    a.   price   /   /   prize   /   /

    b.   proof   /   /   prove   /   /

    c.   teeth   /   /   teethe   /   /

    d.   cease   /   /   sees   /   /

    e.   strife   /   /   strive   /   /

    f.   hiss   /   /   his   /   /

D.   Read each of the sentences below twice, using word (a) in the first reading and word (b) in the second. Then read again and use either (a) or (b), while another member of the class tries to identify in each case the word you pronounced.

    1. (a. back) (b. pack) Now I must go _____.

    2. (a. bear) (b. pear) You can't eat a whole _____.

    3. (a. mob) (b. mop) The leader kept the _____well in hand.

    4. (a. fast) (b. vast) The patient has shown _____improvement.

    5. (a. feel) (b. veal) He spoken on "The _____of the Future."

6. (a. few) (b. view)   We have a _____ on the hilltop.

7. (a. safe) (b. save)   Nothing will make a careless man _____.

8. (a. cold) (b. gold)   Are you getting _____?

9. (a. cave) (b. gave)   Under great pressure they _____ in.

10. (a. back) (b. bag)   Put your coat on your _____.

11. (a. dime) (b. time)   There's no _____ to lose.

12. (a. bed) (b. bet)   When he moved, he lost his _____.

13. (a. dead) (b. debt)   We must never forget the _____.

14. (a. feed) (b. feet)   He was off his _____.

15. (a. grade) (b. great)   The child was put in a _____ school.

16. (a. led) (b. let)   A traitor _____ the enemy in.

17. (a. seal) (b. zeal)   Her _____ is well known.

18. (a. ice) (b. eyes)   You need good _____ to skate well.

19. (a. loss) (b. laws)   You can't avoid the _____ of the land.

20. (a. peace) (b. peas)   A meal without _____ is disappointing.

21. (a. place) (b. plays)   Put yourself in her _____.

22. (a. race) (b. raise)   I'll _____ you to the top.

23. (a. bridges) (b. breeches)   Don't burn your _____.

24. (a. ridge) (b. rich)   It was grown on _____ land.

25. (a. ether) (b. either)   The doctor wouldn't give her _____.

Your teacher may wish to use the above drill as a test of your ability to distinguish between voiced and voiceless sounds when you hear them. If so, take a piece of paper and number the lines from 1 through 25. The teacher will read each sentence, inserting one of the two test words. You should decide which one he or she used and write (a) or (b) on your paper opposite the number of the sentence.

E. There follows an exercise that will give you a chance to work on the special type of medial /t/ that is pronounced "somewhat like a /d/." (See end of Section I of this lesson.) Remember that, in English, the tongue tip touches the tooth ridge rather than the upper teeth to form /t/ or /d/.

1. Read the sentences, paying particular attention to the underlined parts of the words.

a. What's hurting you?

b. She's getting the potatoes.

c. It's a pity you waited so long.

d. There's not enough water to matter.

e. Betty hoped to stay later at the party.

f. They have better butter at Ralph's.

2. Several members of the class should answer these questions by complete statements.

a. At what age is a person at his or her best? (forty, thirty)?

b. What can be described as "pretty"?

c. What do you think of the atom bomb?

d. What kinds of foods (books, clothes, movies, music) do you like better than others?

F. Using the words listed below, describe some of the things that might happen in preparing for a picnic or that might take place on a picnic. This exercise is intended to give you practice in using aspirated consonants.

picnic	tennis	pear	basket	cold drinks
take	croquet	peach	people	table cloth
cook	tea	apple	towel	potato salad
plates	coffee	barbecue	park	potato chips

napkins	milk	pie	plan	clean
paper	cups	car	play	ice cream

G. Let the members of the class and the teacher ask one another questions about their amusements, living arrangements, and so on. Each question and answer should include the name (or a substitute for the name) of the person addressed: "Have you seen a good movie lately, Natalie?" "Oh yes, Mr. Liebmann, I saw a wonderful one last night." The instructor should listen carefully to see that proper intonation is used for direct address. (See Lesson 6, end of Section II.)

H. The passage that follows contains a great many final voiced consonants. A number of useful activities can be based on it.

1. Make sure you can read the passage and then draw a circle around each of the final voiced consonants.
2. Your instructor will call on students to read each sentence naturally. If the instructor thinks that any of the final voiced consonants sound too much like their voiceless counterparts, see if you can improve their pronunciation by more vibration of the vocal cords, less aspiration, and a longer preceding vowel.
3. Answer the questions that follow the exercise. It is helpful to answer them in complete sentences.
4. Your instructor may want to ask additional questions about James and Three Rivers so as to make sure that you can pronounce final voiced consonants even when your attention is focused on the meaning of what you are saying.

1. ðə pléys ɪz kóld θríy rívərz, / bɪkóz ɪts lówkeytɪd hwɛɛr ə léyk ɪz fórmd

bay θríy stríɣmz.   2. ðɛər ər hándrədz əv kátɪdžɪz an ðə šórz əv ðə léyk.   3. ðə

how téəl sərvz vɛ́rɪ gúd fúɣd.   4. džéymz əz spɛ́nt fáɪv sámərz ðɛ́ər / ən nówz

ɛ́vrɪbadɪ.   5. dʊrɪŋ ðə déy hiy swímz ən slíɣps; / æt náyt iy dǽnsɪz ən hǽz fán.

6. ðɪs yíər hiy əz déytɪd twɛ́əlv dífrənt gə́rlz.   7. hiy dráyvz ɪz ówld yúwzd

kár / ən hǽndəlz ɪt vɛ́rɪ wɛ́əl.   8. ɪf ɪz frɛ́ndz ər bórd, / híy ólwɪz hǽz gúd aydíəz fər θíŋz tə │dúw.   9. hiy tráyz tə fərgét │ ɪz │ stə́dɪz, / ən nɛ́vər

│ówpənz ə │búk.   10. hiy fíəlz ðət vey│kéy│šənz šʊd biy │sɛ́vrəl yíərz lɔ́ŋ.

   a.   Why is the place called Three Rivers?

   b.   What is to be seen at Three Rivers?

   c.   Is the hotel a good place to eat?

   d.   Who spends his summers at Three Rivers?

   e.   Why does he know everybody who goes there?

   f.   How does James spend his time?

   g.   What things does he like best to do?

   h.   Does he have a steady girl friend?

   i.   Is he ever bored?

   j.   What transportation does he use?

   k.   What does he think about?

   l.   Is he ready to go back to his studies?

LESSON 10

L, R, and Syllabic Consonants

I. The Formation of /l/ and /r/

/l/ and /r/ are unusual sounds in a number of ways: in how they are formed, in their effect on preceding vowel sounds, in their relationship to spelling, and so on. In Lesson 18, which deals with spelling, we shall see that letters representing vowels are very often pronounced differently before *l* and *r* than they are before other consonants: compare *alter* /ɔltər/ and *after* /æftər/, *car* /kar/ and *cab* /kæb/. As is well known, native speakers of many Asian languages frequently confuse /l/ and /r/ in their pronunciation of English: *fried rice* can sound like /flayd lays/. During the historical development of a number of languages, including English, /l/ and /r/ have sometimes replaced each other. When the French word *colonel* entered English, it came to be pronounced /kərnəl/, but it is still spelled *colonel;* in Spanish it is spelled and pronounced *coronel*.

The basic reason for these peculiarities of /l/ and /r/ may be that they are formed with more movement of the speech organs than are most other consonant sounds. The word we shall use in this manual as a cover term for both /l/ and /r/ is *liquid*. In describing a liquid, dictionaries use some such definition as "a vowel-like consonant, such as /l/ and /r/, produced without friction." Most other consonants are made with the speech organs in a more or less fixed position, as we saw in Lesson 8. But the two liquids—along with the glides

/w/ and /y/—are characterized by extensive movements of the speech organs from one position toward or to another. Thus the glide /w/, as an element in diphthongs such as /ow/ and /aw/, begins in the position of /o/ or /a/ and then moves toward the back of the mouth as the back of the tongue is raised and the lips are rounded. In /ɔy/ or /ay/, the glide /y/ begins in the position of /ɔ/ or /a/ and then moves toward the front of the mouth. (See Lesson 2, Section II.)

Speakers of English normally produce /l/ as the tip of the tongue moves to or away from the *tooth ridge,* just behind the upper teeth. Note that in many other languages /l/ is made with the tongue tip approaching the upper teeth themselves. In English, as the tongue tip reaches for and then touches the tooth ridge, the sides of the tongue are lowered so that the air goes out *laterally* over the sides.[1] In order to learn to distinguish /l/ from /r/, it is important to remember that for the usual /l/ *the sides of the tongue do not touch anything.* /l/ is a voiced sound, which means that the vocal cords vibrate continuously as it is produced. The movement that characterizes /l/ is more extensive when the /l/ *follows* a vowel sound, as in *call* /kɔl̲/, than when it *precedes* a vowel sound, as in *lie* /l̲ay/. For an initial /l/ as in *lie,* the sound begins with the tongue tip already touching the tooth ridge and the middle of the tongue relatively high in the mouth. This latter type of /l/ is sometimes called a "clear" /l/ as contrasted with the "dark" /l/ in *call.*

Pronounce *coal* /kowl/, *fool* /fuwl/, *pull* /pʊl/, *like* /layk/, *long* /lɔŋ/, being certain that your speech organs take the proper positions.

The /r/-sound is somewhat more complex. In certain parts of England, and the East and South of the United States, the sound hardly seems to be pronounced at all except at the beginning of a word or syllable. A large majority of English-speaking people, however, pronounce it with both sides of the tongue touching the back part of the tooth ridge and the back teeth. *It is important to note that the tongue tip does not touch anything;* the middle of the tongue, including the tip, is lower than the sides, and the air goes out through the channel formed between the middle of the tongue and the roof of the mouth. The lips are slightly open. The liquid, the characteristic /r/-sound, is produced as the speech organs move to this position from a vowel, as in *are* /ar/, or away from this position to a vowel, as in *red* /rɛd/. In whatever direction the movement may end, *it always begins by a motion toward the back of the mouth.* More than any other factor, it is this retroflex (toward the back) motion that gives the American-English /r/ its typical sound. The tongue tip rises a little and is curved backward, while the sides of the tongue slide along the back part of the tooth ridge as along two rails.

---

[1]It has been shown that some speakers make a unilateral /l/, with the air going out over only one side of the tongue.

Pronounce the vowel /a/. As you do so, curve the tip of your tongue up and slide the sides of the tongue backward along the tooth ridge, and you should have no difficulty in producing a perfect American /r/.

When /r/ follows a vowel, as in *or* /ɔr/, the entire movement is in a backward direction. When /r/ precedes a vowel, *right* /rayt/, the backward movement is very brief, and is almost immediately reversed as the tongue moves forward again to the vowel position. In addition, the lips may be rounded.

Many speakers of German, French, and certain other languages use a "uvular" r̲, made by vibrating the uvula (the little flap of flesh that hangs down at the entrance of the throat) or by the friction produced as the air passes between the uvula and the raised back portion of the tongue. This type of r̲ is also a liquid characterized by movement of the speech organs, but to produce it the tongue slides a little forward, rather than backward, and the muscles of the soft palate are tensed. Students who find it difficult to avoid this type of r̲ in English should concentrate on the *backward* movement of the tongue and making the uvula and soft palate (the soft back part of the roof of the mouth) remain motionless and relaxed.

The trilled r̲, typical ∪f such languages as Arabic, Spanish, and Italian, can best be avoided by concentrating on the sliding of the sides of the tongue along the tooth ridge, by keeping the tongue tip comparatively inactive, and by being very careful that the tip does not approach closely the roof of the mouth or upper teeth.

Japanese and Chinese students, in particular, sometimes have difficulty in distinguishing between /l/ and /r/. They should spend a great deal of time pronouncing such pairs of words as *grass* /græs/ and *glass* /glæs/, *crime* /kraym/ and *climb* /klaym/, *free* /friy/ and *flee* /fliy/, *red* /rɛd/ and *led* /lɛd/, making the tip of the tongue touch the tooth ridge for /l/ and stay away from the roof of the mouth and teeth for /r/. In a sense, /l/ and /r/ are made in exactly opposite ways: for /l/ the tongue tip touches the tooth ridge and the air goes out over the sides; for /r/ the sides of the tongue touch the tooth ridge while the air goes out over the middle and tip.

II. /l/ and /r/ after Front Vowels

In Lesson 2 we classified /iy/, /ɪ/, /ey/, /ɛ/, and /æ/ as front vowels; /a/, /ɔ/, /ow/, /ʊ/, and /uw/ as back vowels; and /ə/ as a central vowel. If the reasons for this classification are not clear to you now, it might be well to review that lesson at this point.

The movements that characterize both /l/ and /r/, especially when they *follow* a vowel sound, are produced quite far back in the mouth. As a result, it is a more complicated process and takes more time to pass from a *front* vowel to /l/ or /r/ than from a *back* vowel to either of these two liquid sounds. Compare *ill* and *all, ear* and *or.* As the tongue moves back from the position of the front vowel, it passes through the middle, central zone where /ə/ is formed. In doing so, it produces a centering glide that is heard as /ə/. We may say that,

No such /ə/ is heard between a back vowel and /l/ or /r/, since the movement of the tongue takes place primarily in the back of the mouth without passing through the central zone. We pronounce *wall* as /wɔl/, but *well* as /wɛə̲l/. Similarly, in the case of words in which /r/ follows a vowel, we hear *car* /kar/ without the intermediary /ə/ and *care* /kɛə̲r/ with it.

These combinations of front vowels followed by the centering glide /ə/ constitute, of course, a type of diphthong. Some phoneticians call them "centering diphthongs." In this manual we recognize five of these centering diphthongs and transcribe them as follows.

	Elements	*Transcription*	*Examples*
1.	/iy/ + /ə/	/iə/	*seal* /siəl/
2.	/ɪ/ + /ə/	/ɪə/	*fill* /fɪəl/
			fear /fɪər/
3.	/ey/ + /ə/	/eə/	*tale* /teəl/
4.	/ɛ/ + /ə/	/ɛə/	*well* /wɛəl/
			wear /wɛər/
5.	/æ/ + /ə/	/æə/	*shall* /šæəl/

There is a considerable amount of dialectal variation in the use of these centering diphthongs. The five listed above are those that are normally heard in the most widely spoken dialects of American English. In these dialects /iə/ and /eə/ occur only before /l/, not before /r/. Note that in transcribing these same two diphthongs we omit the /y/ glide. This is because the transcriptions of *seal* as /siyəl/ and of *tale* as /teyəl/ might give students the mistaken impression that such words are pronounced as two syllables. /æə/ is fairly widely used before /r/ and is so represented in many dictionaries, but it appears to be increasingly replaced by /ɛə/: *care* /kɛə̲r/. (Further information about vowels before /l/ and /r/ is given in Lesson 17, Section IV.)

The deliberate insertion of /ə/ in the pronunciation of front vowels before /l/ or /r/ will usually help a student to produce an /l/ or /r/ that "sounds American," and will enable her or him to avoid pronouncing such words as *will, bell,* and *feel* with an unnaturally pure vowel and with the tongue too high. The mispronunciation of words like these is a prominent feature of many a foreign accent. Think of them as /wɪə̯l/, /bɛə̯l/, and /fiə̯l/, rather than as /wɪl/, /bɛl/, and /fiyl/.

Though the centering glide /ə/ is inserted in such words as *hill* /hɪə̯l/ or *hillside* /hɪ́ə̯lsàyd/, in which the /l/ is final or followed by another consonant sound, usually no such glide is inserted in words like *hilly* /hɪ́lɪ/, in which the /l/ is followed by a vowel sound. The same is true for words with /r/: *merry* /mɛ́rɪ/ without /ə/, but *where* /hwɛə̯r/ with /ə/.

III. Syllabic Consonants

Most of us are accustomed to thinking that every syllable must include at least one vowel, yet in words such as *little, sudden,* and *wouldn't* there are only consonant sounds in the final syllable. These are known as syllabic consonants, since they may make up a syllable without the accompaniment of vowels. In phonetic transcription, syllabic consonants may be indicated by drawing a short vertical line below them: *little* /lɪtl̩/, *sudden* /sədn̩/, *wouldn't* /wʊdn̩t/. They are difficult for most foreign students to pronounce; in place of /lɪtl̩/ we frequently hear /lɪtəl/ or /lɪl/; in place of /wʊdn̩t/ the student may say /wʊdənt/ or /wʊnt/.

Syllabic consonants occur when a syllable ends in /t/, /d/, or /n/, and the next syllable is *unstressed* and contains an /l/ or /n/. This may be expressed by an equation:

$$\left.\begin{array}{l} /t/ \\ /d/ \\ /n/ \end{array}\right\} + \text{unstressed syllable containing} \left\{\begin{array}{l} /l/ \\ /n/ \end{array}\right\} > \text{syllabic consonant.}$$

All the necessary conditions are present, for example, in *saddle* and *cotton,* and we have the pronunciations /sædl̩/ and /katn̩/. In *lieutenant* /luwtɛ́nənt/, there is a /t/ followed by an /n/, but the /n/ is in a stressed syllable, so no syllabic consonant results.

It is easy to remember the four consonants that are involved in syllabic consonants: /t/, /d/, /n/, and /l/. They are the four that are formed with the tip of the tongue touching the tooth ridge.[2] Indeed, it is the fact that the four are

---

[2]In rapid conversational speech, syllabic consonants may occur in two other cases where stops and continuants have the same points of articulation: (1) between /p/ or /b/ and /m/, as in *stop 'em* /stapm̩/; and (2) between /k/ or /g/ and /ŋ/, as in *I can go* /aykŋ̩gow/. Since the alternate pronunciations, /stapəm/ and /aykəngow/ do not sound "foreign," these two cases are not important for the purposes of this text. Some phoneticians also transcribe as syllabic consonants such combinations as the /l/ after the /s/ in *pencil,* /pɛnsəl/ or /pɛnsl̩/, and the /l/ after the /p/ in *apple,* /æpəl/ or /æpl̩/, where the points of articulation are not quite identical (or in technical terms, where the two sounds are not homorganic). In these cases also, however, either alternate pronunciation is perfectly normal American English.

all made with the tongue tip in the same position that causes the formation of syllabic consonants. What happens is that, in pronouncing *cotton,* for example, the tongue tip goes to the tooth ridge to form /t/, *and just stays there to pronounce the following* /n/. There should not even be a brief separation of tip and tooth ridge between /t/ and /n/. If the tongue tip breaks contact and moves from its fixed position for even a fraction of a second, it will result in the insertion of an /ə/ between the two consonants. In a word such as *cotton,* an /ə/ in the second syllable is definitely an element of "foreign accent."

You will remember that the formation of a stop, such as /t/ or /d/, usually requires two movements: a *closure,* or stopping of the outflow of air, and then a *release* of the air. (See Lesson 9, Section III.) Before a syllabic consonant, in words like *little* and *sudden,* the closure for the stop takes place normally, as the tongue tip makes contact with the tooth ridge. But the release is quite unusual, since the tongue tip, which normally makes the release by moving away from the tooth ridge, must in this case remain in its position for the formation of the following syllabic consonant. Before syllabic /l/ the release is made by a sudden lowering of the *middle and sides*—not the *tip*—of the tongue; this permits the air imprisoned by the preceding closure to rush out and make an /l̩/. Before syllabic /n/ the release is made by a sudden opening of the velum, which allows the imprisoned air to escape through the nose. (The velum is the soft part of the palate, at the back of the roof of the mouth. When drawn up, it closes the nasal passages, and all escaping breath must come out through the mouth; when relaxed and open, the breath may come out through either nose or mouth. See Figure 8, p. 93.

So, when you wish to pronounce a word like *little* /lɪtl̩/ or *sudden* /sədn̩/, bring the tongue into contact with the tooth ridge sharply and definitely for the /t/ or /d/. Then, *as you force the tongue tip to remain where it is,* make the release that will produce /l/ or /n/. You may find it helpful at the beginning to pronounce the first syllable completely, /lɪt/, and to pause on the /t/ in order to feel and maintain the pressure of the tongue tip in its proper position before you go on to make the release and pronounce the last syllable, /l̩/. In the same way, try *important,* /ɪmpɔ́rt/, pause, /n̩t/; and *sentence,* /sɛnt/, pause, /n̩s/.

It should be noted that the /t/ which precedes a syllabic /l/, as in *little,* is the "/d/-like /t/" discussed at the end of Section I, Lesson 9.

IV. Exercises

A. This drill is intended to furnish you with an opportunity for extensive and careful practice in the formation of /r/. It begins with the combinations in which most students usually find it easiest to make an American /r/, and then moves on to more difficult combinations. Pronounce each item three or four times, more if necessary, keeping in mind the instructions given in Section I. Try to master each step in the exercise before you go on to the next one. Start with (a), then proceed to (b), and so on.

<table>
<tr><td>(a)</td><td>(b)</td><td>(c)</td></tr>
<tr><td>1. ar</td><td>1. kar</td><td>1. farm</td></tr>
<tr><td>2. ɔr</td><td>2. fɔr</td><td>2. bɚn</td></tr>
<tr><td>3. ɪer</td><td>3. sɚr</td><td>3. gɚl</td></tr>
<tr><td>4. ɛɚr</td><td>4. hɪɚr</td><td>4. mə́ðɚr</td></tr>
<tr><td>5. ər</td><td>5. ðɛ́ɚr</td><td>5. fáðɚr</td></tr>
</table>

<table>
<tr><td>(d)</td><td>(e)</td><td>(f)</td></tr>
<tr><td>1. mɔ́rnɪŋ</td><td>1. ara</td><td>1. mɛ́rɪ</td></tr>
<tr><td>2. bárgɪn</td><td>2. arow</td><td>2. kǽrɪ</td></tr>
<tr><td>3. wɚk</td><td>3. ariy</td><td>3. mɔ́rəl</td></tr>
<tr><td>4. wɔ́rmɚr</td><td>4. ərə</td><td>4. fyúrɪ</td></tr>
<tr><td>5. bɔ́rdɚr</td><td>5. ɔrɛ</td><td>5. ɛ́rɚr</td></tr>
</table>

<table>
<tr><td>(g)</td><td>(h)</td><td>(i)</td></tr>
<tr><td>1. riy</td><td>1. rɪd</td><td>1. rəf</td></tr>
<tr><td>2. rey</td><td>2. reyn</td><td>2. rowl</td></tr>
<tr><td>3. ra</td><td>3. rɛk</td><td>3. rayd</td></tr>
<tr><td>4. row</td><td>4. rǽpɪŋ</td><td>4. rawz</td></tr>
<tr><td>5. ruw</td><td>5. rɪfɚr</td><td>5. rúwlɚr</td></tr>
</table>

<table>
<tr><td>(j)</td><td>(k)</td><td>(l)</td></tr>
<tr><td>1. gruw</td><td>1. θrown</td><td>1. ɛ́vrɪ</td></tr>
<tr><td>2. frow</td><td>2. brɪŋ</td><td>2. əpréyz</td></tr>
<tr><td>3. drɔ</td><td>3. kreyt</td><td>3. bɪfrɛ́nd</td></tr>
<tr><td>4. prey</td><td>4. prɪpɛ́ɚr</td><td>4. dɪkríys</td></tr>
<tr><td>5. triy</td><td>5. gráwndɪd</td><td>5. bɪgrə́dž</td></tr>
</table>

<table>
<tr><td>(m)</td><td>(n)</td></tr>
<tr><td>1. a large farm</td><td>1. a greater artist</td></tr>
<tr><td>2. shorter working hours</td><td>2. frequent arrivals</td></tr>
<tr><td>3. to further your purposes</td><td>3. to cross the border</td></tr>
<tr><td>4. forever and ever</td><td>4. a brown dress</td></tr>
<tr><td>5. the wrong room</td><td>5. to bring under control</td></tr>
</table>

B.   Your instructor will pronounce the following geographical names with an "American accent." Imitate him or her as closely as possible, paying special attention to the formation of /r/.

1. Berlin	8. Ferrara	15. Rio de Janeiro
2. Turkey	9. Prague	16. Cairo
3. Hiroshima	10. Tripoli	17. Paris
4. Peru	11. Burma	18. Rumania
5. Smyrna	12. Florida	19. Warsaw
6. Florence	13. Madras	20. France
7. Karachi	14. Teheran /tɪərán/	21. Argentina

C.   These two exercises are particularly for Oriental students.

1.   Pronounce each pair of words several times, remembering the differences be-
     tween /l/ and /r/ as described in the last paragraph of Section I. In each case
     the two words sound exactly alike, except for /l/ and /r/.[3]

a. late, rate	e. alive, arrive	i. believe, bereave
b. cloud, crowd	f. liver, river	j. blight, bright
c. glue, grew	g. play, pray	k. blush, brush
d. lime, rhyme	h. glass, grass	l. fly, fry

2.   Read the following paragraph, and then tell a fellow student what happened to
     Richard and Grace Robinson.

> Richard and Grace Robinson planned to attend a Broadway play while
> they were in New York. The traffic that night was very heavy, so they
> were late getting to the theater. Because they arrived late, the usher told
> them they would have to stand at the rear of the auditorium until the end
> of the first scene. The play was so bad that they decided to leave. Since
> it was really too late to go anywhere else, they went back to the hotel
> and watched television.

D.   In the light of what you learned in Section II of this lesson, determine which of
     the following words would be pronounced with an /ə/ inserted between the vowel
     sound and /l/ or /r/. Then transcribe all the words in phonetic symbols, and check
     them with your instructor's transcription. Finally, pronounce your transcriptions,
     taking particular care with combinations such as *well,* in which a front vowel pre-
     cedes /l/.

| 1. bar | 3. hair | 5. care |
| 2. for | 4. ear | 6. beer |

---

[3]Note to the teacher: In order to maintain a minimal distinction between the two words, help
the students to pronounce each word with the same intonation: ⌣late, ⌣rate (rather than with a series
intonation: ╱late, ╱rate).

7.	bear	15.	will	23.	fell
8.	they're	16.	tell	24.	ball
9.	we're	17.	coal	25.	shall
10.	fur	18.	kill	26.	help
11.	sir	19.	real	27.	pool
12.	word	20.	self	28.	spelled
13.	heard	21.	full	29.	failed
14.	verb	22.	milk	30.	she'll

E. Three of the items in the following exercise are not pronounced with a syllabic consonant, but all the others usually are. Which are the three exceptions? Draw a line under the syllabic consonants in the other 30 words (see Section III); then pronounce the entire exercise. Your instructor should pronounce this material with you, before you try to work on it alone.

1.	little	12.	hospital	23.	gardening
2.	didn't	13.	travel	24.	certainty
3.	student	14.	curtain	25.	penalty
4.	couldn't	15.	oriental	26.	finally
5.	article	16.	bottle	27.	fertilize
6.	tunnel	17.	saddled	28.	ordinary
7.	Latin	18.	broadened	29.	ventilate
8.	harden	19.	attention	30.	monotonous
9.	idle	20.	battleship	31.	bread and butter
10.	important	21.	suddenly	32.	bright and early
11.	mountain	22.	sentences	33.	salt and pepper

F. The following passage contains many /l/'s and /r/'s, as well as some syllabic consonants. It can be used in the same way as Exercise H in Lesson 9.

1. Make sure you can read it, and then underline any words you may find troublesome.

2. Your instructor will call on students to read each sentence naturally and may call attention to any pronunciation problems he or she hears.

3. Answer the questions that follow the passage and any additional questions the instructor may ask in order to make sure you can pronounce key items even when your attention is concentrated on the meaning of what you are saying.

1. džíəl mártn̩ lívz ɔ́l yíər ráwnd ɪn θríy rívərz, / wɪð ər fáðər / ən máðər / ən túw lítl̩ sístərz. 2. ræðər ðæn rɪméyn áydl̩ ɪn ðə sə́mər, / šiy wɔ́rks æz ə

wéytrɪs æt ðə howtél.   3. dʊrɪŋ ðə skúwl yɪər / šiyz ə styúwdn̩t æt ə níərbay

yuwnɪvə́rsɪtɪ.   4. šiy ɪnténdz tə biy ə fárməsɪst, / láyk ər faðər.   5. híy

ównz ðə mártn̩ drə́gstɔr ɪn θríy rívərz.   6. džíəl stárts wərk bráyt n̩ ə́rli ɪn ðə

mɔ́rnɪŋ, / ən sə́mtaymz də́zənt fínɪš əntíəl léyt æt náyt.   7. sévrəl əv ər fréndz

ɔ́lsow wə́rk æt ðə howtél.   8. ɔldów ðɪ áwrz ər lɔ́ŋ, / ðə wə́rkərz hæv ə sə́rtn̩

əmáwnt əv fríy táym ɪn ðɪ æftərnúwn / tə ɡów swímɪŋ, / pléy ténɪs, / ər džə́st lówf.

9. ðey ríylɪ láyk tə spénd ðɛər sə́mərz wə́rkɪŋ æt ðə howtél.   10. ɪts ə ɡud

wéy tʊ ə́rn mə́nɪ, / míyt píypəl, / ən hæv ə lítl̩ fə́n æt ðə séym táym.

a.   What is Jill's last name?

b.   Who are the members of her family?

c.   How does she spend her summers?

d.   Do you think it's necessary for her to work in the summer?

e.   Give a reason for your answer to the previous question.

f.   What are Jill's reasons for wanting to work?

g.   What are her working hours?

h.   What free time does she have?

i.   Is she an ambitious student?

j.   What do you think her future will be like?

k.   Would you enjoy the kind of summer work that Jill does?

l.   Why, or why not?

G. 1. As you answer these questions, use the intonation that is normal for a series. (See Lesson 6, p. 63–64.)

    a. What do you usually eat for breakfast?

    b. What languages do you speak?

    c. What courses are you taking now?

    d. What countries have you visited?

    e. What kinds of ice cream have you tried in this country?

2. Make questions in which you present the following ideas as alternatives with *or;* for example, ''Is the food better in the *United States,* or in *your native country?*'' Be careful with the intonation of the questions. (See Lesson 6, p. 64.)

a. interesting, boring	f. January, June
b. a real fire, a false alarm	g. morning, afternoon
c. just beginning, ending	h. long, short
d. this school, the school you last attended	i. easy, difficult
e. Monday, Tuesday, Wednesday	j. music, art

H. This lesson ends with a speed and rhythm drill. Read it at normal conversational speed, and try to observe an even, regular sentence rhythm. (See Lesson 4, Section I.) The material is well suited for individual recording.

1.   a. I found it.

    b. I've told you I found it.

    c. I've told you already that I found it.

    d. I've told you already that I found it at the movies.

    e. I've told you already that I found the money at the movies.

    f. I've told you already that I found the money at the movies on Sunday.

2.   a. I'm surprised!

    b. I'm surprised you believed it!

    c. I'm surprised you believed such a story!

    d. I'm surprised you believed such an incredible story!

    e. I'm surprised that anyone believed such an incredible story!

    f. I'm surprised that anyone believed such an incredible story as that!

3. a. He knóws éverything.

    b. He appéars to knów éverything.

    c. He sómetimes appéars to knów éverything.

    d. He sómetimes appéars to knów éverything when he léctures.

    e. He sómetimes appéars to knów éverything when he léctures so cónfi-
        dently.

    f. He sómetimes appéars to knów éverything when he léctures so cónfi-
        dently to his clásses.

I. Outside of class, read aloud several pages of simple, conversational material, con-
    centrating your attention on the pronunciation of /l/ or /r/, whichever you find more
    difficult.

LESSON 11

Front Vowels

I. Vowel Substitutions

A common—and very serious—mistake made by students of English is the substitution of one vowel for another in the stressed syllable of a word: for example, the pronunciation of *leaving* as /lívɪŋ/ instead of /líyvɪŋ/. Such a substitution is serious because it often completely changes the meaning of the word. It may be polite to tell your friend, "/ay howp yuw wownt liyv naw/"; but "/ay howp yuw wownt lɪv naw/" may not be appreciated.

The usual causes for mistakes of this sort seem to be:

1. The speaker gives the letters that represent vowels the sounds these letters would have in her native language. The French tend to pronounce *aid* as /ɛd/ instead of /eyd/.
2. The speaker is deceived by the inconsistencies of English spelling. Usually ar is pronounced /ar/, as in *car, far,* and *part;* therefore *war* is sometimes wrongly pronounced as /war/ instead of /wɔr/.
3. The speaker cannot hear, and consequently cannot reproduce, the difference between two sounds, either because the two do not exist in his own language, or because they do not regularly serve to distinguish between words in it. Both /ey/ and /ɛ/ are heard in Spanish, but there are very few cases of two Spanish words that are exactly alike except that one contains

/ey/ and the other /ɛ/. As a result, the student from Mexico often mispronounces *change* as /tšɛndž/ instead of /tšeyndž/.

Lessons 11, 12, 17, and 18 attack the problem of stressed vowel substitutions. They are intended to give you practice in hearing and reproducing the differences between vowels that are frequently confused, to give you an opportunity to make stronger associations between vowel sounds and their usual spelling, and to call your attention to certain common words in which the vowel sounds are spelled in an unusual way.

II. The Vowel /iy/ as in be<u>a</u>t

The material that follows is based on the vowel chart as explained in Lesson 2. (It would be well at this point to review that explanation, particularly Figure 3 on page :131.)

You may remember that /iy/ is the vowel which is pronounced farthest toward the front of the mouth, with the jaw most nearly closed. *The sides of the tongue are pressed tightly against the upper bicuspid (two-pointed) teeth and the palate (roof of the mouth).* The tongue tip may *press the cutting edge* of the lower front teeth. *Upper and lower teeth almost touch. The lips are spread somewhat by muscular force. The air escapes through a very narrow opening between the tongue blade (the part just behind the tip) and the upper tooth ridge.* In general, /iy/ is made with noticeable tension. Although the tongue is already very high in the front of the mouth when you begin this sound, the tongue normally moves farther up before beginning the next sound; therefore, this sound is symbolized as a vowel plus a glide: /iy/.

This is the vowel heard in *she* /šiy/, *seem* /siym/, *leave* /liyv/, *chief* /tšiyf/, and so on. Say these words carefully, then pronounce the vowel in each of them alone: /šiy/, /iy/; /siym/, /iy/; and so on. As you pronounce, make sure that your tongue, teeth, and lips take the position described in the preceding paragraph.

III. /ɪ/ as in b<u>i</u>t

The vowel that follows /iy/ on the vowel chart, as we move away from the front of the mouth, is /ɪ/. To change /iy/ to /ɪ/, *the jaw relaxes and drops very slightly, the pressure of the sides of the tongue against the upper bicuspids is relaxed, and the forced spreading of the lips disappears.* The tongue tip may merely *touch the back* of the lower front teeth. To see what happens to lips, jaws, and tongue, it is good to watch your mouth in a hand mirror as you form /iy/ and /ɪ/. *Most important of all, the opening between the tongue blade and the palate becomes wider and rounder.* This means that the place where the tongue and palate are closest together moves a little farther back in the mouth.

Pronounce *sheep* /šiyp/, then *ship* /šɪp/. Now pronounce only the vowels of the two words: /iy/, /ɪ/, /iy/, /ɪ/, /iy/, /ɪ/. Can you feel the essential differences in the position of the speech organs clearly? Form an /iy/-sound; then, without interrupting the flow of breath, try to make the /iy/ change to an /ɪ/ by appropriate movements of the tongue, jaw, and lips.

The /ɪ/-sound is the vowel of *big* /bɪg/, *king* /kɪŋ/, and *city* /sítɪ/. In some languages this sound does not exist. In others it may be heard occasionally, but does not differentiate words from similar words containing /iy/. Students who learned these other languages first will probably have difficulty in distinguishing clearly between *leave* /liyv/ and *live* /lɪv/. Very often they will use, instead of /iy/ or /ɪ/, a vowel halfway between the two, which will make *leave* sound like *live*, or *live* like *leave,* to an American ear.

The use of /iy/ for /ɪ/ or of /ɪ/ for /iy/ is, in fact, by far the most common and troublesome of the vowel substitutions we spoke of at the beginning of this lesson.

IV. /ey/ as in b<u>ai</u>t

Moving downward and backward on the vowel chart from /ɪ/, we come to /ey/. *The jaw drops just a little more.* The tongue tip may touch the *bottom* of the front teeth without pressure. *The sides of the tongue press slightly against the sides of the upper bicuspids. The passage through which the air escapes between the middle of the tongue and the palate grows wider. The lips are open and relaxed.*

Perhaps the characteristic which best distinguishes /ey/ is that *it ends with a definite upward and forward movement of the tongue.* The complete vowel begins in the position described in the preceding paragraph, then moves upward and forward toward the /ɪ/ position as the tongue is pushed nearer the palate and upper front teeth. The diphthongization of /ey/ is much more discernible than that of /iy/, and it is also much greater in most varieties of British English than in American English.

The degree of diphthongization is greatest in words where /ey/ is:

1. Final: *day* /dey/.
2. Followed by a final voiced consonant: *made* /meyd/.

3. Pronounced with a slide at the end of an intonation pattern:

It's the hand of fate.   /ɪts ðə hænd əv feyt/

The /ey/-sound is the vowel heard in *say* /sey/, *plain* /pleyn/, and *came* /keym/. It is most often confused with /ɛ/ and /æ/. Can you see the difference between /ey/, /ɪ/, and /iy/ in your mirror?

V. /ɛ/ as in b_et_

After /ey/ on the chart comes /ɛ/; but, unlike /ey/, /ɛ/ is not usually diph-thongized. To form /ɛ/, *the jaw is once more lowered just a little. For the first time, the tongue exerts no pressure at all.* The tongue tip may touch the spot where the lower front teeth join the tooth ridge; *the sides touch the tips of the upper bicuspids. The air-escape passage is as wide as the roof of the mouth itself.*

The /ɛ/-sound is the vowel of *yes* /yɛs/, *edge* /ɛdž/, and *end* /ɛnd/. It is not so clear a sound as /ey/, from which it must be carefully distinguished. Make sure you have understood and seen the chief differences: /ɛ/ is not diphthongized, and in forming it the sides of the tongue touch lightly the tips of the upper bicuspids without pressure. For /ey/ there is enough pressure to narrow the air passage somewhat.

VI. /æ/ as in b_at_

The last of the front vowels is /æ/. *To form it the jaw is lowered quite a bit, until the mouth is almost as wide open as it can be without making a muscular effort.* Remember that this is the last front vowel that can be made; when we move on to /a/, the sides and tip of the tongue will no longer touch the upper or lower teeth at all. *For /æ/, the lightest possible contact is made between tongue tip and lower tooth ridge, and between sides of tongue and the tips of the upper bicuspids or even of the first molar teeth just behind the bicuspids.* In other words, the passage through which the air escapes is as wide and deep as it can be and still remain a passage formed by the tongue rather than by the cheeks.

The /æ/-sound is the vowel of *am* /æm/, *black* /blæk/, and *cap* /kæp/. It is easily confused with /a/, /ɛ/, or even /ey/. Before you go on to the next section of this lesson, it would be well to go over the entire series—/iy-ɪ-ey-ɛ-æ/—many times with your mirror, checking your way of forming the sounds with the physiological descriptions of how they should be formed.

VII. Exercises

A. 1. Listen carefully as your instructor pronounces a prolonged /iy/ several times: /iy—, iy—, iy—/. Imitate the pronunciation of the vowel, watching your lips, tongue, teeth, and so on, in a hand mirror and trying to make your speech organs assume the exact position described in the appropriate section of this lesson.

2. Listen, then imitate, as your instructor pronounces the following material. If the instructor indicates that the vowel in any word does not sound quite right, correct yourself by making your speech organs assume more exactly the desired position.

(a)	(b)	(c)
1. biy	1. these dreams	1. riyd, rɪd
2. miy	2. green trees	2. hiyt, hɪt
3. friy	3. weak tea	3. sliyp, slɪp
4. iytš	4. meet in the street	4. miyt, mɛt
5. iyst	5. please teach me	5. fiyd, fɛd
6. šiyp	6. a deep sleep	6. siyt, sɛt
7. siyk		
8. niyd		
9. fiyt		
10. kwiyn		

B. The instructions for Exercise A apply also to Exercises B, C, D, and E.

1. /ɪ—, ɪ—, ɪ—/

2.

(a)	(b)	(c)
1. bɪt	1. this city	1. sɪt, siyt
2. fɪks	2. a quick finish	2. lɪp, liyp
3. kɪs	3. which gift	3. stɪk, steyk
4. rɪŋ	4. six inches	4. mɪs, mɛs
5. trɪp	5. to visit my sister	5. sɪns, sɛns
6. wɪn	6. sip the milk	6. bɪt, bɛt
7. lɪft		
8. ɪts		
9. ɪf		
10. ɪŋk		

C. 1. /ey—, ey—, ey—/

2.   (a)   (b)   (c)
        1. pey   1. straight pay   1. pleyn, plæn
        2. sey   2. a date at eight   2. greys, græs
        3. grey   3. a famous flavor   3. geyt, gɛt
        4. eyt   4. the baby's name   4. bleyd, blɛd
        5. eydž   5. made me late   5. teyk, tɪk
        6. reyn   6. bake a cake   6. leyd, lɪd
        7. leyd
        8. weyt
        9. peynt
       10. pleyz

D. 1. /ɛ—, ɛ—, ɛ—/

2.   (a)   (b)   (c)
        1. stɛp   1. send them   1. bɛd, bæd
        2. tɛn   2. her best dress   2. mɛn, mæn
        3. lɛg   3. a red head   3. lɛt, leyt
        4. prɛs   4. several presents   4. rɛst, reyst
        5. nɛkst   5. when I left   5. wɛəl, wɪəl
        6. lɛŋθ   6. help the men   6. pɛk, pɪk
        7. frɛš
        8. ɛg
        9. ɛnd
       10. ɛdž

E. 1. /æ—, æ—, æ—/

2.   (a)   (b)   (c)
        1. bæk   1. narrow path   1. bænd, bɛnd
        2. bæŋk   2. past master   2. læst, lɛst
        3. fæst   3. half a glass   3. sæd, sɛd
        4. glæd   4. a happy fancy   4. æd, ɛd
        5. pæs   5. a grand family   5. hæt, hat
        6. plænt   6. a black cat   6. sæk, sak
        7. ræg
        8. æz
        9. æsk
       10. ækt

F. It is suggested that five steps be carried out in doing each of the two parts of the following drill: (1) be sure that the students understand the meaning of all the words; (2) let the teacher read across the columns, as the students imitate; (3) have the students read collectively and individually across the columns; (4) let the teacher dictate ten words selected at random from the drill, and have the students write down the words they hear; (5) let the students pick out certain words and try to pronounce them so well that the teacher can recognize them.

1. iy   ɪ   ɛ

	iy		ɪ		ɛ
a.	peak	b.	pick	c.	peck
d.	dean	e.	din	f.	den
g.	deed	h.	did	i.	dead
j.	least	k.	list	l.	lest
m.	heed	n.	hid	o.	head
p.	feel	q.	fill	r.	fell

2. ey   ɛ   æ

	ey		ɛ		æ
a.	bait	b.	bet	c.	bat
d.	pain	e.	pen	f.	pan
g.	bake	h.	beck	i.	back
j.	laid	k.	led	l.	lad
m.	lace	n.	less	o.	lass
p.	shale	q.	shell	r.	shall

G. Many of the following sound combinations do not make up English words. First, pronounce them in imitation of your instructor. Then the instructor will dictate twenty or more combinations chosen from the list at random, while you try to copy down the sounds in symbols.

1.	šiy	11.	riym	21.	fiyt
2.	šɪ	12.	rɪm	22.	fɪt
3.	šey	13.	reym	23.	feyt
4.	šɛ	14.	rɛm	24.	fɛt
5.	šæ	15.	ræm	25.	fæt
6.	šiyp	16.	liyv	26.	siyg
7.	šɪp	17.	lɪv	27.	sɪg
8.	šeyp	18.	leyv	28.	seyg
9.	šɛp	19.	lɛv	29.	sɛg
10.	šæp	20.	læv	30.	sæg

H. Before reading each sentence below, pronounce the two words in parentheses in contrast. Then read each of the sentences twice, using word (a) in the first reading and word (b) in the second. Then read the sentence again using either (a) or (b), while another member of the class tries to identify in each case the word that you pronounced.

1. (a. wean) (b. win)   It's time to _____ the child.

2. (a. feel) (b. fill)   He doesn't seem to _____ the need.

3. (a. peak) (b. pick)   He walked confidently toward the _____.

4. (a. dean) (b. din)   I can't study because of the _____.

5. (a. heed) (b. hid)   We always _____ our mistakes.

6. (a. sheep) (b. ship)   You can't get a _____ into such a small place.

7. (a. bit) (b. bet)   I'd like to make a little _____ on that horse.

8. (a. pin) (b. pen)   Keep the _____where you can reach it.

9. (a. pig) (b. peg)   I caught the _____ with both hands.

10. (a. rain) (b. wren)   The _____ descends gently from the clouds.

11. (a. dale) (b. dell)   A great many flowers grow in the _____.

12. (a. laid) (b. led)   Who could have _____ the child there?

13. (a. date) (b. debt)   I'll never forget that old _____ of mine.

14. (a. mate) (b. mat)   The dog was asleep by his _____.

15. (a. cane) (b. can)   The cook has a _____ in her hand.

16. (a. mess) (b. mass)   In the street was a tangled _____ of cars.

17. (a. pet) (b. pat)   It's not wise to _____ a tiger.

18. (a. ten) (b. tan)   She's very proud of her _____ shoes.

19. (a. peck) (b. pack)   You'll need a whole _____ of cards.

20. (a. shell) (b. shall)   You'll shell more peas than I _____.

If the instructor so wishes, the above drill may be used as a test of your ability to distinguish between the front vowel sounds. Take a piece of paper and number the lines from 1 through 20. The instructor will read each sentence, inserting one of the two test words. You should decide which one was used and write (a) or (b) on your paper opposite the number of the sentence.

I.   Read these sentences aloud, making as clear a distinction as possible between the vowels of the words in italics.

1. Either *read* the book or get *rid* of it.

2. Didn't you buy *it* to *eat*?

3. I didn't *seek* to be *sick*.

4. *Each* foot *itches*.

5. *List* at *least* the most important ones.

6. She *dipped deeply* into the sack.

7. Don't *grin* at my *greenness*.

8. They *begged* a *big* meal.

9. There was a sharp noise as the ball *met* his *mitt*.

10. The living influenced us more than the *dead did*.

11. Can you *lift* what's *left*?

12. You'll get *wet* if you *wait*.

13. *Tell* us a *tale*, Grandma.

14. There's a *gate* to *get* through.

15. I hope long dresses are a *fading fad*.

16. Bankers *lend* money on *land*.

17. He *said* he was *sad*.

18. His bad *leg* made him *lag* behind.

19. The hen *sat* where he *set* her.

20. You've certainly *met* your *match*.

J.   Read these sentences with two different intonation patterns: (1) so as to create suspense between the two parts of the sentence, and (2) without suspense. (See Lesson 6, Section II.)

1. If you do that again, I'll punish you.
2. You push a little button, and the food comes out.
3. I opened the door, and there was the "ghost."
4. When he heard the answer, he was horrified.
5. If it happens here, it will be the ruin of us.
6. Until you see me, make no move.
7. If I'd known that, I could have made ten dollars.
8. Smoke one of these, and you'll never smoke again.

K.   American children delight in asking one another riddles they consider funny. The four typical examples that follow can help you learn to read phonetic transcriptions and give you practice in question-and-answer intonation. When you become familiar with the riddles, you may even want to try them out on a friend.

1. a. hwáy dəz ə stórk stænd / an ównlı wən lɛ́g?

    b. bıkɔ́z ðə wɔ́tərz kówld?

    a. bıkɔ́z ıf iy líftıd bówθ lɛ́gz / hiyd fɔl dáwn.

2. a. hwáts gréy, / hæz fɔ́r lɛ́gz /, ən ə trə́ŋk?

    b. ən ɛ́ləfənt, / əv kɔ́rs.

    a. ɔr ə máws / gówıŋ an ə trı́p.

3. a. hwát táym ɪz ɪt / wɛn ðə klák stráyks θərtíyn?

    b. méybɪ wən pǽst twéəlv?

    a. ɪts táym tə rɪpéər ðə klák.

4. a. hwáy dɪd ðə gə́rl klówz ər áyz / wɛn šiy lʊ́kt ɪn ðə mírər?

    b. šiy dídn̩t láyk wat šiy sɔ́?

    a. bɪkɔ́z šiy wántɪd tə síy wat šiy lʊ́kt láyk / wɛn šiy wəz slíypɪŋ.

L. Read aloud several pages of English, concentrating your attention on the correct formation of the front vowel with which you seem to have most difficulty.

LESSON 12

Central and Back Vowels

I. The Vowel /a/ as in pot

You have no doubt noticed that when a physician wishes to have a clear view into your mouth and throat, he or she asks you to say "Ah." That is, of course, the sound of our vowel /a/. The physician knows that the formation of /a/ requires the mouth to be opened more widely than for any other sound. The tongue is also positioned lower in the mouth than for any other vowel. That is what gives the doctor an unobstructed view of your throat.

It might be well here to refer again to the vowel chart in Lesson 2 (Figure 3).

In order to form /a/, *the jaw is lowered more than it would be in a normal relaxed position, lowered so far as to require a slight muscular effort. As a consequence, the lips are also wide open, about an inch apart for most speakers,* and two upper front teeth and several lower teeth are probably visible. Verify this with your mirror. *The tongue tip lightly touches a point as low on the floor of the mouth as it can reach, so low that in compensation the back of the tongue must be raised just a little in the throat.*

In most varieties of American English, /a/ is the vowel of *father* /fáðər/, *box* /baks/, and *calm* /kam/. It is most often confused with /ə/ and /æ/. What are the essential differences in the formation of /æ/ and /a/? Check your answer with the description of /æ/ in Lesson 11 and by watching the formation of the two vowels in your mirror.

II. /ɔ/ **as in b<u>ough</u>t**

In moving from /a/ to /ɔ/, we are starting up the back portion of the vowel chart. The most important thing to watch with this vowel is the position of your lips. The value of a front vowel—/iy/, /ɪ/, /ey/, /ɛ/, or /æ/—is largely determined by the tongue; that is, by the shape and size of the air-escape passage between the tongue and the roof of the mouth. On the other hand, it is the lips—the size and shape of the opening between them—that have most influence in forming the central and back vowels. For /a/ this opening is about an inch and a half across, one inch from top to bottom, and shaped as in Figure 9.

Figure 9. Lip position for /a/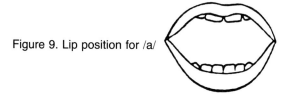

For /ɔ/ the opening is usually about one inch or less across, and half an inch from top to bottom. The lips are somewhat protruded (pushed forward). Normally little is to be seen of the teeth. (See Figure 10.) In order for the lips

Figure 10. Lip position for /ɔ/

to assume this position for /ɔ/, *the jaw is raised a little. The tongue remains in approximately the same position as for* /a/, *but it is "bunched" a little more toward the back of the mouth.*

The /ɔ/-sound is the vowel of *all* /ɔl/, *saw* /sɔ/, *cause* /kɔz/, and *cross* /krɔs/. It is easily confused with /a/, /ow/, and /ə/.

III. /ow/ **as in b<u>oa</u>t**

In order to produce an /ow/, *the lips form the shape of the letter* <u>o</u>. *This requires that they be protruded and rounded more than for* /ɔ/. *The resulting opening is a little circle about half an inch in diameter.* (See Figure 11.) *The jaw has been raised still more, and the "bunching" of the tongue in the back*

Figure 11. Lip position for /ow/

of the mouth is greater. The tongue tip probably no longer touches the floor of the mouth.

Like /ey/, the /ow/-sound is *diphthongized,* much more so in British than in American English. This means that during the pronunciation of the sound the lips close slightly and lose their forced rounding, and the back of the tongue moves upward and backward. The sound is, therefore, symbolized as a vowel plus a glide: /ow/.

The /ow/-sound is the vowel found in *go* /gow/, *cold* /kowld/, *coast* /kowst/, *soul* /sowl/, and *snow* /snow/. It is sometimes confused with /ɔ/ and /uw/. What are the essential differences between /ow/ and /ɔ/? Can you see them with your hand mirror?

IV. /ʊ/ as in p<u>u</u>t

Until now, in order to make the classification of vowels as simple as possible, we have assumed that the progression from /ow/ through /ʊ/ to /uw/ was perfectly regular: that as we moved from one vowel to another up the back part of the vowel chart we merely raised the jaw, rounded the lips, and pulled the tongue backward a little more each time. Actually, the relationship between the back vowels is more complex; the regular progression will account for /ɔ/, /ow/, and /uw/, but not altogether for /ʊ/.

To form /ʊ/, the lips are less rounded and protruded than in the production of /ow/. The opening between them is wider across than for /ow/, but a good bit smaller in distance from upper to lower lip. The teeth may be visible: *the tips of the lower teeth approach the backs of the upper ones.* (See Figure 12.) *Though the tongue tip touches nothing, the tongue itself is pulled back and up, more than for /ow/, until its sides touch the upper tooth ridge.*

The /ʊ/-sound is the vowel of *book* /bʊk/, *full* /fʊl/, and *could* /kʊd/. It is most often confused with /uw/ and /ə/.

Figure 12. Lip position for /ʊ/

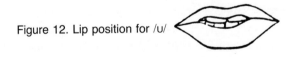

V. /uw/ as in boot

Like /iy/ at the other extreme of the chart, the /uw/-sound requires tension for its production. It is pronounced with a slight upward and backward movement of the tongue after the sound is begun. It is, therefore, symbolized as a vowel plus a glide: /uw/. This diphthongization, however, is much less discernible than in the /ow/-sound. *The lips should be rounded and protruded as much as possible, leaving a little circular opening about the size of a pencil.* The teeth are not visible. (See Figure 13.) *The tip of the tongue is drawn quite far back and touches nothing, but the sides of the tongue press firmly for some distance along the upper tooth ridge.*

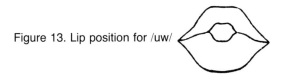

Figure 13. Lip position for /uw/

The /uw/-sound is the vowel of *too* /tuw/, *soon* /suwn/, and *blue* /bluw/. It is easily confused with /U/. Form the two sounds carefully before your hand mirror until you can see and feel clearly the essential difference: (1) in the rounding and protrusion of the lips; (2) in the pressure exerted by the tongue; and (3) in the visibility of the teeth.

This would be an excellent place, in fact, to go through the entire series– a-ɔ-ow-U-uw–before your mirror, fixing in your mind the distinguishing characteristics of the formation of each vowel.

VI. /ə/ as in but, and /ər/ as in bird

The only remaining vowel sound is the central, neutral, relaxed /ə/, which is not properly a part of either the front or back series. It has already been described at some length in Lessons 2 and 3 in connection with its very frequent use in unstressed syllables. However, it may be well to add a few more details, by way of comparison, now that you have a clearer understanding of the physiology of the other vowel sounds.

The /ə/-sound *is formed with the lips slightly parted almost their entire length.* (See Figure 14.) *There is no tension or effort anywhere. The tongue lies relaxed on the floor of the mouth, and usually neither its sides nor its tip touches anything.*

It is the vowel of *cut* /kət/, *jump* /džəmp/, and *dull* /dəl/. Owing to its position in the center of the vowel chart, it may be confused with any of the

Figure 14. Lip position for /ə/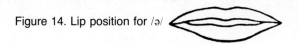

other vowels, though this seems to happen most often with /a/, /ɔ/, and /ʊ/. To change an /ə/ to /a/, all that is needed is to open the mouth wider. To change /ə/ to /ʊ/, narrow the lip opening by putting some pressure on the corners of the mouth, touch the sides of the tongue against the upper tooth ridge, and move the teeth closer together.

The combination /ər/ is a complex sound, which, because it includes the liquid, /r/, is characterized by movement rather than by a fixed position of the speech organs. Though many regional variations of the sound occur, the student from abroad may safely pronounce /ər/ as the symbols indicate—begin it as an ordinary /ə/ and end it as an /r/. *But very little pure /ə/ is heard; even as the /ə/ is formed, it begins to change into an /r/, moving backward in the mouth with the sides of the tongue sliding along the tooth ridge and with the tongue tip curving upward without touching anything.* Practice this with *word* /wərd/, *verb* /vərb/, and *turn* /tərn/.

VII. Exercises

A. 1. Listen carefully as the instructor pronounces a prolonged /a/ several times: /a—, a—, a—/. Imitate the pronunciation of the vowel, watching your lips, tongue, teeth, and so on, in a hand mirror and trying to make your speech organs assume the exact position described in the appropriate section of this lesson.

2. Listen, then imitate, as your instructor pronounces the following material. If the instructor indicates that the vowel in a word does not sound quite right, correct yourself by making your speech organs assume more exactly the desired position.

	(a)		(b)		(c)
1.	ad	1.	start shopping	1.	hat, hət
2.	aks	2.	a garden party	2.	stak, stək
3.	arm	3.	a hot-rod car	3.	kap, kəp
4.	drap	4.	lock the shop	4.	nat, nɔt
5.	gad	5.	stop the clock	5.	rak, ræk
6.	klak	6.	from top to bottom	6.	lak, læk
7.	lat				
8.	martš				
9.	gard				
10.	dark				

B.   The instructions for Exercise A apply also to Exercises B, C, D, E, F, and G.

   1.   /ɔ—, ɔ—, ɔ—/

   2.   (a)   (b)   (c)
         1.   sɔ   1.   tall corn   1.   lɔ, low
         2.   pɔ   2.   small talk   2.   bɔl, bowl
         3.   drɔ   3.   across the walk   3.   kɔst, kowst
         4.   ɔl   4.   a horse's stall   4.   strɔŋ, strəŋ
         5.   ɔf   5.   a soft cloth   5.   nɔrs, nərs
         6.   krɔs   6.   along the wall   6.   tɔk, tək
         7.   lɔ
         8.   sɔlt
         9.   kɔld
        10.   bɔrn

C.   1.   /ow—, ow—, ow—/

   2.   (a)   (b)   (c)
         1.   now   1.   both soldiers   1.   flow, flɔ
         2.   ðow   2.   an open coat   2.   kowt, kɔt
         3.   θrow   3.   those snows   3.   nowz, nɔz
         4.   owld   4.   wrote a note   4.   kowl, kuwl
         5.   owd   5.   his own show   5.   rowz, ruwz
         6.   bown   6.   knows the road   6.   powl, puwl
         7.   smowk
         8.   powst
         9.   nowt
        10.   howps

D.   1.   /ʊ—, ʊ—, ʊ—/

   2.   (a)   (b)   (c)
         1.   fʊt   1.   a good book   1.   fʊl, fuwl
         2.   pʊl   2.   she could cook   2.   šʊd, šuwd
         3.   tʊk   3.   put in sugar   3.   wʊd, wuwd
         4.   hʊd   4.   stood by a brook   4.   pʊt, pət
         5.   nʊk   5.   look at the woman   5.   tʊk, tək
         6.   šʊr   6.   took a look   6.   lʊk, lək
         7.   pʊš
         8.   bʊš
         9.   wʊl
        10.   wʊlf

E. 1. /uw—, uw—, uw—/

    2.   (a)   (b)   (c)
        1. truw   1. a loose tooth   1. šuwt, šət
        2. huw   2. through the school   2. suwn, sən
        3. gluw   3. whose shoe   3. luwk, lʊk
        4. fuwd   4. a blue moon   4. spuwk, spowk
        5. spuwl   5. choose the boot   5. tšuwz, tšowz
        6. fruwt   6. move into the room   6. suwp, sowp
        7. luwz
        8. pruwv
        9. truwθ
        10. guws

F. 1. /ə—, ə—, ə—/

    2.   (a)   (b)   (c)
        1. əp   1. mother tongue   1. šət, šat
        2. əs   2. trouble with bugs   2. klək, klak
        3. həm   3. young love   3. kəm, kam
        4. hənt   4. ugly duckling   4. kət, kɔt
        5. ləŋ   5. wonderful company   5. nən, nuwn
        6. kəp   6. above the cut   6. lək, lʊk
        7. dəst
        8. wəns
        9. rəb
        10. brəš

G. 1. /ər—, ər—, ər—/

    2.   (a)   (b)   (c)
        1. ərθ   1. the girl's birth   1. wərm, wɔrm
        2. ərdž   2. early bird   2. wərd, wɔrd
        3. fər   3. a thirsty herd   3. stər, stɪər
        4. sər   4. the curves merge   4. wər, wɛər
        5. stərn   5. her earnings   5. bərn, barn
        6. θərd   6. stern words   6. lərk, lark
        7. hərt
        8. wərθ
        9. bərst
        10. ərb

H. Did you every try to read lips as the deaf must learn to do in order to understand what is said to them? The back vowels and certain consonants are rather easy to recognize by sight. Before doing the following exercise, it would be well to review the pictures of the lip position for the back vowels and /ə/ and to reread, if necessary, the material in Lesson 8 on the point of articulation of /f/ and /p/. Watch in your hand mirror as you form the sounds. In class your instructor will form some of the combinations below with lips, tongue, and so on, without actually uttering any sound. Try to recognize each combination and write down its number.

1.	a	7.	fa	13.	pa
2.	ɔ	8.	fɔ	14.	pɔ
3.	ow	9.	fow	15.	pow
4.	ʊ	10.	fʊ	16.	pʊ
5.	uw	11.	fuw	17.	puw
6.	ə	12.	fə	18.	pə

I. The drills below are to be carried out like Exercise F of the preceding lesson: (1) the teacher makes sure that the meaning of all words is understood; (2) the teacher reads across the columns and the class imitates the teacher; (3) the students read across the columns as a group and individually; (4) the teacher dictates ten or more words selected at random; (5) the students pick out certain words and try to pronounce them so well that the teacher can identify them by letter.

1.

	a		ə (and /ər/)		ɔ
a.	not	b.	nut	c.	naught
d.	cod	e.	cud	f.	cawed
g.	Don	h.	done	i.	dawn
j.	cot	k.	cut	l.	caught
m.	are	n.	err	o.	or
p.	barn	q.	burn	r.	born

2.

	ɔ		ow		uw
a.	flaw	b.	flow	c.	flew
d.	Shaw	e.	show	f.	shoe
g.	bought	h.	boat	i.	boot
j.	call	k.	coal	l.	cool
m.	Paul	n.	pole	o.	pool
p.	lawn	q.	loan	r.	loon

3.

	ə		ʊ		uw
a.	luck	b.	look	c.	Luke
d.	cud	e.	could	f.	cooed

g. buck   h. book   i.
j.   k. should   l. shoed
m. putt   n. put   o.
p.   q. pull   r. pool

J. Before reading each sentence below, pronounce the two words in parentheses in contrast. Then read each of the sentences twice, using word (a) in the first reading and word (b) in the second. Then read again and use either (a) or (b), while another member of the class tries to identify in each case the word that you pronounced. The teacher may also give the drill as a test of your ability to distinguish between back vowels.

1. (a. cat) (b. cot)   Would you call it a _____?

2. (a. shack) (b. shock)   He had a _____ in the woods.

3. (a. map) (b. mop)   The _____ was hanging on the wall.

4. (a. far) (b. fur)   Is it _____ from the zoo?

5. (a. doll) (b. dull)   She's wearing a _____ hat.

6. (a. bomb) (b. bum)   One _____ can cause a lot of damage.

7. (a. lock) (b. luck)   We depend on our _____ to avoid burglars.

8. (a. barn) (b. burn)   Take good care of that _____.

9. (a. hall) (b. whole)   Shall we paint the _____ floor?

10. (a. naught) (b. note)   I wrote a _____ on the slip of paper.

11. (a. cost) (b. coast)   The _____ is high along the shore.

12. (a. faun) (b. phone)   Do you have a _____ at your house?

13. (a. awed) (b. owed)   The speaker _____ every person there.

14. (a. horse) (b. hearse)   The _____ was followed by a line of cars.

15. (a. balks) (b. bucks)   The pony _____ badly.

16. (a. boat) (b. boot) I'm sure such a _____ will float.

17. (a. foal) (b. fool) She loves that _____ dearly.

18. (a. took) (b. tuck) I _____ the money in my pocket.

19. (a. pull) (b. pool) To have no _____ is a misfortune in Hollywood.

20. (a. school) (b. skull) A _____ can teach many lessons.

If possible, tape record the above drill. You might make notes of the word you intend to use in each sentence 1-a, 2-b, 3-b, and so on. Then record, following your notes, and put the latter away where you cannot see them for several days. After an interval long enough to allow yourself to forget which word you used in each sentence, listen to the recording and write down what you hear. Finally, compare your original notes with the record of what you later heard. You might also have another student listen to your tape and make notes of what he or she hears. Did you in every case hear the word you originally intended to use? Did the other student always hear the same word you heard? Are you now making your back vowels with enough clarity to be understood regularly?

K. Read these sentences aloud, making as clear a distinction as possible between the vowels of the words in italics.

1. A *black* cat *blocked* my way.

2. His story only *adds* to the *oddness* of what happened.

3. You'll be *hot* without a *hat*.

4. The sea is *becoming calm*.

5. It fell *suddenly* on the *sod*.

6. The *ducks* swim under the *dock*.

7. We heard a *shot* and *shut* the door.

8. I think he *heard,* though he's *hard* of hearing.

9. When they *woke,* they took a *walk*.

10. Every man brought his own *bowling ball*.

11. I *saw* her *sew* it.

12. The tiger's *claws closed*.

13. It was a noisy *war* of *words*.

14. All was *done* before *dawn*.

15. I *stole* up behind the *stool*.

16. The results will be *known* by *noon*.

17. We made a *rush* for the *bushes*.

18. The child has *good blood*.

19. He just *stood* and looked at his *food*.

20. *Soon* the *sun* will come out.

L.   All the sentences in each of the following groups have the same rhythm and intonation. Sentence stresses are marked. Go through each group several times until you
can produce that particular pattern rapidly and smoothly.

1.   a.   The bíll has góne to Cóngress.
     b.   The Sénate's slów to páss it.
     c.   The séssion's néarly óver.
     d.   Deláy would cáuse us tróuble.
     e.   We néed to knów the réason.

2.   a.   Spríng is the prélude to súmmer.
     b.   Whát is the náme of the áctor?
     c.   Róbert is táller than Állen.
     d.   Whén is the lády expécted?
     e.   Whó has the cóurage to trý it?

3.   a.   The inflátion may léad to a depréssion.
     b.   It's a fáshion I réad of in the pápers.

    c. I can gíve you the ánswer in a mínute.

    d. I'll repéat the suggéstion as I héard it.

    e. You can sée in a móment that he néeds it.

4. a. When the cát's awáy, the míce will pláy.

    b. If the príce is ríght, I'll búy the cár.

    c. Though the níghts are cóld, it's wárm todáy.

    d. As you súrely knów, it's tíme for lúnch.

    e. Since he séems surprísed, you'd bétter spéak.

The above drill is also suitable for taping.

M. Below are some English proverbs. Practice saying them, paying particular attention to the back vowels and /ə/. Do you have proverbs with similar meanings in your own language?

1. ɔ́l ðət glítərz / ɪz nát go̊wld.

2. túw ménɪ kúks spɔ́yl ðə brɔ́θ.

3. íyzɪ kə́m, / íyzɪ gɑ́w.

4. ə nyúw brúwm swíyps klíyn.

5. ɪts névər túw léyt tə lə́rn.

N. Read aloud several pages of English, concentrating your attention on the correct formation of the central or back vowel with which you have most difficulty.

LESSON 13

Consonant Substitutions: Part 1

I. Consonant Substitutions

You should be familiar by now with the idea of vowel substitutions, and will probably understand immediately what is meant by the similar phrase "consonant substitutions." The latter refers, of course, to that type of speech error in which one consonant is incorrectly used in place of another: the pronunciation of *those* as /dowz/ instead of /ðowz/, of *days* as /deys/ instead of /deyz/.

A very large number of such substitutions involve the replacement of a voiced consonant by its voiceless counterpart, or vice versa. We have already treated this type of error in Lessons 8 and 9. In Lessons 13 and 14, we shall work on several common and troublesome consonant substitutions of other kinds, in which the error is not due to incorrect voicing. However, a knowledge of the system of consonant classification and the effect an initial or final position may have on a consonant sound—the material of Lessons 8 and 9—is basic in attacking the problem before us.

II. /θ/, /t/, and /s/; /ð/, /d/, and /z/

The English sounds /θ/ and /ð/ occur in very few of the other important tongues of the modern world. Naturally, most students of English as a second language have trouble with the two consonants and often try to replace them in conversational speech by other, more familiar sounds. The most frequent substitutes for /θ/ and /ð/ seem to be /t/ and /d/, respectively, though /s/ and /z/ are sometimes heard also. If you will check back for a moment and think of the points of articulation of these six sounds, you will note how close together they all are.

The consonants /ð/ and /θ/, of course, make up a voiced-voiceless pair. In the formation of both, the cutting edges of the upper and lower front teeth are aligned and brought close to one another without touching. The tongue is advanced toward the slit-like opening between the upper and lower teeth until its tip makes light contact with the back of both sets of teeth. For /θ/, both initial and final, the air is forced out between the tongue and the teeth with considerable pressure. In fact, the /θ/-sound is merely the noise of this air escaping through its narrow passage. For /ð/, there is less pressure and consequently less sound of escaping air, the latter being largely replaced by vibration of the vocal cords. /ð/ is usually a somewhat shorter sound than /θ/. Practice with *teeth* /tiyθ/ and *teethe* /tiyð/, *thigh* /θay/ and *thy* /ðay/, and make the contrast as clear as possible.

When /t/ is substituted for /θ/, as when a Scandinavian or German pronounces *thing* as /tɪŋ/ in place of /θɪŋ/, it means that a stop has been substituted for a continuant. The speaker has interrupted the outflow of breath completely by a brief but firm contact of the tongue against the tooth ridge, rather than allowing the air to escape continuously between the tongue and the teeth. Exactly the same thing happens when /d/ replaces /ð/, as when *the* is pronounced /də/ instead of /ðə/. Both substitutions can be avoided by *making a longer but a less firm contact with the tongue, and by making this contact between the teeth rather than against the tooth ridge*.

When /s/ is substituted for /θ/, or /z/ for /ð/, as when the traditional Frenchman speaking English pronounces *think* as /sɪŋk/ instead of /θɪŋk/, the problem is primarily with the place of articulation rather than the manner of articulation. The substitutions can be avoided by *advancing the tip of the tongue and allowing the air to escape between it and the teeth, rather than farther back between the blade of the tongue* (the part just behind the tip) *and the hard palate*.

In spite of the ease with which substitutions of /t/ for /θ/ and of /d/ for /ð/ can be corrected when the speaker makes a conscious effort to form them well, they may continue for years to mark his or her English as "foreign-sounding" at times when concentrating on the thought he or she wishes to express rather than on the position of the tongue. *This kind of error is especially persistent in the short, unstressed words of a sentence.* The combinations *of the* and *knew that* are good examples. To eliminate incorrect /d/'s when such phrases are used unselfconsciously, the student may need to make a considerable disciplined effort. Drills such as those in this lesson may help, especially Exercises A-3 and B-3, in which attention is fixed on the formation of a good /ð/ or /θ/ at the beginning, then gradually transferred to the meaning of what is being said.

III. /dž/ and /y/

The substitution of /dž/ for /y/ is often noted, for example, in the speech of students whose mother tongue is Spanish. In Argentina /dž/ (or /ž/) has replaced /y/ altogether in words like *yo* and *suya*. In most of Latin America and in Spain this substitution can be heard in words spoken with emphasis. By way of contrast, Scandinavians who learn English tend to make the opposite substitution; in a word like *jump* they are likely to replace dž/ by /y/, and pronounce /y̲əmp/ instead of /d̲ž̲əmp/. Since the manner in which these two consonant sounds are made in English has not yet been fully explained in this manual, we shall examine them in some detail.

Up to now we have considered /y/ principally as a glide, a semi-vowel, that occurs *after* a vowel sound in diphthongs such as /ɔy/ and /ay/. In these diphthongs the /y/ begins in the position of /ɔ/ or /a/ and then moves toward the *front* of the mouth. (See Lesson 10, Section I.) /y/ also occurs, however, at the beginning of a syllable and thus *before* a vowel sound, as in *young* /yə́ŋ/ and *onion* /ə́nyən/. In this position it is usually thought of as a consonant. It is still formed as a glide, characterized by movement from one position to another. But the movement of /y/ as a consonant is in the direction opposite to its movement as a semi-vowel: it begins in the front of the mouth, in the position of /i/ or /ɪ/, and then quickly moves *backward* toward the position of the following vowel. This means that the consonant /y/ cannot very well be pronounced alone or separated from the following vowel.

On the other hand, /dž/ is classified as an affricate. An affricate is a stop (see Lesson 8, Section II) followed by a slow separation of the organs of speech, which makes the last part of the sound a continuant. As the symbol indicates, /dž/ is a combination of /d/ and /ž/. It is voiced, as are both the sounds of which it is composed. You may remember that the voiceless counterpart of /ž/ is /š/. Both /ž/ and /š/ are normally produced by the sound of air rushing through a long shallow channel between the blade of the tongue and the hard palate. (See Figure 8 in Lesson 8.) At the sides, the channel is closed by contact between the sides of the tongue and the tooth ridge. The lips are somewhat protruded and rounded. For the production of /dž/ the position is similar, except that for a moment at the beginning of the sound, while forming the initial /d/, the tongue touches the tooth ridge all around, thus blocking altogether the escape of air. When a little pressure has built up, the tip of the tongue (but not the sides) moves away from the tooth ridge, opening the channel for the outrush of air.

If you compare the descriptions of /dž/ and /y/, you will note that the essential difference is *this contact at the beginning of /dž/ between the tongue and the upper tooth ridge.* For /y/, *no part of the tongue touches the roof of the mouth; only light contacts are made between the tongue tip and lower teeth and between the sides of the tongue and the upper bicuspids.* Contrast *jet* /dž̲ɛt/ and yet /y̲ɛt/ and keep your tongue away from your palate and tooth ridge for /y/.

IV. /š/ and /tš/

For reasons that need not be explained here, there is a tendency to substitute /š/ for /tš/ in certain positions, even on the part of students whose mother tongue has a /tš/-sound. Thus *question* is frequently mispronounced as /kwɛsš̲ən/ instead of /kwɛstš̲ən/ by speakers of various language backgrounds.

Since /š/ and /tš/ are the voiceless counterparts of /ž/ and /dž/, they are naturally formed in much the same way, described above, as these latter consonants. Only, in the production of /š/ and /tš/, there is more sound of the outrush of air to make up for the lack of voicing. When /š/ is substituted for /tš/, it simply means that the brief contact between the tongue tip and upper tooth ridge, necessary for /t/, has been omitted. Compare *sheep* /š̲iyp/ and *cheap* /tš̲iyp/, *washer* /waš̲ər/ and *watcher* /watš̲ər/.

V. Exercises

A. 1. Listen carefully as your instructor pronounces a prolonged /θ/ several times: /θ—, θ—, θ—/. Imitate the pronunciation of the consonant, making sure that you make light contact between the tongue tip and the back of the upper and lower teeth.

   2. Listen, then imitate, as your instructor pronounces the following material. Finally, try to pronounce each word or phrase to his or her satisfaction.

   (a)

1. θɔ	4. θɪŋk	7. truwθ
2. θæŋk	5. θərd	8. mənθ
3. θɛft	6. θrow	9. ɔ́θər
		10. mɛ́θəd

(b)

1. arithmetic
2. thick and thin
3. a thrilling thing
4. beneath his thumb
5. the fourth of the month
6. through the theater

(c)

1.	θɪk, tɪk	6.	pæθ, pæt	11.	θɪk, sɪk
2.	θiym, tiym	7.	šiyθ, šiyð	12.	θæŋk, sæŋk
3.	θrɛd, trɛd	8.	lowθ, lowð	13.	θəm, səm
4.	θɪn, tɪn	9.	tiyθ, tiyð	14.	mawθ, maws
5.	feyθ, feyt	10.	íyθər, íyðər	15.	tɛnθ, tɛns

3. After you have an opportunity to look at this exercise to be sure you understand all of the words, repeat this drill as rapidly as you can after your instructor. Do not read from the printed page; just imitate what you hear. Each
sentence contains at least one /θ/, but you should *not* concentrate on these
sounds. Think only of the meaning of the sentence. The instructor will tell
you if you mispronounce a /θ/, and you can try again. The drill is intended to
help you begin to make the /θ/-sound well when your attention is directed
toward the thought of what you are saying.

a.	I'm thirsty.	k.	I'm thinking hard.
b.	I'm methodical.	l.	I'm very thankful.
c.	I'm through with it.	m.	I'm third in the class.
d.	I'm quite thrilled.	n.	I'm three years older.
e.	I'm thoroughly satisfied.	o.	I'm a thousand miles from home.
f.	I'm always faithful.	p.	I'm not a thief.
g.	I'm having a birthday.	q.	I'm at the theater.
h.	I'm in the bathtub.	r.	I'm going south.
i.	I'm healthily tanned.	s.	I'm losing my teeth.
j.	I'm almost pathetic.	t.	I'm anything you say.

B. The instructions for Exercise A apply also to this exercise.

1. /ð—, ð—, ð—/

2.
        (a)   (b)

(a)				(b)	
1.	ðæn	6.	suwð	1.	father and mother
2.	ðiyz	7.	briyð	2.	get them together
3.	ðɪs	8.	lɛ́ðər	3.	smooth feathers
4.	ðaw	9.	béyðɪŋ	4.	either this or that
5.	ðəs	10.	rǽðər	5.	the weather
				6.	then and there

(c)

1.	ðow, dow	6.	tayð, tayd	11.	riyð, riyθ
2.	ðey, dey	7.	lowð, lowd	12.	klowð, klowz
3.	ðɛn, dɛn	8.	ə́ðər, ə́dər	13.	siyð, siyz
4.	ðowz, dowz	9.	wə́rðɪ, wə́rdɪ	14.	sayð, sayz
5.	ðɛər, dɛər	10.	ðay, θay	15.	tiyð, tiyz

3.   a.   I knew that you'd rather not.

        b.   I knew that you'd answer these letters.

        c.   I knew that you'd be absent this afternoon.

        d.   I knew that you'd gather up your things.

        e.   I knew that you'd give clothing.

        f.   I knew that you'd change those grades.

        g.   I knew that you'd investigate further.

        h.   I knew that you'd speak at the beginning of the hour.

        i.   I knew that you breathed easily.

        j.   I knew that it bothered you.

        k.   I knew that you were smothering.

        l.   I knew that the reverse was the case.

        m.   I knew that you'd ask that question.

        n.   I knew that the water was smooth.

        o.   I knew that you were younger than that.

        p.   I knew that you liked the idea.

        q.   I knew that you loathed the place.

        r.   I knew that you disliked bathing.

        s.   I knew that you had them already.

        t.   I knew that they were fun though difficult.

C. 1. Imitate as your teacher pronounces the syllables /dža/ and /ya/ several times. For /dža/, be sure the tip of the tongue touches the tooth ridge; for /ya/, avoid such contact carefully.

2. The exercise below may be carried out as similar drills done previously: (a) the teacher makes sure that the meaning of all words is understood; (b) he or she reads down the columns, then across them, and the class imitates the pronunciation; (c) the students read across and down, in a group and individually; (d) the teacher dictates several words selected at random; (e) the students pick out certain words and try to pronounce them so well that the teacher can identify them by letter.

	dž		y
a.	Jew	b.	you
c.	juice	d.	use (noun)
e.	jet	f.	yet
g.	jarred	h.	yard
i.	joke	j.	yoke
k.	jail	l.	Yale

3. Read these sentences aloud, making as clear a distinction as possible between the /dž/ and /y/ of the italicized words.

a. He has been *jeered* at for *years*.

b. You can't make *jam* with *yams*.

c. *You lie;* it was in *July*.

d. The oranges are *juiceless* and *useless*.

e. Please *yell* when the mixture *jells*.

D. The instructions for Exercise C also apply to this exercise.

1. /šow-tšow, šow-tšow, šow-tšow/

2.

	š		tš
a.	sheep	b.	cheap
c.	ship	d.	chip
e.	shatter	f.	chatter
g.	mush	h.	much
i.	mashing	j.	matching
k.	washer	l.	watcher

3. a. The baby shouldn't *chew* her *shoe*.

b. Merchants try to *catch* all the *cash* they can.

    c. I never *wished* to see such a *witch*.

    d. He uses *crutches* since his foot was *crushed*.

    e. You were *cheated* when you bought that *sheet*.

E.   Your instructor will dictate some of the words from the exercise below for you to recognize and write down. Then you should choose certain of them, not in any fixed order, and try to pronounce them well enough so that he or she can identify them. In the phonetic transcription of each word, marks of length, /:/, and aspiration, /ʰ/, have been added where appropriate (see Lesson 9) in order to help you pronounce more clearly.

1.	dead	/dɛ:d/	8.	sink	/sʰɪŋk/	15.	die	/day/
2.	death	/dɛθʰ/	9.	zinc	/zɪŋk/	16.	thy	/ðay/
3.	debt	/dɛt/	10.	think	/θʰɪŋk/	17.	thigh	/θʰay/
4.	thread	/θʰrɛ:d/	11.	heart	/hart/	18.	sigh	/sʰay/
5.	dread	/drɛ:d/	12.	hard	/ha:rd/	19.	breath	/brɛθʰ/
6.	tread	/tʰrɛ:d/	13.	hearth	/harθʰ/	20.	bread	/brɛ:d/
7.	threat	/θʰrɛt/	14.	tie	/tʰay/	21.	breadth	/brɛ:dθʰ/

F.   This exercise is a review of the consonants that have been practiced in this lesson, and it can be used in different ways. (1) Combine the introductory phrases on the left with each item on the right to practice all of the sentences. (2) Your instructor will call out a letter, and you are to make a sentence by combining one of the introductory phrases on the left with the phrase that corresponds to that letter. (3) When your instructor says "think," you are to use only the phrase "He thought that he should . . ." to make sentences, and when your instructor says "wish," you are to use only the phrase "She wished that she could . . ." to make sentences.

      a. wash the car.

      b. thank the teacher.

      c. watch television.

He thought that he should . . .   d. use the telephone.

      e. go to the theater.

      f. joke about the matter.

She wished that she could . . .   g. shut the door.

      h. breathe deeply.

      i. tell the truth.

      j. choose something else.

G. This exercise is to be carried out like similar exercises done earlier.

    1. (a. thought) (b. taught)   I would never have _____ that.

    2. (a. booth) (b. boot)   That _____ is too small.

    3. (a. thinking) (b. sinking)   Are you _____ or just lying there?

    4. (a. truth) (b. truce)   We must have the _____ at all costs.

    5. (a. They've) (b. Dave) _____ sat there for hours without moving.

    6. (a. these) (b. d's)   Can you pronounce _____ perfectly?

    7. (a. soothe) (b. sued)   He declared he'd _____ her.

    8. (a. teething) (b. teasing)   I believe the child is only _____.

    9. (a. jail) (b. Yale)   My son just got out of _____.

    10. (a. jet) (b. yet)   The color is not _____ black.

    11. (a. joke) (b. yolk)   I see no _____ in that egg.

    12. (a. jeers) (b. cheers)   Don't let their _____ disturb you.

    13. (a. shin) (b. chin)   He hit me on the _____.

    14. (a. share) (b. chair)   Don't take my _____ from me.

    15. (a. dish) (b. ditch)   Put the ashes in the _____.

    16. (a. washing) (b. watching)   What are you _____ so carefully?

H. The sentences in each of the following groups have the same rhythm and intonation. Repeat each group until you can produce that particular pattern rapidly and smoothly.

    1. a. Can you ánswer it for me?

          b. Won't you téll us about it?

          c. Is he shówing it to them?

    d. You're antágonizing him?

    e. You presénted me to her?

2. a. Tóm is a gréat bíg bóy.

    b. Whích is the síxtéenth flóor?

    c. Thís is a óne-mán shów.

    d. Whát was in lást níght's néws?

    e. Whó has the bést báss vóice?

3. a. It's a lóng tíme since I have séen you.

    b. It's a góod thíng that he's an áthlete.

    c. There's a réal réason for precáutions.

    d. It's a lóng wáy to San Francísco.

    e. She was quíte háppy to be chósen.

4. a. It's nót wíse to téll them what you léarned.

    b. There's nó wáy to bríng it to the shóre.

    c. A níce cúp of cóffee would be góod.

    d. A lóud "nó" was áll that he could sáy.

    e. My óld shóes are pléasant to put ón.

It would be instructive to tape the above exercise.

I.   This exercise about jogging provides an opportunity to use the consonant sounds discussed in this lesson in a communicative situation. It can be done in the same way as the exercises in Lessons 9 and 10 about summers in Three Rivers.

1. In ríysənt yíərz / džägıŋ əz kəm tu endžɔ́y gréyt pæpyəlǽrıtı / ın ðə yuwnáytıd stéyts / ən ın mátš əv ðə rést əv ðə wɔ́rld.   2. ıt ız džədžd tə hæv mɛ́nı ədvǽntıdžız.   3. ðey séy ðət ıt ımprúwvz yur bríyðıŋ, / strɛ́ŋθənz yur θáyz, / ən hɛ́əlps yu kəntrówl yur wéyt.   4. yuw kən kəmbáyn ıt wıð bərd

watšɪŋ, / ər wɪð džəst θíŋkɪŋ súwðɪŋ θɔ́ts.   5. ɪf yuw əv ríytšt ə sə́rtn̩ éydž, /

féyθfʊl dzágɪŋ wɪəl kíyp yuw yə́ŋ.   6. yuw kən íyvən tšúwz tə lísən tə ↑

myúwzɪk / æz yuw džág əlɔŋ ðə pǽθ.   7. bət dzágɪŋ ɪz nát wɪðáwt ɪts ↑

dísədvæntɪdžɪz ən déyndžərz.   8. ɪt méyks yuw vέrɪ θə́rstɪ, / ɪkspówzɪz yuw

tə θréts frəm dɔ́gz ən ə́ðər džágərz, / ən méy líyd tʊ ə hárt ətæk.   9. lísənɪŋ

tə džǽz, / yuw mey féal tə híər ən əprówtšɪŋ ɔ́təməbiəl.   10. ðə kwέstšən

ɪz, / hwáy wéyst ɔ́l ðǽt énərdžɪ / wεn yuw kʊd biy dúwɪŋ ə yúwsfʊl džáb tə gét

yʊr έksərsayz?
_____

a. How would you define jogging?
b. Are you yourself a jogger?
c. What are the advantages of jogging thought to be?
d. Are there both physical and mental advantages?
e. Do you think that jogging will keep you young?
f. Is jogging better for the old or for the young?
g. Is it a dangerous sport?
h. Why, or why not?
i. Do you think jogging is just a passing fad?
j. Would you rather jog than do a useful chore?

J. Read aloud several pages of English, concentrating your attention on avoiding whichever of the consonant substitutions treated in this lesson you have noticed in your own speech.

Consonant Substitutions: Part 2

I. /b/, /v/, /w/, and /hw/

These four sounds—/b/, /v/, /w/, and /hw/—form a group within which are made several different substitutions not due to incorrect voicing. Students whose original tongue was Spanish, Japanese, Korean, or Pilipino tend to confuse /b/ and /v/, because of the lack of a clear distinction between the two consonants in those languages; it may seem to an American ear that such students pronounce *visit* as /bízɪt/ instead of /vízɪt/. Scandinavians, Central Europeans, Iranians, members of the Arabic-speaking group, and some others often substitute /v/ for /w/, give *we* the improper sound of /viy/ in place of /wiy/. Latin Americans may prefix a /g/ to words that begin with /w/; *would* /wʊd/ thus becomes /gwʊd/. Since /hw/ does not exist in many languages and may be becoming less common even in American English, there is a rather general tendency to replace it by /w/; *where* /hwɛər/ becomes /wɛər/, *white* /hwayt/ becomes /wayt/.

These substitutions are easily made because all four of the sounds—/b/, /v/, /w/, and /hw/—are produced far forward in the mouth, largely with the lips, the teeth, and the tip of the tongue.

You may remember that /b/ is a voiced stop, made between the lips. For an initial or medial /b/, the lips close firmly, the pressure of air trying to escape builds up briefly behind them, and then the air is released by a sudden opening of the lips: try it with *berry* /bɛ́rɪ/. In the production of a final /b/, the last part of the process, the explosive release of the air as the lips open, is usually not heard. (See Lesson 9, Section III.) Can you pronounce *rob* /rab/, and allow the sound to end while your lips are still closed?

By way of contrast, /v/ is a voiced continuant, made between upper *teeth* and lower lip. It thus differs from /b/, both in place and in manner of articulation. The cutting edge of the upper teeth touches lightly the lower lip, and the air escapes smoothly, without being stopped even momentarily. It should be clear, then, that what is necessary in order to avoid the substitution of /b/ for /v/ is to touch the lower lip *lightly* against the *teeth* rather than *firmly* against the *upper lip. Very, berry;* /vɛ́rɪ/, /bɛ́rɪ/; light touch against upper teeth, firm closure of lips.

Like /y/, /w/ is a glide used both as a vowel and as a consonant. We have seen (Lesson 12, Sections III and V) that in transcription /w/ is written *after* the vowels /o/ and /u/ to represent upward movement toward the *back* of the mouth. When used as a consonant, *before* a vowel as in *went* /wɛnt/ and *once* /wəns/, the sound begins with the lips somewhat protruded and rounded in the /u/-position. The lips then *open* and the speech organs move on quickly to the position for the following vowel, whatever it may be. In avoiding the substitution of /v/ for /w/, it is most important to protrude the lips and keep the lower lip away from the upper teeth. If this lip even brushes the teeth, the /w/ will have some of the /v/-quality about it and may be misunderstood. Contrast *wine* /wayn/ and *vine* /vayn/, *west* /wɛst/ and *vest* /vɛst/.

The remaining sound in this group, /hw/, is a consonantal glide. It is sometimes known as the "candle-blowing sound," because we make it by emitting a little puff of air through the rounded and protruded lips, just as we do when we want to blow out a candle or match. No such puff of air accompanies the formation of /w/. You can see the difference between these two sounds if you will hold a lighted match about two inches from your lips as you pronounce *witch* /wɪtš/ and *which* /hwɪtš/. *Witch* should hardly cause the flame to flicker, but a strongly produced *which* should blow it out.

It should be pointed out that the substitution of /w/ for /hw/ cannot be regarded as an error. Many, perhaps most, American speakers make the substitution, especially when pronouncing rapidly such words as *which, where, what, why,* and *when* in unstressed positions. In the dominant form of British English, /w/ for /hw/ is customary even in stressed words like *whale* and *white*. Such substitutions can sometimes result in misunderstanding, however, and it is certainly worthwhile for the student of American English to be aware that there can be a difference in the pronunciation of such pairs of words.

II. /f/

/f/ is a relatively uncommon sound, particularly in the Austronesian languages of Asia and the Pacific area. In the major Philippine languages it occurs only in loan words. In some forms of Japanese writing, the same symbols are used for both /f/ and /h/. Naturally, then, some students of English have problems in producing the sound.

The most common substitution for /f/ seems to be /p/; for example, Filipinos usually refer to their national language as Pilipino, and the important Korean city of Pusan is often written as Fusan. The differences between /f/ and /p/ parallel those we have already noted between /v/ and /b/. In both cases there are differences both in place and in manner of articulation. /f/ is labiodental, formed between the upper teeth and the lower lip, but /p/ is bilabial, formed between the upper and lower lips. And /f/ is a continuant, whereas /p/ is a stop. In order to avoid the substitution of /p/ for /f/, then, it is necessary to touch the lower lip *lightly* against the upper *teeth* rather than *firmly* against the upper *lip*. Contrast *fat* /fæt/ and *pat* /pæt/, *suffer* /sə́fər/ and *supper* /sə́pər/.

If you have ever listened closely to a Japanese pronouncing the name of beautiful Mount Fuji, you have probably heard another substitution for /f/. Before /uw/, as in *Fuji,* Japanese normally pronounce the sound spelled with the letter f as a consonant very similar to or identical with /hw/. The lips are rounded and protruded, the lower lip touches neither the upper teeth nor the upper lip, and there is noticeable aspiration. See if you can pronounce Fuji, Fukuy, and Fukuoka that way. However, in pronouncing English words such as *fool* /fuwl/, *foot* /fʊt/, and *fist* /fɪst/, make your *lower lip* touch your *upper teeth lightly*.

III. Final /m/, /n/, /ŋ/, and /ŋk/

At the end of words, there is often confusion between /m/, /n/, /ŋ/, and /ŋk/. /m/, /n/, and /ŋ/ form a group of consonants known as nasals, a classification that we have not so far discussed. In the productions of other consonants (orals) the air escapes through the mouth; for the nasals it comes out through the nose. It is the soft palate (velum) that determines which way the air will escape. When the velum is drawn up, it closes the nasal passage and forces the air out through the mouth. When the velum is relaxed, the breath stream may pass out through mouth or nose. To produce a nasal consonant, the velum is relaxed and at the same time the passage through the mouth is blocked at some point by the tongue or lips, so that all the air is forced out through the nose. In

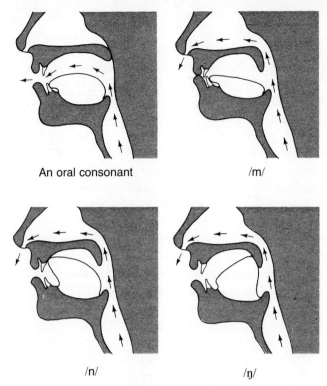

An oral consonant   /m/

/n/   /ŋ/

Figure 15. Air escape for an oral consonant and
the nasal consonants

English, nasals are voiced. The diagrams in Figure 15 should help you visualize the essential differences between an oral consonant and the nasals /m/, /n/, and /ŋ/.

It will be seen that for /m/ the outflow of air through the mouth is blocked by the closing of the lips, for /n/ it is blocked by the tongue's touching the tooth ridge, and for /ŋ/ by the tongue's bunching in the back of the mouth and pressing against the palate.

In Spanish, words ending in <u>m</u> are extremely rare, but words with a final <u>n</u> are very common. The first man is not called Ada<u>m</u> but Adá<u>n</u>, and the preferred spelling for the name of the Jewish patriarch Abraha<u>m</u> is Abrahá<u>n</u>. There is therefore a strong tendency for Spanish speakers, when they begin the study of English, to substitute final /n/ for final /m/. A word such as *from* thus becomes /fran/ and *dim* /di<u>m</u>/ may become *din* /di<u>n</u>/. The problem can be overcome by *closing the lips firmly* for the final /m/: *some* /sə<u>m</u>/, *came* /key<u>m</u>/, and *bloom* /bluw<u>m</u>/.

On the other hand, speakers of certain widespread dialects of Spanish regularly pronounce as /ŋ/ the final consonants that are pronounced as /n/ in Standard Castilian. The same is true of the speakers of several Chinese dialects, in which /ŋ/ replaces the final /n/ of Standard Mandarin. Such speakers find it hard not to carry this habit over into English. In their mouths *rain* /reyn/ becomes / reyŋ/, and *seen* /siyn/ becomes /siyŋ/. To avoid this substitution, it is only necessary to make sure that the *tongue tip and blade* touch the *tooth ridge all around* with enough *firmness* to block the escape of air through the mouth. Note the clear contrast in tongue positions for *ran* /ræn/ and *rang* /ræŋ/, *sin* /sɪn/ and *sing* /sɪŋ/.

Still another group of students—among whom are many native speakers of German, Yiddish, and Russian—often add a /k/ to words that should end with an /ŋ/-sound: for example, they pronounce *doing* /dúwɪŋ/ as /dúwɪŋk/. One of the reasons for this is probably a feeling on the part of the speaker that the final g of a word like *doing* should be pronounced. Since /g/ is a voiced sound, a person in whose native language final voiced consonants are not common will tend to substitute for /g/ its voiceless counterpart, /k/. It should be understood clearly that the g of the ending -ng is silent; the g changes the preceding n from /n/ to /ŋ/, but it is not itself pronounced. You may be able to realize this fact better if you will note the contrasting pronunciations of *singer* and *finger*. The former is /síŋər/; the g is silent, though it affects the sound of n. The latter is /fíŋgər/; the g not only changes the n, but is also pronounced itself. Can you hear the difference between /ŋ/ and /ŋg/? At the end of a word -ng always has the sound of /ŋ/, as in *singer*.

You may have noticed that /ŋ/, /g/, and /k/ are all formed with the tongue in the same position, bunched high in the back of the mouth so as to touch the soft palate. Two of these, /g/ and /k/, are oral stops. To produce them, the velum is drawn up, preventing the escape of air through the nose. The tongue momentarily blocks the passage of air through the mouth, then releases it explosively. The other, /ŋ/, is a nasal continuant. The velum is relaxed, allowing the air to pass out through the nose. The tongue, which blocks the passage through the mouth, remains in its position until the end of the sound. There is no explosive release of breath. The substitution of /ŋk/ for /ŋ/ may be avoided, then, by taking care that there shall be no explosive release, no aspiration, at the end of a word like *rang*. The tongue should remain pressed against the palate until the sound is completely finished. Contrast *rang* /ræŋ/ and *rank* /ræŋk/, *sing* /sɪŋ/ and *sink* /sɪŋk/.

IV. /h/

The problem with /h/ is not usually substitution, but omission. It is another of those English sounds that do not occur in certain other languages, notably

French, Italian, and Portuguese. In Spanish a sound similar to /h/ exists, but it is represented by the letter j; the letter h̲ is always silent. This means that speakers of one of these Latin languages may have difficulty in producing /h/, and find it natural simply to ignore the sound. On the other hand, once they become aware of /h/, they may tend to insert the sound where it does not belong: /ɪts may h̲ównlɪ howp/ for "It's my only hope."

This tendency is probably strengthened by the fact that in a few common English words the h̲ really should be left silent: *heir* /ɛər/, *honor* /ánər/, and *hour* /awr/. Either pronunciation, with or without /h/, is possible for *herb,* /ərb/ or /hərb/; *homage* /hámɪdž/ or /ámɪdž/; and *humble,* /hə́mbəl/ or /ə́mbəl/. Furthermore, native speakers of English frequently omit the /h/ of little words such as *he, him, his, her, have, has,* and *had, when these are in an unstressed position* in the sentence: *Téll him nów* /tɛ́əl ɪm náw/; *we have dóne it* /wiy əv də́n ɪt/.

Except in the cases mentioned above, initial h̲'s should be sounded. Even with *he, him,* etc., it is certainly not necessary to omit the h̲ in order to avoid a "foreign accent."

The /h/-sound is a voiceless continuant, and no particular position of the tongue and lips is required to produce it. With the speech organs in the position of the vowel that is to follow /h/, the breath is forced through the partially closed vocal cords and out of the mouth with sufficient strength to make a rushing sound (as if the speaker were panting for breath): *home* /h̲owm/, *house* /h̲aws/.

V. Exercises

A. 1. Listen carefully as your instructor pronounces a prolonged /v/ several times: /v—, v—, v—/. Imitate the pronunciation, making sure that your lower lip lightly touches your upper teeth.

2. Listen, then imitate, as your instructor pronounces the following material. Finally, try to pronounce each word or phrase to his or her satisfaction.

a.						
1.	veyn	6.	vízɪt	11.	ɪnvéyd
2.	vɛst	7.	vílɪdž	12.	ɪnváyt
3.	vɔys	8.	ləv	13.	kə́vər
4.	vyuw	9.	breyv	14.	ɪlɛ́vən
5.	hɛ́vi	10.	sɛ́vən	15.	peyvd

b. 1. various vegetables   3. never vexed
    2. overly virtuous   4. verify the victory

5.	a vicious savage	9.	an oval table
6.	a big vote	10.	a back vowel
7.	a vivid blue	11.	a bold visitor
8.	a very bad verdict	12.	a beautiful valley

3. After you have an opportunity to look at this exercise to be sure you understand all of the words, repeat this drill as rapidly as you can after your instructor, without looking at the printed page. Concentrate on the *thought* of the sentences, and depend upon your instructor to call to your attention any /v/ that is mispronounced.

a. I've sealed the envelope.

b. I've had very little vacation.

c. I've prevented an accident.

d. I've never tried to write verse.

e. I've read Volume I.

f. I've just left my favorite class.

g. I've developed several vices.

h. I've spilled gravy on my vest.

i. I've never even seen it.

j. I've lost some valuable papers.

k. I've never driven a Cadillac.

l. I've learned all vowels are voiced.

B. 1. Imitate as your teacher pronounces /wiy/, /wiy/, /wiy/; /wow/, /wow/, /wow/. Be sure your lips are rounded and protruded, and that you keep your lower lip away from your teeth as you pronounce /w/.

2. a.

1.	wey	6.	kwáyət	11.	wéyt
2.	wɔl	7.	swɪm	12.	əwéyt
3.	wɛnt	8.	ɔ́lweyz	13.	kwɛ́stšən
4.	wər	9.	bɪwɛ́ər	14.	wɛ́stərn
5.	kwɪk	10.	bɪtwíyn	15.	wúmən

b.

1.	within a week	7.	a vast world
2.	gone with the wind	8.	a loving wife
3.	wish me well	9.	vile weather
4.	waste away	10.	win over
5.	awaken at once	11.	a wicked villain
6.	without vigor	12.	the seven wonders of the world

3. After reading this exercise to be sure you understand all of the words, repeat
    the drill after your instructor, without looking at the printed page. Concentrate
    on the *thought* of the sentences, and depend upon your instructor to call your
    attention to any mispronounced /w/'s.

    a. I wish I were wiser.

    b. I wish I had a sandwich.

    c. I wish I weighed less.

    d. I wish I knew more words.

    e. I wish I could find work.

    f. I wish I were widely read.

    g. I wish we had won.

    h. I wish we were through.

    i. I wish you would warn us.

    j. I wish you would reward us.

    k. I wish the window were open.

    l. I wish to ask a question.

C. 1. With your hand before your lips, pronounce the name of the letter y̲ /w̲ay/ and
        the word /h̲way/ several times. You should be able to feel the puff of air with
        which /hway/ is produced.[1]

    2. a. 1. hway   5. hwayt   9. hwayn
            2. hweyl   6. hwɪp   10. ɛ́vrɪhwɛər
            3. hwɛn   7. hwiyl   11. hwɛnɛ́vər
            4. hwɪtš   8. əhwáyl   12. hwiyt

        b. 1. the white whale   7. wash his whiskers
            2. which wharf   8. a wild whistle
            3. the whip whistled   9. whisk away
            4. a whiff of whiskey   10. while the wind whirled
            5. whine and whimper   11. whether we want it or not
            6. wherever you wish   12. when she winked

    3. a. I know what you want us to do.

        b. I know what we're to study.

---

[1]Note to the teacher: The chief purpose of this drill is to help students *hear* the difference
between /w/ and /hw/. Because many native speakers of English do not distinguish between the
two sounds in their own speech, little time should be spent trying to make sure that all students
learn to *produce* the distinction automatically.

   c.   I know what a whirlwind is.

   d.   I know what you whispered.

   e.   I know nowhere to look.

   f.   I know where the laboratory is.

   g.   I know when we make recordings.

   h.   I know when I pronounce it right.

   i.   I know all your whims.

   j.   I know which bus to take.

   k.   I know why the wheels turn.

   l.   I know why we're doing this.

D. This section deals with /f/. As it is less commonly mispronounced than some of the other sounds we have been studying, many members of a particular class may have no difficulty with it. The following communicative activities may help to decide how much time should be spent in practicing /f/ with a particular group. Activity 1 can serve as a way of determining if problems with /f/ are common in the class. If they are found to be common, Activity 2 can provide additional practice. A good way for a teacher to encourage a student to try to correct a faulty pronunciation by repeating a word is for the teacher to cup his or her hand behind the ear as if to indicate inability to hear what the student said.

  1. a. The teacher asks if the following are used for food or for fuel: gasoline, margarine, coal, butane, snails, fodder, wood, straw, fowls, fish, fruit, kerosene.

      b. Ask how many there are of the following: seasons in a year, cents in a nickel, quarters in a dollar, people in a quintet, states in the United States, hours in a day and night, cards in a deck for playing bridge, weeks in a year, numbers in half a hundred.

  2. a. Ask the class as a group to list as many towns and cities as they can whose name begins with the sound of /f/.

      b. Ask students to explain what fauna and flora are.

      c. Ask them what their favorite foods are.

      d. Ask if there is a difference in meaning between *further* and *farther*.

E. 1. Imitate your teacher's pronunciation of /ræm/, /ræn/, /ræŋ/, /ræŋk/ several times. Be sure that your lips meet firmly for /m/, that your tongue touches your tooth ridge for /n/, that it touches your soft palate for /ŋ/, and that only /ŋk/ has an explosive release.

2.   This exercise is to be carried out similarly to previous exercises of the same kind. (For example, Lesson 11, Exercise F.)

	m		n		ŋ		ŋk
a.	tam	b.	tan	c.	tang	d.	tank
e.	clam	f.	clan	g.	clang	h.	clank
i.	brim	j.		k.	bring	l.	brink
m.		n.	ban	o.	bang	p.	bank
q.	some	r.	son	s.	sung	t.	sunk
u.	bum	v.	bun	w.	bung	x.	bunk
y.	hum	z.	Hun	aa.	hung	bb.	hunk

3.   Read these sentences aloud, making as clear a distinction as possible between the /m/, /n/, /ŋ/, and /ŋk/ of the italicized words.

a.   They *ran* and *rang* the bell.

b.   A new *gang* war *began*.

c.   I think he's *kin* to the *king*.

d.   It's *pinching* my *chin*.

e.   Come *on;* get *along*.

f.   A pilot must *win* his *wings*.

g.   What are you *doing* with the *ink?*

h.   The Titanic's passengers *sang* as the ship *sank*.

i.   Are you *ordering drinks?*

j.   I *think* the *thing* is possible.

k.   The chains *clank* and *clang*.

l.   The flowers are *dropping* their *pink* petals.

m.   What a *dumb thing* to have *done!*

n.   We had to spend *some time* away *from home*.

o.   She's *done some singing on television*.

p.   That car *can* turn *on* a *dime*.

q.   The waitress *came, bringing* his *rum*.

4.   Try to explain what *ram, ran, rang,* and *rank* mean.

F.   1.   Imitate your teacher's pronunciation of /huw/ /huw/ /huw/; /hey/, /hey/, /hey/. You should be able to feel the strong puff of air at the beginning of each of these syllables.

2. a.
1. haws
2. huw
3. how
4. hɪər
5. heyt

6. howld
7. hɔrs
8. hiyt
9. hə́rt
10. əhɛ́d

11. pərhǽps
12. bɪhéyv
13. bɪháynd
14. hə́ŋgrɪ
15. hǽmbərgər

b.
1. hard-hearted
2. high-handed
3. the whole of history
4. Uncle Henry

5. a happy home
6. my only hope
7. hurricane winds
8. an entire ham

3. After going over this exercise to be sure you understand all of the words, repeat the drill after your instructor without looking at the printed page. Concentrate on the *thought* of the sentences and depend upon your instructor to call your attention to the omission of any /h/'s that should not be omitted, or to the insertion of any /h/'s where they do not belong.

a.   I hear you've been in the hospital.

b.   I hear you've heard from home.

c.   I hear you're going away for the holidays.

d.   I hear you know how to manage a horse.

e.   I hear you hope to be able to hire an electrician.

f.   I hear you've been hesitating to ask for help.

g.   I hear he's been misbehaving.

h.   I hear he always has high grades.

i.   I hear he's not happy here.

j.   I hear he habitually hides his errors.

k.   I hear he has a beautiful head of hair.

l.   I hear it has already happened.

m.   I hear they're holding open house.

n.   I hear I must meet the American history and institutions requirement.

o.   I hear that instructor is often hard to please

G.   This exercise is to be carried out like similar exercises done previously.

b	v	w
1. bail	2. veil	3. wail
4. buy	5. vie	6. Y
7. bile	8. vile	9. wile

10. bet	11. vet	12. wet
13.	14. vine	15. wine
16. best	17. vest	18. west

H. In order to help fix in your mind the position in which the consonants studied in these last two lessons and the back vowels are formed, another lip-reading exercise is included here. Your instructor will form some of the combinations below with his or her lips, tongue, and so on, without actually uttering any sound. Try to recognize each combination and write down its number.

1. ba	2. va	3. wa	4. ða	5. da
6. bow	7. vow	8. wow	9. ðow	10. dow
11. bə	12. və	13. wə	14. ðə	15. də

I. This exercise is to be carried out like similar exercises previously done.

1. (a. bow) (b. vow) He made a _____ to greet us cordially.

2. (a. boat) (b. vote) The candidate received a large _____.

3. (a. bat) (b. vat) A _____ is used in making beer.

4. (a. veil) (b. wail) A _____ is a sign of sorrow.

5. (a. verse) (b. worse) It couldn't possibly be _____.

6. (a. vines) (b. wines) Californians should know about _____ .

7. (a. fan) (b. pan) You don't need a _____ for that.

8. (a. fashion) (b. passion) Do you know about my new _____?

9. (a. leaf) (b. leap) That's a beautiful _____.

10. (a. food) (who'd) We saw _____ served.

11. (a. sum) (b. sun) How can the _____ be so large?

12. (a. clam) (b. clan) Do you know what a _____ is?

13. (a. ton) (b. tongue) Does it weigh as much as a _____ ?

14. (a. sin) (b. sing) Don't urge me to _____ .

15.   (a. stun) (b. stung)   Your remarks _____ me.

16.   (a. wing) (b. wink)   The waiter gave me a _____ .

17.   (a. sing) (b. sink)   The child won't _____ in the water.

18.   (a. bang) (b. bank)   I wouldn't _____ on the door, if I were you.

19.   (a. hitch) (b. itch)   I hope no _____ will develop.

20.   (a. heart) (b. art)   Put your _____ in your work.

21.   (a. heating) (b. eating)   I won't live there because of the _____ arrangements.

J.   In English the most popular type of humorous verse is certainly the limerick. A limerick has five lines. The first, second, and fifth lines each have three stresses (not necessarily placed according to the usual rules for sentence stress) and rhyme with one another. The third and fourth lines have only two stresses each and likewise rhyme with each other. The rhythmic pattern is very strong and regular.

   The four well-known limericks that follow are very suitable for small-group activities designed to give you a surer control of rhythmic patterns. One good sequence for such activities might be:

a.   The teacher divides the class into four groups and assigns each group of you a limerick to prepare.
b.   The members of each group then read the limerick that has been assigned to you and try to help one another understand its meaning.
c.   Each group locates and marks the stresses in its limerick.
d.   The teacher comes to each group in turn and reads the assigned limerick to you line by line while the members listen and imitate.
e.   The students in each group practice reading their limerick, or reciting it from memory, with each student pronouncing one line and one of you following another in order around the circle. You should try to keep the overall rhythm of the verse as regular as possible.
f.   Each group recites its limerick for the entire class.
g.   If facilities are available, the groups can record their limericks on tape.

1.   I'd rather have fingers than toes;
     I'd rather have ears than a nose;
        And as for my hair,
        I'm glad it's still there.
     I'll really be sad when it goes.

2. As a beauty I'm not a star;
    There are others more lovely by far;
    But my face—I don't mind it,
    For I am behind it.
    The people out front get the jar!

3. An amoeba named Sam and his brother
    Were having a drink with each other.
    But while they were quaffing
    They split their sides laughing,
    So each of them now is a mother.

4. A medical student named Lees,
    Worn down by B.A.'s and M.D.'s,
    Collapsed from the strain.
    Said his doctor, "It's plain
    You are killing yourself by degrees."[2]

K. Read aloud several pages of English, concentrating your attention on avoiding whichever of the consonant substitutions treated in this lesson you have noticed in your own speech.

---

[2]The limericks are adapted from somewhat different versions in *The World's Best Limericks* (Peter Pauper Press), *A Treasury of Laughter* (edited by Louis Untermeyer), and H.A. Gleason's *Workbook in Descriptive Linguistics* (Henry Holt and Company).

LESSON 15

Consonant Clusters

I. Phonotactic Rules

Sounds can be difficult for language learners to pronounce not only because of the way they are formed when they stand alone, but also because of the position they occupy in relation to other sounds in words or sentences. Every language has its own set of rules (sometimes called *phonotactic* rules) governing such features as the positions in which each sound can be used, the vowels that can appear together, and the order in which consonants can follow one another without intervening vowels. These rules always greatly restrict the number of sound sequences that can actually be used as words in a given language. Though you may have never seen the word *ndiyo* (Swahili for "yes") before, you know that it cannot be English because of the order in which the sounds follow one another. No real language would permit the combination *Btfsplk*, which is the impossible name that an American humorist gave to one of his characters.[1] Though the individual sounds that make up that name are easy for the speakers of most languages to pronounce in isolation, the sounds are arranged in a way that violates the phonotactic rules of all known languages. Therefore no one can pronounce the name easily without inserting two or three vowels.

---

[1] Al Capp in his widely read comic strip, *Li'l Abner*. Joe Btfsplk walked around under his own little black cloud and always brought terrible misfortune to anyone with whom he came in contact.

Some of the phonotactic rules of English are shared with other languages, but no two languages have precisely the same set of rules. And each time a student of English has to learn a word whose sounds are in positions that the mother tongue does not permit, the student has more or less of a problem in pronouncing the word. The reverse is, of course, also true. A native speaker of English has trouble pronouncing the Swahili word *mtoto* /mtóto/ "child", because the rules of English require that an initial /m/ be followed by a vowel. For similar reasons English speakers have problems with *ngalan* /ŋálan/ "name" and *maaari* /ma'á'ari/ "possible" in Pilipino, or *Pferd* /pfɛrt/ "horse" in German, or *Gdynia* /gdíynya/ "name of city" in Polish.

A somewhat simplified formula for the syllable structure of English is (C)(C)(C)V(C)(C)(C)(C). This is read as meaning that the only obligatory element in an English syllable is V: that is to say, a vowel sound. The vowel may, optionally, be preceded by as many as three C's, consonant sounds. It may be followed by up to four consonant sounds. An example of the most elaborate permitted syllable would, then, be *strengths,* pronounced as /strɛŋkθs/.

This syllable structure of English is relatively complicated; the great majority of syllables of most languages are much simpler than the longer syllables that English allows. The formula for the syllable structure of Japanese, for example, is (C)(y)V(n). There must be a vowel sound, which may be preceded by a consonant sound. If a second consonant sound precedes the vowel, it can only be /y/, and the only consonant sound permitted after the vowel is /n/. Thus, most Japanese words are made up of a series of simple CV's: *sayonara, sukiyaki,* and so on.

All this means that native speakers of Japanese, like the native speakers of most other languages, do not find it easy to pronounce the more elaborate consonant clusters of English. When English words such as *strike* and *guest* are borrowed into Japanese, they have to be reconstituted according to the Japanese formula: *strike* becomes *sutoraiku,* and *guest* becomes *gesuto.*

The phonotactic rules that cause most trouble to language students may be those that govern consonant clusters—that is, sequences of two or more consonants within one syllable. In this lesson we will consider in some detail the consonant clusters that English permits. Initial and final clusters will be identified, and opportunities will be given to practice those that occur most frequently. We will also discuss ways in which the pronunciation of words and phrases may be affected by unfamiliar clusters, as well as ways in which the pronunciation of consonant clusters can be made easier. In the next lesson, Lesson 16 entitled "The Sandhi of Spoken English," we will look at other pronunciation problems that are related to the phonotactics of English.

II. Consonant Clusters in Initial Position

The table that follows lists, with examples, all of the consonant clusters that are permitted in initial position in an English word or syllable.[2] The items are arranged according to the final element of each cluster, in alphabetical order.

Initial Consonant Clusters Permitted in English

(Two-Consonant Clusters)

1. /sf/ sphere /sfɪər/	26. /tw/ twelve /twɛəlv/
2. /sk/ sky /skay/	27. /θw/ thwart /θwɔrt/
3. /bl/ blue /bluw/	28. /by/ beauty /byúwtɪ/
4. /fl/ fly /flay/	29. /dy/ due /d(y)uw/
5. /gl/ glad /glæd/	30. /fy/ few /fyuw/
6. /kl/ clear /klɪər/	31. /gy/ gewgaw /gyúwgɔ/
7. /pl/ play /pley/	32. /hy/ hue /hyuw/
8. /sl/ sleep /sliyp/	33. /ky/ cure /kyʊr/
9. /sm/ small /smɔl/	34. /my/ mute /myuwt/
10. /sn/ snow /snow/	35. /ny/ new /n(y)uw/
11. /sp/ speak /spiyk/	36. /py/ pure /pyur/
12. /br/ bring /brɪŋ/	37. /ty/ tune /t(y)uwn/
13. /dr/ drink /drɪŋk/	38. /vy/ view /vyuw/
14. /fr/ free /friy/	
15. /gr/ great /greyt/	
16. /kr/ cross /krɔs/	*(Three-Consonant Clusters)*
17. /pr/ price /prays/	39. /skl/ sclerosis /sklɪrówsɪs/
18. /šr/ shrink /šrɪŋk/	40. /spl/ split /splɪt/
19. /tr/ tree /triy/	41. /skr/ scratch /skrætš/
20. /θr/ three /θriy/	42. /spr/ spring /sprɪŋ/
21. /st/ still /stɪəl/	43. /str/ street /striyt/
22. /dw/ dwell /dwɛəl/	44. /skw/ square /skwɛər/
23. /gw/ Gwen /gwɛn/	45. /sky/ skew /skyuw/
24. /kw/ quick /kwɪk/	46. /spy/ spew /spyuw/
25. /sw/ sweet /swiyt/	47. /sty/ stew /st(y)uw/

Some of the clusters on the list—such as /gw/ (number 23), /θw/ (27), /gy/ (31), and /skl/ (39)—are so rare that even a native speaker of English

---

[2]Much of the data in the tables in this lesson is drawn from Betty Jane Wallace, "A Quantitative Analysis of Consonant Clusters in Present-Day English," unpublished dissertation, University of Michigan, 1951.

might spend a lifetime without ever needing to use them. Many of the clusters made up of a consonant plus /y/ or /w/ (22–38) are permitted by the phonotactic rules of many other languages, so that native speakers of those languages seem to have little or no trouble with them when learning English.

Four of the clusters, which include an alveolar consonant (see Lesson 8, Figure 8) followed by /y/ as part of the diphthongal vowel /yuw/, are regularly heard in extensive regions of the United States, but not in other regions. These four are /dy/ (29) as in *due,* /ny/ (35) as in *new,* /ty/ (37) as in *tune,* and /sty/ (47) as in *stew.* Note that the /y/ with which these clusters are transcribed is written between parentheses in the list as (y) in order to indicate that the inclusion or omission of the /y/ is optional. For a student of English, either pronunciation—/yuw/ or /uw/—is equally acceptable in words of this type.

For a large group of students the numerous clusters ending in /l/ or /r/ (3–8, 12–20, 39–43) are quite difficult. The basic reason here is that speakers of Chinese, Japanese, Korean, and a number of other languages have trouble pronouncing /l/ and /r/ in any position. In their language /l/ and /r/ are not distinguished from one another as they are in English. Thus their *play* /pley/ may sound like *pray* /prey/, and/or their *pray* may sound like *play.* Once they master the pronunciation of /l/ and /r/ in other positions, as in *lay* and *ray,* they should find it relatively easy to pronounce *play* and *pray.* The production of /l/ and /r/ has already been discussed in some detail in Lesson 10, Section I. If you are still having problems with the two sounds, it would be well to review that discussion at this point.

It may be worth noting that all three-consonant initial clusters (39–47) are put together according to a very limited formula. The first sound is always /s/. The second sound is always one of the three voiceless stops that exist in English: /p/, /t/, or /k/. And the third sound is always one of the four glides and liquids of the language: /w/, /y/, /l/, or /r/. The nine combinations of these sounds that actually occur are indicated by the arrows in Figure 16.

consonant 1   consonant 2   consonant 3

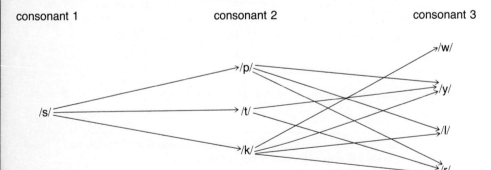

Figure 16. Formula for initial three-consonant clusters

III. Initial Clusters Beginning with /s/

The most troublesome initial clusters for the largest number of students seem to be those consisting of an initial /s/ followed by one or more other consonants. This large group includes /sf/, /sk/, /sl/, /sm/, /sn/, /sp/, /st/, and /sw/, as well as all nine of the three-consonant clusters. Typical examples are *spirit* /spírɪt/, *stop* /stap/, *string* /strɪŋ/, *scrap* /skræp/, and *square* /skwɛər/. All these words violate the phonotactic rules of a number of important languages, including Chinese, Spanish, and Iranian. Speakers of these languages often try to make initial-/s/ clusters easier to pronounce by placing a vowel—/ɛ/ or /ɪ/—before the /s/, thus splitting the clusters into two separate syllables: /es-pírɪt/, /ɛs-táp/, /ɪs-tríŋ/, and so on. This type of mispronunciation can usually be avoided by concentrating on the /s/-sound and consciously lengthening it: /s:pírɪt/, /s:tap/, /s:trɪŋ/.

Some students make a different type of error in pronouncing the /sl/, /sm/, and /sn/ clusters. They substitute a /z/-sound for the /s/. In other words, they begin voicing for the /l/, /m/, or /n/ too soon. Thus, *smoke* sounds like /zmowk/. Again, the way to avoid this is to concentrate on lengthening the /s/-sound without voicing it, and then to pronounce the following consonant very rapidly: /s:mowk/.

IV. Consonant Clusters in Final Position

The following table lists the consonant clusters that are permitted at the end of an English word or syllable. The items are arranged as in the table of initial consonant clusters: alphabetized, first, according to the final element in each cluster and, then, according to each preceding element in turn. The most frequently used clusters are marked with an asterisk (*). Particular attention should, of course, be paid to these marked clusters.

Final Consonant Clusters Permitted in English

(Two-Consonant Clusters)

1.	/lb/ bulb /bəlb/	8.	/ŋd/ longed /lɔŋd/
2.	/rb/ barb /barb/	*9.	/rd/ marred /mard/
3.	/bd/ robbed /rabd/	10.	/ðd/ bathed /beyðd/
4.	/gd/ tagged /tægd/	11.	/vd/ lived /lɪvd/
*5.	/ld/ filled /fɪəld/	*12.	/zd/ caused /kɔzd/
6.	/md/ seemed /siymd/	13.	/žd/ rouged /ruwžd/
*7.	/nd/ cleaned /kliynd/	*14.	/lf/ self /sɛəlf/

Final Consonant Clusters Permitted in English (continued)

15.	/nf/ Banff /bænf/	55.	/rv/ curve /kərv/
16.	/rf/ scarf /skarf/	56.	/bz/ cabs /kæbz/
17.	/rg/ berg /bərg/	*57.	/dz/ beds /bɛdz/
18.	/lk/ milk /mɪəlk/	58.	/gz/ bags /bægz/
*19.	/ŋk/ ink /ɪŋk/	*59.	/lz/ fills /fɪəlz/
*20.	/rk/ dark /dark/	*60.	/mz/ seems /siymz/
21.	/sk/ ask /æsk/	*61.	/nz/ cleans /kliynz/
*22.	/rl/ girl /gərl/	*62.	/ŋz/ things /θɪŋz/
23.	/lm/ film /fɪəlm/	*63.	/rz/ cars /karz/
24.	/rm/ arm /arm/	64.	/ðz/ bathes /beyðz/
25.	/ln/ kiln /kɪəln/	65.	/vz/ loves /ləvz/
*26.	/rn/ turn /tərn/		
*27.	/lp/ help /hɛəlp/		*(Three-Consonant Clusters)*
28.	/mp/ camp /kæmp/		
29.	/rp/ harp /harp/	66.	/lbd/ bulbed /bəlbd/
30.	/sp/ wasp /wasp/	67.	/rbd/ barbed /barbd/
31.	/fs/ laughs /læfs/	68.	/rld/ curled /kərld/
*32.	/ks/ likes /layks/	69.	/lmd/ filmed /fɪəlmd/
*33.	/ls/ else /ɛəls/	70.	/rmd/ armed /armd/
*34.	/ps/ stops /staps/	71.	/lnd/ kilned /kɪəlnd/
*35.	/rs/ nurse /nərs/	72.	/rnd/ learned /lərnd/
*36.	/ts/ eats /iyts/	73.	/lvd/ shelved /šɛəlvd/
37.	/θs/ baths /bæθs/	74.	/rvd/ carved /karvd/
38.	/rš/ harsh /harš/	75.	/dzd/ adzed /ædzd/
39.	/ft/ laughed /læft/	76.	/nzd/ bronzed /branzd/
*40.	/kt/ liked /laykt/	77.	/džd/ judged /džədžd/
*41.	/lt/ felt /fɛəlt/	78.	/mpf/ nymph /nɪmpf/
*42.	/nt/ ant /ænt/	79.	/lfs/ Alf's /æəlfs/
*43.	/pt/ stopped /stapt/	80.	/rfs/ serfs /sərfs/
*44.	/rt/ art /art/	81.	/lks/ milks /mɪəlks/
*45.	/st/ passed /pæst/	*82.	/ŋks/ links /lɪŋks/
*46.	/št/ washed /wašt/	*83.	/rks/ works /wərks/
47.	/dθ/ width /wɪdθ/	84.	/sks/ asks /æsks/
48.	/fθ/ fifth /fɪfθ/	85.	/lps/ helps /hɛəlps/
*49.	/lθ/ wealth /wɛəlθ/	86.	/mps/ camps /kæmps/
50.	/nθ/ month /mənθ/	87.	/rps/ harps /harps/
51.	/pθ/ depth /dɛpθ/	88.	/sps/ wasps /wasps/
*52.	/rθ/ earth /ərθ/	89.	/fts/ lifts /lɪfts/
53.	/tθ/ eighth /eytθ/	90.	/kts/ acts /ækts/
*54.	/lv/ twelve /twɛəlv/	91.	/lts/ belts /bɛəlts/
		*92.	/nts/ prints /prɪnts/

Final Consonant Clusters Permitted in English (continued)

93. /pts/ accepts /əksɛ́pts/
94. /rts/ hearts /harts/
95. /sts/ tests /tɛsts/
96. /dθs/ widths /wɪdθs/
97. /fθs/ fifths /fɪfθs/
98. /lθs/ filths /fɪəlθs/
99. /nθs/ months /mənθs/
100. /pθs/ depths /dɛpθs/
101. /rθs/ births /bərθs/
102. /tθs/ eighths /eytθs/
103. /ltš/ Welsh /wɛəltš/
104. /ntš/ pinch /pɪntš/
105. /rtš/ march /martš/
106. /lft/ delft /dɛəlft/
107. /mft/ triumphed /tráyəmft/
108. /rft/ surfed /sərft/
109. /lkt/ milked /mɪəlkt/
110. /ŋkt/ linked /lɪŋkt/
111. /rkt/ worked /wərkt/
112. /skt/ asked /æskt/
*113. /rnt/ burnt /bərnt/
114. /lpt/ helped /hɛəlpt/
115. /mpt/ camped /kæmpt/
116. /rpt/ carped /karpt/
117. /spt/ clasped /klæspt/
118. /dst/ midst /mɪdst/
119. /kst/ taxed /tækst/
120. /lst/ pulsed /pəlst/
121. /nst/ sensed /sɛnst/
122. /pst/ lapsed /læpst/
*123. /rst/ forced /fɔrst/
124. /tst/ blitzed /blɪtst/
125. /ršt/ marshed /maršt/
126. /tšt/ watched /watšt/
127. /rθt/ berthed /bərθt/
128. /lfθ/ twelfth /twɛəlfθ/
129. /ŋkθ/ length /lɛŋkθ/
130. /ksθ/ sixth /sɪksθ/
131. /lbz/ bulbs /bəlbz/

132. /rbz/ barbs /barbz/
133. /ldz/ holds /howldz/
134. /ndz/ lends /lɛndz/
135. /rdz/ cards /kardz/
136. /rgz/ bergs /bərgz/
137. /rlz/ curls /kərlz/
138. /lmz/ films /fɪəlmz/
139. /rmz/ arms /armz/
140. /lnz/ kilns /kɪəlnz/
141. /rnz/ learns /lərnz/
142. /lvz/ selves /sɛəlvz/
143. /rvz/ carves /karvz/
144. /ldž/ bulge /bəldž/
*145. /ndž/ change /tšeyndž/
146. /rdž/ large /lardž/
(Four-Consonant Clusters)

147. /ldžd/ bulged /bəldžd/
148. /ndžd/ changed /tšeyndžd/
149. /rdžd/ charged /tšardžd/
150. /mpfs/ nymphs /nɪmpfs/
151. /lkts/ mulcts /məlkts/
152. /ŋkts/ instincts /ɪ́nstɪŋkts/
153. /mpts/ tempts /tɛmpts/
154. /rpts/ excerpts /ɛ́ksərpts/
155. /ksts/ texts /tɛksts/
156. /rsts/ thirsts /θərsts/
157. /lfθs/ twelfths /twɛəlfθs/
158. /ŋkθs/ lengths /lɛŋkθs/
159. /ksθs/ sixths /sɪksθs/
160. /ŋkst/ amongst /əmə́ŋkst/
161. /mpst/ glimpsed /glɪmpst/
162. /ltst/ waltzed /wɔltst/
163. /ntst/ minced /mɪntst/
164. /rtst/ quartzed /kwɔrtst/
165. /ltšt/ filched /fɪəltšt/
166. /ntšt/ pinched /pɪntšt/
167. /rtšt/ marched /martšt/
168. /rmpθ/ warmth /wɔrmpθ/
169. /rldz/ worlds /wərldz/

Students should not be alarmed by the large number of permitted final clusters in the above list. Many of them are included in the table merely to give an overall picture of those that exist. Though the 169 final clusters are almost four times as numerous as the 47 initial clusters, an even larger proportion of the final ones than of the initial ones are quite rare in actual use. A glance over the list will show that the great majority of the items marked with an asterisk—those that are quite common—are two-consonant clusters, which are also relatively easy to pronounce. Only six of the three-consonant clusters and none of the four-consonant clusters are so marked.

In an analysis of 10,000 words, about an hour and a half of recorded speech, the /nt/ final cluster was found to occur over 200 times and the /ts/ cluster over 100 times. However, only 37 final clusters occurred five or more times. This manual concentrates on those 37, and students are advised to do the same.

The table shows that many two-consonant clusters, most three-consonant clusters, and all four-consonant clusters are created when the extremely common endings -s and -ed, and the less common -th, are added to words that already end in one or more consonants. This means that a very large part of the difficulty students have in pronouncing final clusters arises from the need to add one or the other of these three endings. In Lesson 8 we discussed the principles that determine the three different ways in which -s and -ed endings are pronounced. A familiarity with those principles is obviously essential if students are to be able to recognize which clusters are represented by the spelling of words like *eighths* /eytθs/, *worlds* /wərldz/, *changed* /tšeyndžd/, and *asked* /æskt/.

A somewhat similar problem of recognizing clusters from the way they are spelled arises in words like *warmth, prince,* and *amongst.* In the pronunciation of words such as these a voiceless stop (/p/, /t/, or /k/) that is not represented in the spelling of the words is inserted in the final cluster. *Warmth* is pronounced as /wɔrmpθ/ with a /p/. *Prince* comes out as /prɪnts/ with a /t/, and thus rhymes perfectly with *prints. Amongst* sounds like /əməŋkst/ with a /k/. These inserted stops seem to occur most regularly when a voiced nasal continuant—/m/, /n/, or /ŋ/—is present in a final cluster where it is followed by a voiceless sound, usually also a continuant. *Warmth, prince,* and *amongst* all conform to that pattern. In passing from the voiced nasal to the voiceless sound, a speaker is almost forced to produce the voiceless stop that corresponds to the voiced nasal in its point of articulation. It is actually easier to insert /p/ between the /m/ and /θ/ of *warmth* than it is to pass directly from /m/ to /θ/. Most native speakers of English are unaware of the inserted stops and may even deny pronouncing them, but the stops are present in the phonetic transcriptions provided in many good dictionaries. Since their insertion makes the pronunciation of a number of final clusters easier, nonnative speakers would do well to become aware of them. In our table of final clusters, additional examples of inserted stops can be found in *nymph* (78), *Welsh* (103), *length* (129), and *minced* (163).

V. Making Clusters Easier to Pronounce

Even native speakers of English, who have presumably internalized the phonotactic rules of the language, may find the pronunciation of the more complicated consonant clusters difficult. It should be remembered that the final cluster of one word may be followed immediately in the stream of speech by the initial cluster of another word. This can result in the creation of sequences of consonants that are very long indeed. To say *changed streets* involves the production of seven consonant sounds in succession without a single intervening vowel: /-ndžd str-/. Sequences of five or six consonants can easily be found: *learned quickly* /-rnd kw-/, *sixth floor* /-ksθ fl-/, *charged three* /-rdžd θr-/, *walked strangely* /-lkt str-/, and so on. For all speakers of English, then, there is a degree of pressure to find ways, especially in rapid conversation, of making clusters and sequences of consonants easier to pronounce.

Nonnative speakers can profit by some of the ways that are used by native speakers to make clusters more pronounceable. Two of these ways will be discussed here: (1) phonetic syllabication, and (2) the omission of consonants.

The most recommendable of the two for students is the process that has been called "phonetic syllabication." Phonetic syllabication can occur when a word ends in a consonant sound and the following word begins with a vowel, as in the sequences *has it* /hǽz ɪt/, *hide 'em* /háyd əm/, and *give up* /gɪv ə́p/. The two words must be closely related and occur within the same thought group, as is the case with verbs and their objects, two-word verbs, auxiliary verbs and their accompanying main verbs, adverbs modifying adjectives, and so on. (See Lesson 4, Section IV, Thought Groups and Blending.) Under those circumstances the final consonant of the first word can be pronounced at the beginning of the second word: /hǽ-zɪt/, /háy-dəm/, /gɪ-və́p/. In the same way the last consonant of a final cluster can be moved forward and pronounced with the vowel of the following word. *Find out* can become /fayn-dáwt/, *Sixth Avenue* can become /sɪks-θǽvənyuw/, and *changed address* can become /tšéyndž-dədrɛ́s/. Two-consonant clusters are thus reduced to single consonants, three-consonant clusters to two-consonant clusters, and four-consonant clusters to easier three-consonant clusters. Proper use of phonetic syllabication can not only facilitate a student's pronunciation, it can also do much to make his or her English sound more authentic.

The second way to make consonant clusters more pronounceable is simply to omit one of the consonant sounds. Native speakers do this more often than they realize: for example, many very commonly pronounce *arctic* as /ártɪk/, omitting the first c̲. Probably everyone omits the difficult p̲ in *raspberry,* which is normally pronounced /rǽzbɛ̀rɪ/, as well as the d̲ in *handsome,* pronounced /hǽnsəm/. Such omissions happen most frequently and are least noticeable in final three-consonant clusters when the middle consonant, the sound that is omitted, is a voiceless stop: *acts* /ækt̲s̲/ becomes /æk̲s̲/, *lifts* /lɪft̲s̲/ becomes /lɪf̲s̲/, *asked* /æsk̲t̲/ becomes /æs̲t̲/. They may also happen with continuants: *depths* /dɛpθs/ becomes /dɛps/, and *government* /gə̀vərnmənt/ becomes /gə̀vərmənt/. Omissions of this kind should, however, be used with restraint. Too many of them, especially in formal situations, may give hearers the impression that the speaker is somewhat uneducated.

There is still another, a third way of making clusters easier, but the authors of this manual definitely do *not* wish to recommend or even to suggest its use by nonnative speakers. Unfortunately, it is the way such speakers often choose instinctively. That is, to break up the combinations by inserting "finishing sounds," obscure vowels, or even fully sounded vowels between individual consonant sounds: *I don't think so* as /ay downt̲ʰ θɪŋkʰ sow/, *these three* as /ðiyzə̲ θriy/, or the Japanese transformation of *stress* into *sutoresu.* These pronunciations are, of course, the result of attempts to impose the phonetic or phonotactic rules of other languages on English. They are *not* common in the speech of native speakers of English and can make the language quite difficult to understand. (See Lesson 9, Section III, Aspiration at the End of Words.)

To sum up, if an American family serves you delicious Russian *borscht* soup for dinner and you have trouble saying /bɔrs̲t̲/, there is a better chance of your being understood if you will omit the /t/ and call the soup /bɔrs̲/, rather than insert an /ə/ and call it /bɔ́rəs̲t̲/.

VI. Exercises

A.   Your instructor may want to use this exercise as a test (see Lesson 11, Exercise H) to find out how much you profited by the material on /l/ and /r/ in Lesson 10, or how well you have otherwise learned to distinguish between the two sounds. More specifically, the exercise should show whether or not you can apply such general ability as you may have in pronouncing /l/ and /r/ to the special problems of handling them in initial clusters.

If you find you still sometimes have trouble in hearing the difference between the two sounds, or in pronouncing them so that a listener can always hear the difference, it would be advisable to go back and work through the materials in Lesson 10 again. Exercises A, B, and C in that lesson are designed to increase students' mastery of /l/ and /r/, beginning with the positions in which they are easiest to pronounce and then working up to the positions where they are most difficult.

1.   (a. play) (b. pray)   It's time to go _____ now.

2.   (a. crime) (b. climb)   The _____ was quite discouraging.

3.   (a. fleas) (b. freeze)   We had trouble with the _____.

4.   (a. plow) (b. prow)   A _____ is always pointed.

5.   (a. crew) (b. clue)   The captain didn't have a _____ .

6.   (a. fright) (b. flight)   The rabbit was about to take _____.

7.   (a. glass) (b. grass)   Please don't walk on the _____.

8.   (a. blue) (b. brew)   Do you see that speck in the _____?

9.   (a. flames) (b. frames)   The pictures were in _____.

10.   (a. braid) (b. blade)   She showed us how to make a _____.

11.   (a. fly) (b. fry)   These fish don't _____ well.

12.   (a. crash) (b. clash)   There was no warning before the _____.

13.   (a. free) (b. flee)   They wanted to _____ the prisoner.

14.   (a. claw) (b. craw)   The fish wound up in the bird's _____.

15.   (a. glowing) (b. growing)   I saw the light _____.

16.   (a. present) (b. pleasant)   Enjoy the sun while it's _____.

B.   1.   This exercise is particularly helpful for those who have difficulty with initial consonant clusters with the /s/-sound. Pronounce each word, concentrating on

the /s/-sound and lengthening it, if necessary, making sure you do not insert
a vowel sound before it. Then pronounce the words at a more normal speed.

a.	sweater	h.	special	o.	splurge
b.	spiral	i.	slide	p.	sphere
c.	struggle	j.	smile	q.	squint
d.	star	k.	splash	r.	small
e.	spot	l.	spray	s.	sky
f.	snow	m.	scratch	t.	sniffle
g.	schedule	n.	string	u.	scream

2. This exercise gives you an opportunity to practice the use of initial three-
consonant clusters. It approaches them through "build-ups," series of three
words. The first word in each series begins with a glide or liquid: for example,
rap /ræp/. In the second word a voiceless stop is prefixed to the first word,
thus producing a meaningful word beginning with a two-consonant cluster:
trap /træp/. In the third word /s/ is prefixed to the second word, producing a
meaningful word beginning with a three-consonant cluster: *strap* /stræp/. For
the formula see the end of Section II in this lesson. Remember that we are
concerned with the *sounds* that make up the words, not with their *spelling*.

The following procedure is suggested for doing the exercise. First, the
teacher reads each word in all the series and you imitate his or her pronunciation. Then you close your books, and the teacher divides you into two teams
for a contest. The teacher gives the first word of a series. Members of the
teams take turns trying to give words two and three in the same series. A
method of scoring may be to score one point for a team each time a member
of it gives a meaningful word that fits the formula (whether the word is listed
below or not), and to subtract a point from the team's score when a member
gives a word that is not meaningful or that does not fit the formula.

a.	ray, tray, stray	g.	ride, tried, stride
b.	ream, cream, scream	h.	rain, train, strain
c.	lay, play, splay	i.	wire, quire, squire
d.	rye, pry, spry	j.	rip, trip, strip
e.	rig, prig, sprig	k.	rate, trait, straight
f.	you, pew, spew	l.	latter, platter, splatter

C. In the final consonant cluster of each of the words below, there is an inserted
    voiceless stop that is pronounced but that is not shown by the spelling. (See end
    of Section IV of this lesson.) Pronounce the words and try to identify the inserted
    stop.

    1. fence   4. warmth   7. dreamt
    2. ninth   5. strength   8. rinse
    3. lymph   6. month   9. sevenths

D. 1. Read the sequences below several times. Simplify their final consonant clus-
        ters by using phonetic syllabication; that is, pronounce the final consonant of
        the first word as if it were the initial consonant of the second word: *cooks it*
        /kúks it/ as /kúk-sit/.

        a. lóans it   h. fínds 'er   o. must adópt
        b. wórks it   i. cáused 'em   p. don't allów
        c. arránged it   j. retúrned 'em   q. won't ánswer
        d. cúrled it   k. turns aróund   r. can't ówn
        e. lóves 'im   l. looked úp   s. júst a féw
        f. hélped 'im   m. sold óut   t. móst of áll
        g. tóld 'er   n. moved óver   u. lóts of tíme

    2. Read the following sequences that *cannot* be made easier by phonetic sylla-
        bication. Try to pronounce all of the consonant sounds in them.

        a. don't know   k. that's clear
        b. last minute   l. most boys
        c. thank them   m. it's broken
        d. can't think   n. can't quite
        e. gets back   o. depth from
        f. doesn't rain   p. looked through
        g. think so   q. first quarter
        h. forward march   r. works perfectly
        i. six feet   s. sounds pretty
        j. first floor   t. just three

E.   Because the word *the* occurs so frequently in English, it seems useful to practice sequences with the word *the* preceded by words that contain final consonant clusters. You will notice that, with a little practice, your tongue adjusts itself to various points of articulation for /ð/, depending upon the consonant that precedes it. Practice reading these sequences several times until you can say them smoothly.

1.	changed the room	11.	worked the puzzle
2.	failed the test	12.	fixed the machine
3.	aren't the ones	13.	sort the cards
4.	assumed the worst	14.	since the dance
5.	hopped the fence	15.	understand the word
6.	helped the man	16.	almost the end
7.	worth the trouble	17.	thinks the most
8.	built the house	18.	points the arrow
9.	amazed the people	19.	knows the date
10.	deals the cards	20.	it's the end

F.   1.   Read the sentences below, all of which have singular subjects. Pay particular attention to the pronunciation of the final consonant clusters in the verb forms: /lts/ *consults,* /ks/ *looks.* Then read the sentences again, making the subject of each sentence plural and paying attention to the final consonant clusters of the noun forms: /rz/ *lawyers,* /mz/ *rooms.*

        a.   The lawyer consults many books.

        b.   The room looks empty.

        c.   The example seems easy.

        d.   The instructor writes on the blackboard.

        e.   The teacher smiles at the class.

        f.   The student tells stories.

        g.   The girl sings beautifully.

        h.   The professor answers the questions.

        i.   The girl receives letters every day.

        j.   The picture hangs on the wall.

    2.   Your teacher will read one of the sentences above, sometimes with a singular subject, sometimes with a plural subject. You will tell which he or she is pronouncing. This will give you practice in listening for the -*s* ending. Individual students can continue the exercise.

G. 1. Read the sentences below, all of which have present-tense verb forms. Then read the sentences changing the verbs to the past form. Pay attention to the final consonant clusters that are formed by the addition of the *-ed* ending.

      a. They live on Main Street.

      b. We study very hard.

      c. They ask a lot of questions.

      d. The professor always answers them.

      e. The janitors mop the floor.

      f. The boys laugh a lot.

      g. The waitress serves breakfast.

      h. We arrange the date of the dance.

      i. The twins look alike.

      j. We prepare a list.

   2. Your teacher will read a sentence from the above, sometimes in the present tense, sometimes in the past. You will tell which he or she is pronouncing. This will give you practice in listening for the *-ed* ending. Individual students can continue the exercise.

H. This drill is intended to give you practice in pronouncing difficult combinations of consonants without inserting a "finishing sound." Use phonetic syllabication to make consonant clusters easier where possible. This material is well suited to individual laboratory work.

   1. A large group of students graduates each spring.
   2. I heard that splendid speech you made last night.
   3. He changed his mind and lunched at the student cafeteria.
   4. They answered correctly, and the instructor thanked them.
   5. I request that all books be removed from the desks.
   6. He will need all his strength to catch the others.
   7. The next time you come we must speak Swahili.
   8. Someone's trying to turn my friends against me.
   9. Does she like this part of the United States?
   10. George nudged me and asked if we hadn't watched long enough.
   11. I wonder why that child acts so strangely.
   12. The baby has a big splinter in the skin of his finger.
   13. Thanksgiving comes the last Thursday in November.

14. Do you expect to catch the next train?

15. We'll have to risk using the old screens this year.

I. Read the following paragraph, paying particular attention to final consonant clusters produced by the *-ed* ending.

Clarence, a university student who lives with his aunt in town, often helps around the house. One Saturday, his aunt went downtown, leaving a list of things for Clarence to do. Clarence performed the first three chores with great good will. Then he discovered that his car had a flat tire. He changed it and began to work on the engine. When his aunt arrived home, she found that Clarence had washed the dishes, made his bed, and picked up his clothes. But he hadn't washed the windows, burned the trash, hosed down the front porch, or trimmed the hedge. Clarence confessed that the time had slipped by, and he was very sorry.

With your book closed, talk about all the things that Clarence had done and had not done.

J. Read the following paragraph, paying particular attention to the final consonant clusters produced by the addition of the *-s* ending.

Alice and Ann are twin sisters. When they were little girls, their mother dressed them exactly alike. Now that they are older, they like to wear clothes that are different. Since they go to the same university and have similar features, people sometimes mistake one for the other. If you are well acquainted with them, however, you can tell them apart in many ways. Alice likes to wear bright-colored blouses and skirts; Ann prefers more subdued shades. Ann reads and studies a lot, while Alice spends her time participating in various sports and games. Alice smiles and laughs a great deal and makes friends easily; Ann seems quieter and attracts friends more slowly. They agree on some things, like going to dances and to the movies on weekends. And neither one ever lacks invitations to go out.

With your books closed, tell about the similarities and differences between the twins.

K. Practice reading aloud interesting articles from the newspaper, paying particular attention to the smooth pronunciation of consonant clusters.

The Sandhi of Spoken English

I. What Sandhi-Forms Are

The word *sandhi,* usually pronounced /sǽndìy/ in English, is a borrowing from Sanskrit, in which language it means "placing together." It is used by grammarians to refer to the differences in the pronunciation of words or endings that depend on the environment in which these occur. A well-known example in English is the use of the article *a* /ə/ before nouns that begin with a consonant sound, and of *an* /ən/ before those beginning with a vowel sound: *a morning, an afternoon*. In the case of *a* and *an* the difference in pronunciation is obvious in both the written form and the spoken form of the language. In many other cases, however, the difference is present only in the spoken form. By far the most important example of this in English is the alternative pronunciations of the *-ed* ending as /t/, /d/, and /ɪd/, and of *-s* as /s/, /z/, and /ɪz/.

We are primarily concerned in this manual, of course, with sandhi in the *spoken* language.

The environment that determines when a sandhi-form is used may be present in a single word or it may involve a sequence of two or more words. You may remember that the environment in which the syllabic consonants we studied in Lesson 10 occur is described in the following equation:

$$\left.\begin{array}{c} /t/ \\ /d/ \\ /n/ \end{array}\right\} \ + \text{ unstressed syllable containing } \left\{\begin{array}{c} /l/ \\ /n/ \end{array}\right. > \text{ syllabic consonant}$$

These syllabic consonants are usually heard within a single word: *final* /fáynl̩/, *student* /styúwdn̩t/, *sentence* /séntn̩ts/. But they will also occur if the necessary environment is present in a contraction formed of two separate words: *didn't* /dídn̩t/, or *couldn't* /kúdn̩t/. And they may likewise occur if the environment is produced by a sequence of closely related words such as *night and day* /náyt n̩ déy/.

Another case of a sandhi-form that may occur either within a word or between closely related words is the medial /t/ that sounds "somewhat like a /d/" that we studied in Lesson 9. (We will transcribe it here as a /d̠/.) You may remember that, within a single word, the environment in which it is produced is between voiced sounds, usually vowels, but not at the beginning of a stressed syllable. Thus it is heard in *letter* /lɛ́d̠ər/, *atom* /ǽd̠əm/, and *party* /párd̠ɪ/; but not in *attest* /ətɛ́st/. Examples of the occurrence of this /d̠/-like /t/ between closely related words are *hit 'im* /híd̠ im/ and *right or wrong* /ráyd̠ ər rɔ́ŋ/. If the sentence stress is on the second of the two words, the /t/ is /d̠/-like when it ends the first word: *get up* is pronounced /gɛd̠ ə́p/. The /t/ remains a /t/, however, when it begins the second word: *a test* is heard as /ə tɛ́st/.

In this manual we are concerned both with sandhi within one word (internal sandhi) and with sandhi between words (external sandhi). The same processes are involved in the two positions.

It should be apparent by now that we have already discussed sandhi often in this text, so far without using that term. The various aspects of sandhi that we have dealt with earlier include not only the endings *-ed* and *-s,* syllabic consonants, and the /d̠/-like /t/, but also blending within thought groups, special unstressed forms of words, the insertion of /ə/ between front vowels and /l/ or /r/, the special features of initial and final consonants, the simplification of consonant clusters, and various other kinds of phonetic variation.

The basic reason for all these types of sandhi seems to be the pressure that speakers feel to make the pronunciation of the language easier. The following are the principal processes by which this very human need is met.

1. *Assimilation:* that is, changing the voicing and/or the point of articulation of adjacent sounds so as to make them more similar (for example, in *guessed* /gɛst̠/ the d̠ is devoiced so as to make it more like the voiceless /s/ that precedes it).

2. *Obscuration:* pronouncing a sound with reduced clarity and effort (unstressed vowels are regularly obscured in English).

3. *Omission:* ignoring entirely a sound suggested by·the spelling of a word (the b̠ of *debt* is always omitted).

4. *Insertion:* adding a sound that puts the speech organs in a better position

to pronounce the following sound (the insertion of /ə/ between a front vowel and /l/, as in *well* /wɛəl/, makes it easier to produce the "dark" /l/ that is needed at the end of the word).

There are sandhi-forms in all languages. All native speakers of each language use a great many of these forms in the environments that call for them. It is true that highly literate speakers, influenced by their extensive contact with the written language, tend to make less use of sandhi. In formal situations some sandhi-forms are completely acceptable, other forms less acceptable. However, sandhi-forms are a perfectly natural, very important, even essential part of English. There is absolutely no justification for the fear some nonnative speakers have of using them. Natural use of them may well do more than any other factor to make your English more understandable.

This lesson is designed, then, to enable you to understand sandhi in a fuller perspective by putting together what you may already know about the phenomenon. Information about several aspects of sandhi that we have not yet discussed will be given, and the environments that call for each type will be indicated. You may be sure that all the forms you are asked to practice here can be used in almost any social situation in which you may find yourself.

II. More about Unstressed Function Words

Back in Lesson 4, Section III, we studied a list of 14 "Words Most Frequently Weakened." That list, which you might want to review, is made up of function words which, in their usual unstressed environment, are "weakened" or "reduced." This reduction is accomplished by the obscuration or omission of some of the sounds that are heard when the words are fully stressed: *can* /kǽn/ becomes /kən/, *have* /hǽv/ becomes /əv/, and so on. Though reduction can take place with a great many function words, the list includes only a few of the most common of them, those whose weakening is most necessary if a speaker's English is to sound like English.

Because the reduction of unstressed function words is so pervasive and our information about it is as yet so incomplete, it seems useful to return to the subject in the present lesson. A list of additional words that are often weakened is therefore provided below. The items are alphabetized and divided into the three groups of words that are particularly subject to reduction: particles (short conjunctions, prepositions, and articles that do not take endings), pronouns, and verbal forms.

Supplementary List of Words Subject to Reduction

Word	Stressed Form	Reduced Forms	Example
			(PARTICLES)
1. as	/æz/	/əz/	it's as good as gold /ɪts əz gúd əz gówld/
2. at	/æt/	/ət/	look at the time /lúk ət ðə táym/
3. from	/fram/	/frəm/	came from there /kéym frəm ðέər/
4. than	/ðæn/	/ðən/	better than ever /bέtər ðən έvər/
		/ðn̩/	more than that /mɔ́r ðn̩ ðǽt/
		/n/	less than a mile /lέs n ə máyl/
			(PRONOUNS)
5. he	/hiy/	{ /iy/	he's gone! /iyz gɔ́n/
		{ /ɪ/	I thought he did /ay θɔ́d ɪ dɪ́d/
6. her	/hər/	/ər/	made her glad /méyd ər glǽd/
7. him	/hɪm/	/ɪm/	wish him luck /wɪ́š ɪm lə́k/
8. his	/hɪz/	/ɪz/	break his neck /bréyk ɪz nέk/
9. she	/šiy/	/šɪ/	did she walk? /dɪ́d šɪ wɔ́k/
10. them	/ðɛm/	{ /ðəm/	I saw them /ay sɔ́ ðəm/
		{ /əm/	give them hell! /gɪ́v əm hέəl/
11. what	/hwat/	/wət/	that's what I said /ðǽts wət ay sέd/
12. you	/yuw/	{ /yʊ/	will you sing? /wɪəl yʊ sɪ́ŋ/
		{ /yə/	how do you do /háw də yə dúw/
			(VERBAL FORMS)
13. am	/æm/	{ /əm/	I am sure /ay əm šúr/
		{ /m/	I'm sure /aym šúr/
14. do	/duw/	{ /dʊ́/	how do I know? /háw dʊ áy nów/
		{ /də/	what do they want? /hwát də ðey wánt/
15. must	/məst/	/məs/	we must leave now /wiy məs líyv náw/
16. will	/wɪəl/	{ /wəl/	Jim will work it /džɪ́m wəl wə́rk ɪt/
		{ /əl/	mother will be there /mə́ðər əl biy ðέər/
		{ /l̩/	what will it be? /hwát l̩ ɪt bíy/
17. would	/wʊd/	/əd/	people would like that /píypəl əd layk ðǽt/

You will note that for some of the items on the list (numbers 4, 5, 10, 12, 13, 14, 16) more than one reduced form is given. In fact, a trained phonetician can hear more than one reduced form for all of the items on both this supplementary list and the one in Lesson 4. The different forms correspond to progressively greater degrees of reduction. For example, *Joan will sign it* may be heard as /džówn wɪəl sáyn ɪt/, or /džówn wəl sáyn ɪt/, or /džówn əl sáyn ɪt/, or /džównl̩ sáyn ɪt/. And *he has gone* may be reduced from /hiy hǽz gɔ́n/, to /hiy həz gɔ́n/, to /hiy əz gɔ́n/, to /hiyz gɔ́n/.

The principal factors responsible for the different degrees of reduction seem to be those listed below.

Sentence stress: the less stress, the more reduction. A word with full normal or contrastive stress (see Lesson 6, Section II) should not be reduced.

Frequency of use: the more often a word is used and the more its presence in a given linguistic environment can be assumed, the more reduction. The starred items on the list in Lesson 4 are among the most frequent of all English words, and they are almost always reduced.

Speed of utterance: the faster a speaker talks, for whatever reason, the more reduction.

Formality of situation: the more informal the social situation, the more reduction. Formality is very common in a university classroom, where teachers may deliver (or read) lectures, and students are expected to demonstrate their knowledge and abilities in the most understandable possible language. However, a great deal of formality is inappropriate in most other social environments.

Some authorities insist that there is more reduction before words beginning with consonants than there is before words beginning with vowels. *The* is said to be pronounced /ðə/ before consonants, /ðiy/ before vowels: *the banana* /ðə bənǽnə/, *the apple* /ðiy ǽpəl/. *To* in *to eat* is said to be /tuw íyt/ or /tʊ iyt/; *to dine* is said to be /tə dáyn/. If this distinction is really widely observed in practice, the usage must be dialectal or occur under relatively formal circumstances. A great many well-educated native speakers of English are quite comfortable pronouncing *the* as /ðɪ/ and *to* as /tə/ in all unstressed positions. We think that teachers of English who insist that their students should always pronounce *the, to,* and other unstressed words one way before consonants and another way before vowels are probably wasting both their own and your time.

III. The Disappearing t̲

There is probably more variation dependent on environment in the American English pronunciation of the letter t̲ than in the pronunciation of any other consonant. We have already discussed in Lesson 9 the variant sounds of t at the beginning of words (with aspiration) and at the end of words (usually without aspiration). We have also referred a number of times to the voiced or flapped medial t that sounds somewhat like a /d/. In Section V of this lesson we shall look at cases in which t, along with certain other consonants, is palatalized; that is, it is pronounced with the front of the tongue raised toward the hard palate.

We know that t is often inserted in consonant clusters where the letter is not present in the spelling: *since,* for example, is pronounced as /sɪnts/. Here we will look at cases where exactly the reverse is true; t is present in the spelling but, for all practical purposes, seems to disappear in pronunciation. The pair of words *winter* and *winner* provide a good example. It is probable that for most Americans, most of the time, the two words rhyme perfectly as /wínər/. If someone says /ðə wínər ɪz kə́mɪŋ/, we cannot tell, without more context, whether the remark concerns the season or an athlete.

The environment in which the disappearing t occurs is represented by the following formula:

$$\begin{pmatrix} \text{stressed syllable} \\ \text{ending with } \underline{nt} \end{pmatrix} + \begin{pmatrix} \text{unstressed} \\ \text{syllable} \end{pmatrix} > \underline{t} \text{ not pronounced}$$

You are likely to notice the absence of /t/ first in very common words such as *twenty* /twéni/ and *plenty* /pléni/. Then you may notice that, in informal situations, Californians will tell you that their state capital is /sækrəménow/ (Sacramento) and that /sǽnə mánɪkə/ (Santa Monica) is near Los Angeles. Georgians will explain that their state is on the /ətlǽnɪk/ (Atlantic) coast and that its capital is /ətlǽnə/ (Atlanta).

Other examples are *county* /káwnɪ/, *bountiful* /báwnɪfəl/, and *quantity* /kwánɪtɪ/. The necessary environment is often created when endings such as -ing, -ed, and -er are added to verbs and adjectives: *slanting* /slǽnɪŋ/, *painted* /péynɪd/, and *fainter* /féynər/.

In phonetic terms, the facts explaining the t's disappearance seem to be that the speaker pronounces the stressed /n/ of a word like *plenty,* then introduces the following unstressed vowel by a nasal release of the consonant sound. You will recall that /n/ and /t/ have the same point of articulation—the tooth ridge. To eliminate the /t/ after the /n/ of /pléni/ the tongue tip has only to leave the tooth ridge weakly, with no aspiration.

The disappearing t is much more common in American English than in British English. And in American English it is more informal than, for example, syllabic consonants. You may or may not want to incorporate this type of sandhi-form into your own speech, but you should certainly be prepared to recognize such forms and to understand the words where the forms occur.

IV. Reductions of Verb + <u>to</u>

The unstressed particle *to* is used with great frequency, and its use in a particular linguistic environment is often quite predictable. In other words, the presence of *to* can often be assumed, whether it can be clearly heard or not. It is therefore the kind of word that is inevitably involved in many reductions.

One of *to*'s typical uses is to link auxiliary-like verbs to the main verbs that usually follow them: *want to see* or *ought to grow*. In this environment several well-established reductions occur that are used at times by even the most educated speakers of American English. Writers of popular literature have even invented special spellings, which do not appear in dictionaries, for a number of these reductions.

Full Form	*Spelling of Reduction*	*Pronunciation of Reduction*	*Meaning*
1. going to	gonna	/gə́nə/ (or /gównə/)	intention
2. got to	gotta	/gádə/	necessity
3. has to	hasta	/hǽstə/	necessity
4. have to	hafta	/hǽftə/	necessity
5. ought to	oughta	/ɔ́də/	moral obligation
6. used to	usta	/yúwstə/	former habit
7. want to	wanna	/wánə/	desire

A number of different processes, with most of which we are already familiar, have resulted in the creation of these sandhi-forms. *Wanna* involves omission of the disappearing t̠. In *gotta* and *oughta* there are /d/-like /t/'s resulting from assimilation: the voicing of /t/ after a stressed (and voiced) vowel. *Hasta, hafta,* and *usta* involve assimilation in the opposite direction: the devoicing of the /z/ and /v/ of /hǽz̠/, /hǽv̠/, and /yuwz̠/ to make them more like the voiceless /t/ of the following *to*. The development of *gonna*, the most common of all these forms, seems to involve a combination of processes. We assume that the /ŋ/ of *going* /gówɪŋ/ was first changed to /n/, /gówɪn̠/, a very widespread sandhi-change that we will return to later in this lesson. The /n/ and /t/ of /gówɪn tə/ thus came to be in the environment that results in the disappearing /t/. The /t/ was omitted, and the /ow/ was obscured to /ə/ because of its frequent use in unstressed positions. The steps would therefore be /gówɪŋ tuw/ > /gówɪn tə/ > /gównə/ > /gə́nə/. This is a very good example of how sandhi-changes can accumulate.

It is useful, even necessary if you want to be fully understood, to be familiar with the *meaning* of these reductions of verb + *to*, because the mean-

ing of the reduced form can differ from that of the corresponding full form.
Note these examples.

> 1a. I'm *gonna* be good.   (intention)
>   b. I'm *going to* church.   (destination)
> 2a. What have we *gotta* eat?   (necessity)
>   b. What have we *got to* eat?   (availability)
> 3a. What does she *hafta* say?   (necessity)
>   b. What does she *have to* say?   (provision of explanation)
> 4a. It's what he *hasta* do.   (necessity)
>   b. It's all he *has to* work with.   (availability)
> 5a. You *usta* dance often.   (former habit)
>   b. This is what you *used to* scare us.   (utilization)
> 6a. How much do you *wanna* do it?   (extent of desire)
>   b. How much does he *want to* do it?   (request for renumeration)

In the case of each of the pairs of sentences above, you cannot use in Sentence
b the reduced form found in Sentence a without changing the meaning of Sentence b or making it meaningless.

V. Palatalization across Word Boundaries

In Lesson 8, Section III, we identified the consonants /z/, /s/, /ž/, and /š/ as
palato-alveolars, formed by allowing the air to escape through a narrow passage
between the tongue and the hard palate. The *palato-* in *palato-alveolar* refers
to the hard palate, and *alveolar* refers to the alveolar ridge, the technical term
for the tooth ridge. The hard palate, of course, is that part of the roof of the
mouth just behind and above the tooth ridge. Hard palate and tooth ridge are
thus joined, and there is no obvious way of telling where the one ends and the
other begins. The chief difference between /z, s/ and /ž, š/ is that /z/ and /s/
are made farther forward with the *tip* of the tongue near the tooth ridge, and
that /ž/ and /š/ are made just a little farther back and higher up, with the *blade*
of the tongue near the hard palate. (See Lesson 13, Section III.) Another
closely related sound, /y/, is made with the *blade* of the tongue approaching
the hard palate still farther back and higher up. In other words, there are similarities among all these sounds and they can be produced in a more or less
regular progression by moving the tongue from the tooth ridge backward and
upward to the highest point of the hard palate: /z, s/→/ž, š/→/y/.

  With the above relationships in mind, it is instructive to consider the historical changes in the pronunciation of *-tion,* a very common ending for nouns
in a number of Germanic and Romance languages, including English. The *-ti-*

of the ending was once pronounced /ty/, which required the tongue to move all the way from a dental position for /t/, backward and upward through the positions for /s/ and /š/, to the high palatal position for /y/. Try it, and see how difficult this considerable movement is to make.

We have seen that it is through the development of sandhi-forms that speakers make pronunciations easier. So the movement of the tongue from /t/ to /y/ was shortened. In modern English the two distant sounds of /t/ and /y/ were reduced to the one intermediate sound /š/, as in *nation* /néyšən/ and *position* /pəzíšən/. This change from /ty/ to /š/ is a type of palatalization. Palatalization can be defined as the raising of the tongue toward the hard palate in the pronunciation of a sound.

Various types of palatalization are now completely accepted when they occur within words, as in *fiction* /fíkšən/, *vision* /vížən/, *question* /kwéstšən/, and *region* /ríydžən/. There is no feeling that the pronunciation of the /š/, /ž/, /tš/, and /dž/ in words like these is in any way uneducated or too informal. Even the most careful speakers of American or British English pronounce the words with the palatalized sounds as indicated in our transcription. The same types of palatalization, however, also occur across word boundaries, between words. They result, in fact, in some of the most common sandhi-forms of spoken English. *Miss you* /mís yuw/ becomes /míšuw/, *loves you* /ləvz yuw/ becomes /ləvžuw/, *hit you* /hít yuw/ becomes /hítšuw/, and *did you* /díd yuw/ becomes /dídžuw/.

The formulas for the environments in which such palatalized sandhi-forms occur are given below.

final /-s/ + initial /y-/ > medial /-š-/
final /-z/ + initial /y-/ > medial /-ž-/
final /-t/ or /-ts/ + initial /y-/ > medial /-tš-/
final /-d/ or /-dz/ + initial /y-/ > medial /-dž-/

Unfortunately, there are still some ultraconservative teachers who would insist that palatalizations across word boundaries are errors, or "careless pronunciation." They willingly accept the pronunciation of *nature* as /néytšur/, but may tell you that the only "correct" way to pronounce *ate your* in *ate your lunch* is /éyt yur/. Such advice not only reveals ignorance of the nature and history of palatalization in English; it is simply bad advice.

VI. A Word of Caution

Although English teachers may sometimes be too conservative about the use of sandhi-forms, there are indeed some of these forms that are so informal as to be inappropriate on most occasions. Some may be interpreted as signs of inadequate education. Others label a speaker as having a particular ethnic background or social status. When you are talking with close friends, it may be very satisfying to use the special language of the social group to which you belong. But there are surely many occasions on which it would not be in your best interests to emphasize through your speech a particular ethnic or social background. There are, finally, sandhi-forms that are so very reduced as to lessen the intelligibility of what is said.

It is not easy to draw the line between forms you should be able to use, those you need only to understand, and those you are not likely to find useful or appropriate. Native speakers are far from unanimous in judging such matters, and decisions must necessarily be very subjective. So far in this lesson we have dealt only with forms we think you should be able to use or at least be able to understand. Before ending the lesson, however, we would like at least to call your attention to a few types of forms you are *not* likely to find useful or appropriate. Knowing what some of these are may make it easier for you to pick out the more useful forms when you hear them.

We suggest that accumulations of several reduced forms in quick succession are usually too informal and will lessen the intelligibility of your English. Examples are:

What did you do? as /wədžə dúw/
Why don't you say it? as /wáyowntšə séyɪt/
Did you eat yet? as /džɪytšɛt/

For reasons that are not altogether clear, the contraction *ain't* is widely regarded as so informal as to be bad grammar. Some people will not like hearing you use it.

On the other hand, contractions beginning with /t/, a reduced form of *it*, are too formal for ordinary conversational purposes. Here are some that are appropriate only in poetry or in writing representing old-fashioned speech: *t'is* /tɪz/, *t'were* /twər/, *t'will be* / twɪəl bíy/. It would be a good idea to avoid them, unless you are trying to sound amusing.

We spoke in Lesson 15 of the difficulties that arise in the pronunciation of consonant clusters such as /str-/ in *strip* and /-rmpθs/ in *warmths*. Somewhat surprisingly, native speakers of English often create unnecessary and unexpected consonant clusters by omitting some of the unstressed vowels that are ordinarily heard in words. Examples are: *balloon* as /bluwn/, *believe* as /bliyv/, *below* as /blow/, *collapse* as /klæps/, *correct* as /krɛkt/, *garage* as /gradž/, *parade* /preyd/, *police* as /pliys/, *polite* as /playt/, and *suppose* as /spowz/. Note that they typically have the following pattern:

$$\begin{pmatrix} \text{unstressed} \\ \text{initial syllable} \end{pmatrix} + \begin{pmatrix} \text{stressed} \\ \text{syllable} \end{pmatrix} > \begin{pmatrix} \text{vowel in initial} \\ \text{syllable omitted} \end{pmatrix}$$

We suggest that you avoid, or at least not cultivate, the above pronunciations since they do not make the formation of the words easier or their meaning more understandable. They may also in the minds of many hearers label you as somewhat illiterate.

(There are, however, other words in which vowels that look as though they should be pronounced are regularly omitted by even the most literate speakers. Some of the most common of these are: *average* as /ǽvrɪdž/, *different* as /dɪ́frənt/, *every* as /ɛ́vrɪ/, *interesting* as /ɪ́ntrɪstɪŋ/, *natural* as /nǽtšrəl/, *separate* (adjective) as /sɛ́prɪt/, and *several* as /sɛ́vrəl/. Note that they typically have the following pattern:

$$\left(\begin{array}{c}\text{stressed}\\\text{syllable}\end{array}\right) + \left(\begin{array}{c}\text{two or more successive}\\\text{unstressed syllables}\end{array}\right) > \left(\begin{array}{c}\text{first vowel after stressed}\\\text{syllable omitted}\end{array}\right)$$

You would do well to familiarize yourself with these words.)

The very common pronunciation of the ending *-ing* as /-ɪn/ instead of /-ɪŋ/ was once even more widespread among almost all social classes than it is today. Well-educated lords and ladies (and some not so well educated) spoke of *singing* as /sɪ́ŋɪn/ and *dancing* as /dǽntsɪn/. Today, however, that particular sandhi-form is widely disapproved among educated speakers of English. It has also come to be considered as a mark of certain restricted social and ethnic groups. The considerable change in attitude toward the form may be due to the omnipresence of *-ing* in printed English and to the conscientious efforts of generations of teachers of English to persuade students to "pronounce it as it is written." Somewhat reluctantly, then, we suggest that you have *nothing* /nə́θɪŋ/ to gain by *using* /yúwzɪŋ/ the /-ɪn/-for-/-ɪŋ/ form.

VII. Exercises

A. Each of the following phrases contains an unstressed word or syllable that would normally, in conversation, be reduced to a syllabic consonant, usually /n̩/ or /l̩/. In a few cases the syllabic consonant will be /m̩/ or /ŋ̍/. (See Footnote 2 in Lesson 10.) Repeat each phrase after your teacher, who will pronounce each with the proper syllabic consonant. If there are words you do not understand, ask for an explanation of their meaning. Then, if time permits, make up a sentence using each of the phrases.

1. góod and réady	6. start an éngine	11. díd indéed
2. hárd and fást	7. láid an égg	12. thát will be
3. góod and ángry	8. bíte an ápple	13. it will háppen
4. wént and lóst	9. gét anóther	14. whén will it cóme
5. hít-and-rún	10. hád enóugh	15. had allówed

16. strĭp 'em báre 18. drŏp 'im óff 20. báck and fórth
17. stŏp 'im 19. I can sáy 21. róck and róll

B. Most of these phrases contain words that are pronounced with a /d/ though they are spelled with t̠. In a few cases, however, the conversational pronunciation is /t/. Try to identify these exceptional cases. (See Section I of this lesson.) Then make up a sentence using each of the phrases, and pronounce each sentence in conversational style. Make sure you understand the meaning of all the phrases.

1. hĭt us
2. éat 'em
3. forgét 'er
4. whát are
5. go gét a
6. rĭght or léft
7. the téa

8. get óver
9. beat úp
10. set óff
11. let ón
12. eat úp
13. get óut
14. it̠ ĭsn't

15. that éver
16. a tĭme
17. rĭght ón
18. great évening
19. nŏt at áll
20. do téll
21. so tĭred

C. The sentences below are spelled out in formal style, though they would probably be spoken in very informal, conversational style. Read them as though they were part of an informal conversation, using reduced forms of the articles, prepositions, pronouns, and so on, that are written in italics. Also, feel free to use other sandhi-forms where the environment seems to call for them.

1. *Will you* ask *her what she* wants *to* do this evening?
2. *Do you* think this *would* be *a* good night for going *to a* baseball game?
3. I *am* not sure *she would* like that *at* all.
4. Baseball games *are* boring; *she has* never been *to* more *than* one *or* two *of them*.
5. But I *do* not know *an* outfielder *from a* shortstop.
6. *You must* tell *him that* we *will* buy *the* tickets.
7. Tell *them* we *can* eat when we get *to the* stadium *and are* seated.
8. I *will* bet *he* knows *that* numbers *are a* very important part *of the* game: *the* number *of* strikes, *of* balls, *of* outs, *and* so forth.
9. *You* have *to* keep *the* numbers in mind in order *to* realize *the* drama *of what is* happening.
10. Here baseball is *as* important *as* fishing, *and* more important *than* politics.

D. Each formally written phrase below is followed by four transcriptions showing how the phrase could be spoken with various degrees of informality. For each phrase rearrange the four transcriptions, listing the four in order of their degree of informality, from most formal to most informal (that is, from the transcription with fewest reductions to that with most reductions). As the class makes its decisions, the teacher can serve as secretary, writing the transcriptions on the blackboard. When the four rearranged lists of transcriptions have been written out, the class may wish to discuss the question: "Just how informal should the pronunciation of a nonnative speaker of English be?"

Alternatively, the exercise could well be carried out as a small-group activity.

1. (I would have been gláed.)

    a.   ay ʊdə bɪn glǽd

    b.   ay wʊd əv bɪn glǽd

    c.   aydə bɪn glǽd

    d.   ay wʊd həv bɪn glǽd

2. (Did you éver méet her?)

    a.   džɛ́vər míydər

    b.   dɪdžuw ɛ́vər míyt hər

    c.   džuw ɛ́vər míyd ər

    d.   dɪdžə ɛ́vər míyt ər

3. (Whát did he wánt?)

    a.   hwát dɪd iy wánt

    b.   wə́dɪdɪ wánt

    c.   wə́dɪd iy wánt

    d.   wə́dɪ wánt

4. (Whát will it bé for you?)

    a.   wádl̩ ɪt bíy fər yuw

    b.   hwát əl ɪt bíy fɔr yuw

    c.   wád əl ɪt bíy fɔr yuw

    d.   wə́dl̩ ɪdbíyfəryə

E. 1. Each of the following sentences has in it one or more of the kind of t̲'s that often disappear in conversational speech. First, note where these t̲'s are, if necessary by using the formula given in Section III of this lesson. Then, omitting the disappearing t̲'s, pronounce the sentences several times until you feel

you could understand the words in question if you heard a speaker pronounce
them without the t̪'s.

a.   When we say the harvest is bountiful, we mean it's plentiful.

b.   She writes with a slanting hand.

c.   It's a great advantage to have plenty of money.

d.   I can feel the splinter in my finger.

e.   His paintings are all gigantic.

f.   Be careful in confronting danger.

g.   We used to live in Pontiac, but now we live in Toronto.

h.   The heroine fainted when she saw the phantom.

i.   I became frantic as the voice grew fainter and fainter.

j.   The Mounted Policeman wanted the bounty very much.

k.   Buy a large quantity of bread.

l.   They were all elected to county office.

2.   This exercise will give you practice in associating meaning with a t̪-less pronunciation of certain items. The instructor will ask questions for individual
students to answer. The information needed to ask and answer the questions
is contained in the table below. Choosing an item in the table, the instructor
asks: "What does /bǽnər/ mean when spelled with (or without) a t̪?" The
student answers: "When spelled with a t̪, /bǽnər/ means good-natured teas-
ing," or "When spelled without a t̪, /bǽnər/ means flag."

Pronunciation	*Meaning*	
	SPELLED WITH t̪	SPELLED WITHOUT t̪
a. /bǽnər/	*banter* = good-natured teasing	*banner* = flag
b. /féynər/	*fainter* = harder to hear	*feigner* = someone who pretends
c. /plǽnər/	*planter* = sower of seed	*planner* = maker of plans
d. /wínər/	*winter* = cold season	*winner* = someone who wins
e. /péynɪŋ/	*painting* = using paint	*paining* = hurting
f. /pənɪŋ/	*punting* = poling a boat	*punning* = making plays on words

I. As you know, all multiples of ten—*twenty, thirty,* and so on—end in *-ty* in English. You may have noticed that the t in this *-ty* is pronounced in three different ways, depending on what precedes it: sometimes as a regular alveolar stop, sometimes as a /d/-like /t/, sometimes as a disappearing t.

Your instructor will count by tens from ten through ninety. Imitate the pronunciation, and identify the kind of t heard in each number.

Finally, you could play a game in which the instructor calls out a number from two to nine. Individual students multiply that number by ten and state the result, being careful to pronounce the t suitably. A point could be scored for each *-ty* that is pronounced in the manner that corresponds to its environment.

LESSON 17

Long and Short Vowels

I. Problems of Spelling English

You may remember that Lessons 11 and 12 were designed to help you avoid that type of vowel substitution which is due to inability to hear or reproduce clearly an English vowel that does not exist as a distinctive sound or is formed differently in your mother tongue. This lesson and the one following are aimed at the other types of difficulty students may have in giving the stressed vowel of a word its correct value: vowel substitutions caused by the inconsistencies of English spelling, or the differences between the English and some other system of spelling.

To approach the problem, we must examine such systematic relationships as exist between vowel sounds and the way they are ordinarily spelled. Unfortunately, there seems to be no fully satisfactory way of doing this for students of English as a Second Language, principally because the spelling of English is much less systematic than that of most other languages. There are more than twice as many vowel sounds in English as there are vowel letters in the roman alphabet with which English is written. It has therefore been necessary to devise various combinations of symbols, some of them unsystematic, to represent all the different vowel sounds. The symbols *w* and *y* have had to be used to represent both consonant and vowel sounds. English has borrowed an enormous number of words from other languages, and has often borrowed elements of foreign spelling systems with the words. Attempts at spelling reform have been very limited and relatively unsuccessful in modern English. For English there has never been the equivalent of the *Académie Française* or the *Real Academia Española* to guide the standardization and development of the spelling system. Irregular, nonsystematic spellings therefore abound.

The classical way of explaining the spelling of English vowel sounds has involved dividing them into two groups, called respectively the "long" vowels and the "short" vowels. There have always been serious difficulties, both theoretical and practical, in this system of long and short vowels. Consequently some ESL instructors have felt that the system was not worth explaining, and have asked their students to learn to spell each word individually without regard for patterns of spelling.

During the last fifteen years, however, our interest in the system of long and short vowels and our confidence in its potential usefulness have grown. This has come about partly through the work of a group of linguists known as the "generative phonologists." (See Footnote 3 in Lesson 3.) Through their research they have demonstrated underlying systematic elements in English spelling of whose existence we were not previously aware.

No attempt will be made in this manual to analyze the complex system of rules formulated by the generative phonologists. Still, encouraged by the successes of generative phonology, the authors will here renew the effort made in earlier editions of the manual to relate the system of long and short vowels in a useful way to the problems of learning to pronounce English better.

II. The System of Long and Short Vowels

The system of long and short vowels underlies the diacritical marks used in many dictionaries of English to represent the pronunciation of words. A straight line is placed over long vowels, as in *fāte;* a curved line goes over short vowels, as in *făt*.

The system is based on the assumption that each of the five English vowel letters—a̱, e̱, i̱, o̱, u̱—has two most common sounds *in stressed syllables,* a long sound and a short sound.

Letter	Long Sound		Short Sound	
a	/ey/	lāte	/æ/	păt
e	/iy/	ēve	/ɛ/	ĕnd
i	/ay/	īce	/ɪ/	sĭt
o	/ow/	bōne	/a/	ŏdd
u	/yuw/	cūbe	/ə/	ŭp

As the above transcriptions show, each of the long sounds is a diphthong that includes one or both of the glides /y/ or /w/. The short sounds are transcribed without glides. It is worth noting that the names we give the vowel letters when we spell a word or recite the English alphabet are the same as their *long* sounds. For example, the letter *a* is called /ey/, not /æ/. It may help you remember the short sounds of the vowel letters if you think of them as the nicknames of those letters; thus /ey/ is the name of a̲ and /æ/ is its nickname.

The long vowels are sometimes called "tense," since they are often pronounced with more muscular tension than the short vowels, which are sometimes called "lax."

Each vowel letter is pronounced with its *long* sound
   1. If it is final in the syllable:

          pā-per, shē, fī-nal, nō, dū-ty

   2. If it is followed by an unpronounced e̲, or a consonant plus an unpronounced e̲:

          māke, ēve, dīe, Pōe, ūse

Each vowel letter is pronounced with its *short* sound
   1. If it is followed in the same syllable by a consonant:

          măt-ter, wĕnt, rĭv-er, dŏc-tor, cŭt

It should be remembered that these rules apply only to vowels in *stressed* syllables. We already know that in *unstressed* syllables vowel letters are normally pronounced as /ə/, /ɪ/, or /ʊ/.

We believe that an understanding of the system of long and short vowels, added to what you already know about the predictable pronunciation of unstressed vowels, will enable you to determine the pronunciation of the vast majority of English vowels on the basis of the way they are spelled.

III. Vowel Sounds and Syllable Boundaries

One reason for questioning the usefulness of the system of long and short vowels has been that it does not enable us to predict the pronunciation of a large group of words of more than one syllable such as *éver* and *éven*. It is indeed true that we cannot determine with certainty whether the stressed vowels of such words are pronounced with the long sound /iy/ or the short sound /ɛ/ by looking at their spelling. As we shall explain, however, a knowledge of how long and short vowels are paired can at least help a student to make an informed guess as to their pronunciation.

The problem is to know where one syllable ends and the next syllable begins. For example, if the stressed vowel in *éver* is final in the syllable, the system tells us that the e̲ is pronounced as /iy/. And if the stressed vowel is followed in the same syllable by a consonant, the e̲ is pronounced as /ɛ/. But where is the line drawn between syllables? If you look up the rules for the division of syllables, you find that a consonant between vowel sounds, such as the v̲ in *éver,* is part of the first syllable if the preceding vowel is short, and is part of the second syllable if the preceding vowel is long. This information is of no help to you, of course, as the longness or shortness of the vowel is precisely what you are trying to determine. You will simply have to guess at the facts, which are that the v̲ of *éver* is part of the first syllable; the e̲ is therefore short, and the word is pronounced /ɛ́v-ər/. On the other hand, the v̲ of *éven* is part of the second syllable; it is therefore long, and the word is pronounced /íy-vən/.

An anlysis of how the system of long and short vowels relates to words such as *ever* and *even,* in which there is a stressed vowel followed by a consonant plus an unstressed vowel, has yielded information that should at least greatly improve a student's chances of guessing correctly whether the stressed vowel of such a word has a long or short vowel sound.

Actually, the situation varies depending on the letter that represents the stressed vowel sound. The lists that follow include most of the words of this type that are among the 2,500 most frequently used English words.[1]

THE LETTER i̲ USUALLY HAS A SHORT SOUND.

SHORT /ɪ/: addi̲tion, Bri̲tish, ci̲tizen, ci̲ty, ci̲vil, condi̲tion, consi̲der, conti̲nue, divi̲sion, fami̲liar, fi̲gure, fi̲nish, gi̲ven, i̲mage, indivi̲dual, I̲taly, li̲berty, li̲ly, li̲mit, li̲nen, magni̲ficent, mi̲litary, mi̲nister, mínute, opi̲nion, ori̲ginal, parti̲cular, Phi̲lip, physi̲cian, pi̲ty, posi̲tion, pri̲son, reli̲gious, spi̲rit, suffi̲cient, Virgi̲nia.

LONG /ay/: Chi̲na, cli̲mate, fi̲nal, Fri̲day, pri̲vate, si̲lence, ti̲ny.

THE LETTER e̲ USUALLY HAS A SHORT SOUND.

SHORT /ɛ/: Ame̲rican, be̲nefit, ce̲lebrate, cre̲dit, de̲licate, de̲velop, de̲vil, ele̲ven, e̲nemy, espe̲cial, e̲ver, ge̲neral, ge̲nerous, le̲vel, me̲dicine, me̲mory,

---

[1]An examination of the 2,500 most common English words, as listed in E. L. Thorndike, *The Teacher's Word Book,* reveals that i̲ is short in 79% of the pertinent cases, e̲ in 75%, o̲ in 64%, a̲ in 55%, and u̲ in only 20%. If we examine a larger number of words, thus including more bookish and unusual terms, the proportion of short vowels is: i̲, 70%; e̲, 76%; o̲, 63%; a̲, 45%, and u̲, 10%.

merit, n<u>e</u>cessary, n<u>e</u>ver, p<u>e</u>rish, pr<u>e</u>cious, pr<u>é</u>sent, pr<u>e</u>sident, r<u>e</u>cognize, r<u>é</u>cord, r<u>e</u>gister, r<u>e</u>gular, r<u>e</u>lative, s<u>e</u>cond, s<u>e</u>nate, s<u>e</u>parate, s<u>e</u>ven, sp<u>e</u>cial, t<u>e</u>lephone.

LONG /iy/: conv<u>e</u>nient, <u>E</u>gypt, <u>e</u>qual, <u>e</u>ven, <u>e</u>vil, f<u>e</u>male, f<u>e</u>ver, fr<u>e</u>quent, imm<u>e</u>diate, P<u>e</u>ter, r<u>e</u>cent, r<u>e</u>gion.

THE LETTER <u>a</u> HAS LONG AND SHORT SOUNDS WITH
ALMOST EQUAL FREQUENCY.

SHORT /æ/: <u>a</u>nimal, <u>a</u>venue, b<u>a</u>lance, ch<u>a</u>pel, comp<u>a</u>nion, ex<u>a</u>mine, f<u>a</u>mily, gr<u>a</u>dual, h<u>a</u>bit, im<u>a</u>gine, It<u>a</u>lian, L<u>a</u>tin, m<u>a</u>gic, m<u>a</u>nage, n<u>a</u>tional, n<u>a</u>tural, p<u>a</u>lace, r<u>a</u>pid, s<u>a</u>lary, s<u>a</u>tisfy, S<u>a</u>turday, sh<u>a</u>dow, Sp<u>a</u>nish, st<u>a</u>tue, tr<u>a</u>vel, v<u>a</u>lue, v<u>a</u>nish, w<u>a</u>gon.

LONG /ey/: <u>A</u>sia, b<u>a</u>by, educ<u>a</u>tion, f<u>a</u>mous, f<u>a</u>vor, f<u>a</u>vorite, found<u>a</u>tion, gr<u>a</u>cious, inform<u>a</u>tion, invit<u>a</u>tion, l<u>a</u>bor, l<u>a</u>dy, l<u>a</u>zy, m<u>a</u>ker, n<u>a</u>ked, n<u>a</u>tion, n<u>a</u>tive, n<u>a</u>ture, n<u>a</u>vy, p<u>a</u>per, p<u>a</u>tience, p<u>a</u>tient, popul<u>a</u>tion, pot<u>a</u>to, rel<u>a</u>tion, st<u>a</u>tion, v<u>a</u>por.

THE LETTER <u>o</u> HAS LONG AND SHORT SOUNDS WITH
ALMOST EQUAL FREQUENCY.

SHORT /a/: b<u>o</u>dy, c<u>o</u>lony, c<u>o</u>lumn, c<u>o</u>py, h<u>o</u>liday, h<u>o</u>nest, h<u>o</u>nor, m<u>o</u>del, m<u>o</u>derate, m<u>o</u>dern, m<u>o</u>dest, m<u>o</u>nument, <u>o</u>live, pr<u>o</u>bable, pr<u>o</u>duct, pr<u>o</u>fit, pr<u>o</u>mise, pr<u>o</u>per, pr<u>o</u>perty, pr<u>o</u>vince, R<u>o</u>bert, r<u>o</u>bin, s<u>o</u>lid, Th<u>o</u>mas, v<u>o</u>lume.

LONG /ow/: br<u>o</u>ken, fr<u>o</u>zen, J<u>o</u>seph, l<u>o</u>cal, l<u>o</u>cate, m<u>o</u>ment, m<u>o</u>tion, n<u>o</u>tice, <u>o</u>cean, Oct<u>o</u>ber, <u>o</u>pen, <u>o</u>ver, p<u>o</u>ny, R<u>o</u>man, s<u>o</u>ber, t<u>o</u>tal.

THE LETTER <u>u</u> ALMOST ALWAYS HAS A LONG SOUND.

SHORT /ə/: p<u>u</u>nish, st<u>u</u>dy.

LONG /yuw/: f<u>u</u>neral, f<u>u</u>ture, h<u>u</u>man, h<u>u</u>mor, m<u>u</u>sic, n<u>u</u>merous, opport<u>u</u>nity, pec<u>u</u>liar, p<u>u</u>pil, <u>u</u>niform, <u>u</u>nion, <u>u</u>sual.

It would be well to check over the lists carefully and mark any items that you would have hesitated to pronounce. Almost all students are doubtful regarding certain words like these, in which the spelling gives no clear indication of the pronunciation.

If you need to pronounce unfamiliar words of this kind, you should consult a dictionary whenever possible. If you have to guess, however, you may do so with some degree of certainty when the stressed vowel is <u>i</u>, <u>e</u>, or <u>u</u>. Thus you could be fairly sure that the <u>i</u> of *tibia* is to be given the sound of /ɪ/, and that the <u>e</u> of *senary* is /ɛ/. You could be practically certain that the <u>u</u> of *cuticle* is pronounced as /yuw/.

You may find the preceding explanation easier to remember if you will note that, in the type of word we have been discussing, the letters we associate with front vowels, i̲ and e̲, tend to have their short sound. The letter we associate with back vowels, u̲, usually has its long sound. The middle vowels, a̲ and o̲, may be long or short.

Because of the relationship between the system of long and short vowels and the way syllables are divided, you should also find the system helpful in dealing with the troublesome problem of dividing words by a hyphen at the end of a line of writing. Remember that long vowels usually end a syllable (except when followed by a consonant plus an unpronounced e̲), but short vowels do not end a syllable. If you know how the stressed vowels in *final* /fáynl̲/ and *finish* /fínɪš/ are pronounced, you can be sure that the *n* of *final* goes with the second syllable, *fi-nal;* and that the *n* of *finish* goes with the first, *fin-ish*.

IV. Vowels before l̲ or r̲

Earlier in this manual it was pointed out that /l/ and /r/ are unusual sounds in a number of ways, including their effect on preceding vowel sounds and their relationship to spelling. In fact, the effect of /l/ and /r/ on preceding vowels seems to be, after the regular system of long and short vowels, the most obvious systematic element in the spelling of English. (See Lesson 10, Sections I and II.)

When they come before l̲ or r̲, the vowel letters in a very large number of words are pronounced according to a special variation of the system of long and short vowels. Because of the lowering and backing of the tongue that are involved in producing the two liquid, glidelike consonants, /l/ and /r/ tend by assimilation to make any vowel that precedes them have a more open and/or back sound than it would otherwise have. Thus, a̲ in the position of a short vowel is pronounced /æ/ according to the regular system of long and short vowels: *actor* /ǽktər/. But an a̲ in a short position before l̲ is ordinarily pronounced /ɔ/: *alter* /ɔ́ltər/. An a̲ in a short position before r̲ usually has the sound of /a/ rather than the /æ/ that might have been expected: *cat* /kæt/, *cart* /kart/.

There follows a table that shows how the pronunciation of vowels before l̲ or r̲ varies from the pronunciation they would have according to the regular system of long and short vowels.

Despite the practical usefulness of the system of long and short vowels, you should remember that the words *long* and *short* used in this connection are somewhat misleading. They suggest that "long" vowels take more time to pronounce than do "short" vowels, and that is not always true. It *is* true that a "long" vowel normally lasts longer than a "short" vowel when the two occur in the same linguistic environment; the /ey/ in "We'll take it up" lasts longer than the /æ/ in "We'll tack it up." However, the sound spectrograph

Pronunciation of Vowel Letters before l or r[2]

<u>a</u>

	In Long Position	
Sound according to regular system		/ey/, l<u>a</u>te /leyt/
Before <u>l</u>		/eə/, s<u>a</u>le /seəl/
Before <u>r</u>		/ɛə/, c<u>a</u>re /kɛər/
	In Short Position	
According to system		/æ/, s<u>a</u>t /sæt/
Before <u>l</u>		/ɔ/, <u>a</u>lter /ɔ́ltər/
Before <u>r</u>		/a/, c<u>a</u>r /kar/

<u>e</u>

	In Long Position	
According to system		/iy/, <u>e</u>ven /íyvən/
Before <u>l</u>		(rare)
Before <u>r</u>		/ɪə/, h<u>e</u>re /hɪər/
	In Short Position	
According to system		/ɛ/, m<u>e</u>t /mɛt/
Before <u>l</u>		/ɛə/, w<u>e</u>ll /wɛəl/
Before <u>r</u>		/ə(ər)/, v<u>e</u>rb /vərb/

<u>i</u>

	In Long Position	
According to system		/ay/, m<u>i</u>ne /mayn/
Before <u>l</u>		(same)
Before <u>r</u>		(same)
	In Short Position	
According to system		/ɪ/, h<u>i</u>t /hɪt/
Before <u>l</u>		/ɪə/, h<u>i</u>ll /hɪəl/
Before <u>r</u>		/ə(ər)/, s<u>i</u>r /sər/

---

[2]There is a great deal of dialectal variation in the pronunciation of vowels before l and especially before r. Also a number of relatively rapid changes in the pronunciation of such vowels seem to be taking place. Not surprisingly, then, different phoneticians analyze them in a number of different ways. It is therefore difficult in some cases to determine what the facts really are.

For example, speakers of some dialects are said to use only five different simple vowel sounds in a syllable that ends in r: /ɪ/, /ɛ/, /ə/, /a/, and /ɔ/. It is said that many more speakers, perhaps an increasing majority, limit themselves to six, adding /ʊ/ to the above group. Phoneticians who count syllables differently say that diphthongs are also used before r without constituting two separate syllables: *fire* /fayr/, *our* /awr/, and so on. Phoneticians who recognize the existence of centering diphthongs, as we do in this manual (see Lesson 10, Section 2), speak of combinations such as /ɪər/ in *here* and /ɛər/ in *care*. In parts of the South and East such combinations as /ɪər/ in *we're* and /ɛər/ in *they're* are heard. In other words you may be told that there are anywhere between five and thirteen monosyllabic vowel-+-/r/ combinations, depending on the region being considered and the analysis favored by the phonetician doing the counting.

The authors have not attempted to include all these legitimate variant pronunciations and analyses in the above table. In order to make the table as useful as possible and to avoid being overly influenced by a preference for our own dialects, we have included in all but one case only the pronunciation listed first in Kenyon and Knott's *A Pronouncing Dictionary of American English* for the words we have used as examples. In the case of <u>o</u> in long position before r (as in *more*)

Pronunciation of Vowel Letters before l̲ or r̲² (continued)

o̲	*In Long Position*	
According to system		/ow/, r̲o̲se /r̲o̲wz/
Before l̲		(same)
Before r̲		/ow/ or /ɔ/, m̲o̲re /m̲o̲wr/ or /m̲ɔ̲r/
	In Short Position	
According to system		/a/, h̲o̲t /h̲a̲t/
Before l̲		/ow/, c̲o̲ld /k̲o̲wld/
Before r̲		/ɔ/, f̲o̲r /f̲ɔ̲r/
u̲	*In Long Position*	
According to system		/yuw/, c̲u̲te /k̲yuwt/
Before l̲		(same)
Before r̲		/yʊ/, c̲u̲re /k̲yʊ̲r/
	In Short Position	
No variation (/ə/)		

provides clear visual evidence that ''short'' vowels often last longer than ''long'' vowels. The ''short'' i̲ of *bid* /b̲ɪ̲d/ is a longer sound than the ''long'' i̲ of *bite* /b̲ayt/. In the sentence ''His name is John,'' the ''short'' o̲ of *John* /džạn/ is surely longer than the ''long'' a̲ of *name* /n̲e̲ym/. The vowel of *bid* is longer because it is followed by a voiced consonant, and that of *bite* is shorter because it is followed by a voiceless consonant. (See Lesson 9, Section II.) In the particular sentence cited above, the o̲ of *John* is unusually long because its intonation slides from high to low. (See Lesson 5, Section II.) In other words, being classified as ''long'' or ''short'' according to the system of long and short vowels is only *one* of the several factors that combine to determine the measurable length of a vowel sound.

Despite its problems, the system of long and short vowels is certainly the most helpful way to explain to nonnative speakers of English, logically and with relative simplicity, the systematic relationships that exist between the spelling and the sounds of most English vowels. In view of the large number of pronunciation errors that even advanced students of English make because of their lack of clear associations between vowel sounds and their usual spelling, it is worth your while to familiarize yourself with the theory. You will then be in a position to identify words of irregular spelling more easily, and to concentrate on learning their pronunciation individually.

---

we have given both Kenyon and Knott's first listing /mowr/ and their second listing /mɔr/. Our symbols often differ from the Kenyon and Knott symbols, but the pronunciations we indicate are intended in all cases to be the same as theirs. *A Pronouncing Dictionary of American English,* which describes the midwestern type of English that used to be called General American, is the most authoritative book of its type.

V. Exercises

A.

1.   What English vowel sounds do not exist in your mother tongue?

2.   In your mother tongue, is it possible to find two words of different meaning exactly alike in sound except that one contains an /iy/ and the other an /ɪ/ (such as *seat* /siyt/ and *sit* /sɪt/ in English)? Do /ey/ and /ɛ/ ever constitute the only difference between two words? /ɛ/ and /æ/? /æ/ and /a/? /ɔ/ and /ow/? /ə/ and /a/?

3.   Which English vowels and diphthongs do you have most difficulty in pronouncing?

4.   Do you sometimes make the mistake of pronouncing *up* as /ap/ instead of /əp/? Why? (See Lesson 11, Section I.) Do you ever confuse /ʊ/ and /ə/? Why? Did you ever mispronounce *post* as /past/ instead of /powst/; *wash* as /wæš/ instead of /waš/? If so, can you explain the reason for the mispronunciation?

B.   1.   What are the long and short sounds of a̱, e̱, i̱, o̱, and u̱?

2.   According to the system, should the *stressed* vowels in the following words be long or short?

a. age	i. less	q. dóctor
b. lake	j. nine	r. númber
c. expéct	k. box	s. háppen
d. I	l. just	t. compléte
e. bone	m. escápe	u. begín
f. suppóse	n. cent	v. which
g. ask	o. see	w. go
h. be	p. tie	x. use

Are all of the words in this list actually pronounced according to the system?

3.   Which of the following very common words have stressed vowels that are *not* pronounced according to the system of long and short vowels as explained in this lesson?

a. ány	d. ónly	g. blue
b. búsy	e. race	h. give
c. have	f. was	i. húndred

j.	óther	o.	move	t.	gone
k.	sing	p.	but	u.	no
l.	watch	q.	then	v.	put
m.	both	r.	wáter	w.	these
n.	glass	s.	bóttom	x.	shoe

C. 1. The stressed vowel in each of the words below is followed by a consonant plus an unstressed vowel. You will remember that the spelling is not a sure indication of how such words are pronounced. The pronunciation of each word, however, is given in the table in Section III of this lesson. Can you remember how all these very frequently used words are pronounced? If there are some of the words you are not sure of, look them up in the table, pronounce them, and try to impress their pronunciation on your memory.

a.	ávenue	i.	hóliday	q.	púnish
b.	cívil	j.	línen	r.	récent
c.	clímate	k.	móment	s.	récognize
d.	cólony	l.	náked	t.	récord
e.	convénient	m.	nátive	u.	róbin
f.	dévil	n.	nátural	v.	tíny
g.	évil	o.	númerous	w.	tótal
h.	fínal	p.	próvince	x.	vápor

2. What would be the safest guess as to the vowel sound in the stressed syllable of each of these comparatively rare words?

a.	dívot	f.	lévitate	k.	pícaroon
b.	dúcat	g.	mímic	l.	ríbald
c.	fétus	h.	múcous	m.	sésame
d.	húmic	i.	nématode	n.	síderite
e.	legúminous	j.	pédiment	o.	tídings

Look up each word in a good dictionary and see how often you guessed correctly. Which of the letters a, e, i, o, and u were you *not* asked to guess the pronunciation of in this exercise? Why?

D. The vowels of the following words are pronounced regularly according to the table, "Pronunciation of Vowel Letters before l or r," that appears in Section IV of this lesson. Pronounce the pairs of words several times, and note the systematic changes that result from the presence of the l or r.

1.	save, sale	3.	case, care	5.	bad, bald
2.	mane, male	4.	date, dare	6.	sat, salt

7.	back, balk	14.	gem, germ	21.	pope, pore
8.	áfter, álter	15.	beg, berg	22.	cod, cold
9.	cat, cart	16.	ten, tern	23.	God, gold
10.	had, hard	17.	sick, silk	24.	cot, colt
11.	mete, mere	18.	sit, silt	25.	spot, sport
12.	met, melt	19.	bid, bird	26.	stock, stork
13.	sped, spelled	20.	fist, first	27.	puke, pure

Write the phonetic symbols that represent the vowel of each word.

E. 1. Keeping in mind that long vowels usually end syllables and short vowels do not, divide these words into syllables.

a.	bacon /béykən/	g.	notion /nówšən/	m.	rival /ráyvəl/
b.	frozen /frówzən/	h.	pity /pítɪ/	n.	second /sɛ́kənd/
c.	gather /gǽðər/	i.	promise /prámɪs/	o.	table /téybəl/
d.	mason /méysən/	j.	punish /pə́nɪš/	p.	tinny /tínɪ/
e.	metal /mɛ́tl̩/	k.	pupil /pyúwpəl/	q.	tiny /táynɪ/
f.	motor /mówtər/	l.	risen /rízən/	r.	together /təgɛ́ðər/

2. Why do you suppose the final p̲ of *hop* is doubled when -̲ing is added? Why double the g̲ of *big* when -̲est is added? Why double the b̲ of *rob* when -̲ed is added?

3. In 1982 the world-champion Saint Louis Cardinals baseball team had a relief pitcher named Bruce Sutter. His last name was pronounced /sútwtər/ rather than /sə́tər/. In what way is the pronunciation /súwtər/ unsystematic?

4. The most famous of all comets is known as "Halley's Comet." Would the regular pronunciation of the name be /hǽlɪ/ or /héylɪ/? /héylɪ/ is often heard, though dictionaries give the pronunciation as /hǽlɪ/.

5. The British usually spell the word that indicates a person who takes trips as "traveḻḻer," while Americans tend to prefer spelling it as "traveḻer." Which spelling is more systematic? Why? (Hint: the system of long and short vowels applies only to *stressed* syllables.)

F. The systematic nature of the pairs of long and short vowels is to be seen also when we compare some English words with words that have been derived from them or are related to them in meaning. For example, the long i̲ of *wide* /wayd/ corresponds to the short i̲ of *width* /wɪdθ/. Such correspondences are quite common though not entirely predictable. Usually the more basic word has the long vowel and the derivative word has the corresponding short vowel. Practice the following pairs of words. Then see if you can give the second word of each pair when your teacher gives the first word in random order. The exercise should help you internalize the system according to which long and short vowels are paired.

(a̲ = /ey/ and /æ/)
1. sáne, sánity
2. nátion, nátional
3. gráteful, grátitude
4. gráde, gráduate
5. státe, státic
6. páge, páginate

(e̲ = /iy/ and /ɛ/)
7. méter, métric
8. seréne, serénity
9. supréme, suprémacy
10. repéat, repétitive
11. procéed (verb), procéssion

(i̲ = /ay/ and /ɪ/)
12. míne, míneral
13. líne, línear

14. decíde, decísion
15. títle, títular
16. sublíme, sublímity
17. deríve, derívative
18. wíld, wílderness

(o̲ = /ow/ and /a/)
19. cóne, cónical
20. códe, códify
21. vócal, vócative
22. jóke, jócular
23. phóne, phónic

(u̲ = /yuw/ and /ə/)
24. púnitive, púnish
25. redúce, redúction
26. prodúce (verb), prodúction
27. númeral, númber

G. The members of the class should take turns asking and answering questions about their lives. As they speak, the instructor will listen carefully and encourage them to diphthongize /ey/ and /ow/ slightly in the positions where those two "long" vowels should actually be most lengthened: when the vowel is final as in *slow* /slo̲w/, when it is followed by a final voiced consonant as in *played* /pley̲d/, or when it is pronounced with a slide at the end of an intonation pattern. (See Lesson 11, Section IV.) Key expressions for use in the questions might be *go, show, play, know, say, alone, date, every day, at home, study load, closed section, grade, raise your grade, an "A," enroll, fail, loathe, hate, notes,* and so on.

H. Outside of class prepare several pages of a magazine article for reading aloud by marking the pauses by means of which it can best be divided into thought groups. Then read the article, being careful to blend your words together within thought groups. Try to avoid glottal stops and finishing sounds. (See Lesson 4, Section IV.)

LESSON 18

Regular and Irregular Spellings

I. What Is Regular Spelling?

Any useful consideration of the relationship between speech and writing, between pronunciation and spelling, must take into account the fact that speech is primary and that writing is derived from speech. In the development of both human beings and languages, speech comes before writing. Children normally learn to pronounce words long before they learn to spell them. Languages often exist for hundreds of years before they are reduced to writing. In fact, there are still many languages in the world for which writing and spelling systems have not yet been devised.

So, as the title of this lesson indicates, we will speak—and think—here of regular and irregular spellings, not of regular and irregular pronunciations. The significant question for us is "How regularly do the letters represent the sounds?" rather than "Why don't you pronounce the words the way they are written?"

An ideal, completely regular system of spelling for a language would be one in which there was a perfect correspondence between the pronunciation of all the distinctive sounds of the language and the written symbols used to represent those sounds. There would be a different symbol for every sound, and each symbol would always represent the same sound. It would then always be easy to determine the pronunciation of a word by seeing how it was spelled.

What a help that would be for a foreign student trying to learn to pronounce a new language!

But it would be difficult, perhaps impossible, to find such a completely regular spelling system in actual use in the writing of a well-established, natural language. All widely used spelling systems are more or less irregular, and it must be admitted that English spelling may well be the most irregular of them all.

Some of the reasons for this lack of perfect regularity were referred to at the beginning of Lesson 17. The roman alphabet, originally devised for the spelling of Latin, was not well suited for the writing of Anglo-Saxon, and is an even poorer fit for the spelling of Modern English. The decision to use the roman alphabet for English made it impossible to follow the principle of one-sound-one-symbol in spelling the language. Then, too, the sound system of English has changed faster than its spelling system, thus making the spelling increasingly irregular. Also, the developers of English spelling have not always considered phonetic regularity to be the most desirable feature of the system. They have been very much concerned with having a spelling that would reveal something of the history of words and their relationships to other words. For example, the b̲ in *debt* /dɛt/ serves as an indication that it is derived from the Latin *debitum,* though it results in an irregular spelling. And the irregular silent g̲ in *sign* /sayn/ serves to show that it is related to a whole family of words—*signal, signature, signify,* and so on—in which the g̲ is actually pronounced.

Despite all this, we found in Lesson 17 elements of regular spelling in the basic system of long and short vowels, in the relationship of vowel sounds to syllable boundaries, and in the effect of l̲ and r̲ on the pronunciation of preceding vowel letters. It is true that we did not find anything approaching the ideal regularity of one-sound-one-symbol in any of these three cases. The system of long and short vowels makes each of the five vowel letters represent at least *two* vowel sounds. We must look at the environment in which the letter occurs before we can know which of the two sounds the symbol probably represents in a given word.

The somewhat systematic relationship of vowel sounds to syllable boundaries is found only in the statistical fact that in a certain environment i̲ and e̲ are more regularly given their short sound and u̲ is more regularly given its long sound. The effect of l̲ and r̲ on the pronunciation of preceding vowel letters, though semisystematic, does not always apply. Nonetheless, in all three cases there is regularity of one type or another. These three types of regularity, plus others that will be noted in this lesson, do make it possible to predict the stressed vowel sounds of most English words by seeing the symbols that represent them.

The purpose of this last lesson in the manual, then, is threefold.

1. To summarize and provide more examples of the elements of regularity we have already found. The authors hope you will feel that the different kinds of regularity add up to a total large enough to justify your making an effort to familiarize yourself with the rather complex system. If you are aware of the several forms that regularity in spelling can take, you should be in a better position to recognize the residue of words whose spelling is irregular.

2. To point out some additional features of spelling that are in some sense regular. For example, the combination *igh* represents the sound /ay/ with a high degree of regularity: *high, sigh, might, brighten, delightful,* and so on.

3. To provide you with a classified list of the most common English words whose spelling is misleading: that is to say, words that look as though they might be regularly spelled but that are not pronounced as might be expected. For example, *have* looks as though it should be pronounced /heyv/, with a long a, but it is really pronounced /hæv/, with a short a. You may then be able to impress these words on your memory by using them, which is really the only way of learning to pronounce and spell them.

II. Principal Elements of Regularity

There follows a table showing the principal ways in which letters represent vowel sounds in stressed syllables with some degree of regularity in English.

The first column of the table lists 57 different letter combinations whose pronunciation is largely predictable. These combinations constitute the linguistic environments that can determine the pronunciation of a vowel letter or letters. Combination number 1, for example, is described as "a in long position, normally." This means that, if the a is final in a syllable or if it is followed by an unpronounced e or by a consonant plus an unpronounced e, it is normally pronounced with its long sound of /ey/, as indicated in the second column. (See Lesson 17, Section 2.) When the word *normally* appears as part of the description of the combination, it implies that there are variations of that combination, described subsequently, which are pronounced differently (for example, combinations 2 and 3).

Among the 57 letter combinations are listed the long and short positions for each vowel letter. For most of the vowel letters the list also includes the long and short positions before l and before r. To these items have been added the digraphs—combinations of two letters such as ai, ea, and oo—that repre-

Spelling As an Indication of the Pronunciation of Stressed Vowels in English

Letter Combination	Pronunciation	Examples	Common Exceptions
1. a̲, in long position, normally	/ey/	face /feys/, brave /breyv/, shape /šeyp/, take /teyk/	have /hæv/; water /wɔ́tər/; father /fáðər/
2. a̲, in long position, before l̲	/eə/	sale /seəl/, male /meəl/, pale /peəl/, tale /teəl/	
3. a̲, in long position, before r̲	/ɛə/¹	care /kɛər/, square /skwɛər/, dare /dɛər/, rare /rɛər/	are /ar/
4. a̲, in short position, normally	/æ/	ask /æsk/, man /mæn/, sad /sæd/, chance /tšæns/, bank /bæŋk/, last /læst/, pass /pæs/, bag /bæg/, path /pæθ/, sand /sænd/, fancy /fænsɪ/, master /mæstər/	able /éybəl/, table /téybəl/; change /tšéyndž/, strange /streyndž/; taste /teyst/, waste /weyst/; want /want/, watch /watš/, what /hwat/, wash /waš/, was /waz/; any /ɛnɪ/, many /mɛnɪ/
5. a̲, in short position, before l̲	/ɔ/	all /ɔl/, salt /sɔlt/, ball /bɔl/, talk /tɔk/	half /hæf/; shall /šæl/
6. a̲, in short position, before r̲	/a/	art /art/, star /star/, car /kar/, charge /tšardž/	war /wɔr/, warm /wɔrm/, quarter /kwɔrtər/
*7. a̲i̲, normally	/ey/	plain /pleyn/, raise /reyz/, wait /weyt/, paint /peynt/	again /əgén/, against /əgénst/, said /sɛd/
*8. a̲i̲, before l̲	/eə/	sail /seəl/, tail /teəl/, mail /meəl/, fail /feəl/	
*9. a̲i̲, before r̲	/ɛə/¹	air /ɛər/, chair /tšɛər/, hair /hɛər/, fair /fɛər/	

¹In many parts of the United States, -are and -air are pronounced /æær/ instead of /ɛər/.

Spelling As an Indication of the Pronunciation of Stressed Vowels in English (continued)

	Letter Combination	Pronunciation	Examples	Common Exceptions
*10.	au	/ɔ/	cause /kɔz/, pause /pɔz/, Paul /pɔl/, daughter /dɔ́tər/	laugh /læf/
*11.	aw	/ɔ/	draw /drɔ/, law /lɔ/, saw /sɔ/, paw /pɔ/	
*12.	ay	/ey/	say /sey/, stay /stey/, ways /weyz/, day /dey/	says /sɛz/
13.	e, in long position, normally	/iy/	be /biy/, he /hiy/, she /šiy/, these /ðiyz/, even /íyvən/	
14.	e, in long position, before r	/ɛə/	here /hɪər/, mere /mɪər/, sphere /sfɪər/, sincere /sɪnsɪ́ər/	there /ðɛər/, where /hwɛər/; were /wər/
15.	e, in short position, normally	/ɛ/	best /bɛst/, dress /drɛs/, end /ɛnd/, fence /fɛns/	pretty /prítɪ/
16.	e, in short position, before l	/ɛə/	bell /bɛəl/, else /ɛəls/, help /hɛəlp/, twelve /twɛəlv/	
17.	e, in short position, before r	/ə(ər)/	her /hər/, serve /sərv/, verb /vərb/, perfect /pə́rfɪkt/	
*18.	ea, normally	/iy/	each /iytš/, leave /liyv/, mean /miyn/, please /pliyz/, reach /riytš/, sea /siy/, speak /spiyk/, beast /biyst/, heat /hiyt/, stream /striym/, teach /tiytš/, weak /wiyk/	break /breyk/, great /greyt/; breakfast /brɛ́kfəst/, heaven /hɛ́vən/, heavy /hɛ́vɪ/, measure /mɛ́žər/, pleasant /plɛ́zənt/, pleasure /plɛ́žər/, death /dɛθ/, weather /wɛ́ðər/

	Letter Combination	Pronunciation	Examples	Common Exceptions
*19.	ea, before d	/ɛ/	bread /brɛd/, dead /dɛd/, head /hɛd/, ready /rɛ́di/	bead /biyd/, lead (verb) /liyd/, read (present tense) /riyd/
*20.	ea, before l	/iə/	deal /diəl/, heal /hiəl/, real /riəl/, steal /stiəl/	health /hɛəlθ/
*21.	ea, before r, normally	/ɛə/	clear /kliər/, dear /diər/, ear /iər/, hear /hiər/	bear /bɛər/, tear (rip) /tɛər/, wear /wɛər/
*22.	ea, before r, and another consonant	/ə(ər)/	early /ə́rli/, earth /ərθ/, learn /lərn/, heard /hərd/	heart /hart/
*23.	ee, normally	/iy/	deep /diyp/, feet /fiyt/, free /friy/, green /griyn/	been /bɪn/
*24.	ee, before l	/iə/	feel /fiəl/, wheel /hwiəl/, heel /hiəl/, steel /stiəl/	
*25.	ee, before r	/iə/	beer /biər/, cheer /tʃiər/, deer /diər/, queer /kwiər/	
*26.	ei, normally	/iy/	either /iyðər/, receive /rɪsíyv/, seize /siyz/	veil /veəl/; their /ðɛər/
*27.	ei, before g or n	/ey/	eight /eyt/, neighbor /néybər/, weigh /wey/, reign /reyn/, rein /reyn/, vein /veyn/	height /hayt/
*28.	ew	/yuw/	few /fyuw/	grew /gruw/
*29.	ey	/ey/	they /ðey/, convey /kənvéy/	eye /ay/

Spelling As an Indication of the Pronunciation of Stressed Vowels in English (continued)

Letter Combination	Pronunciation	Examples	Common Exceptions
30. i, in long position	/ay/	die /day/, lie /lay/, drive /drayv/, arrive /ərayv/, pile /payl/, smiled /smayld/, fire /fayr/, desire /dızáyr/	give /gıv/, live (verb) /lıv/; iron /áyərn/
31. i, in short position, normally	/ı/	big /bıg/, sing /sıŋ/, fish /fıš/, since /sınts/	sign /sayn/; island /áylənd/
*32. i, in short position, before gh, ld (final), or nd (final)	/ay/	high /hay/, night /nayt/, child /tšayld/, wild /wayld/, wind (verb) /waynd/, find /faynd/, mind /maynd/	wind (noun) /wınd/
33. i, in short position, before l	/əl/	ill /ıəl/, will /wıəl/, milk /mıəlk/, until /əntíəl/	
34. i, in short position, before r	/ə(ə)r/	bird /bərd/, first /fərst/, girl /gərl/, sir /sər/	
*35. ie, normally	/iy/	chief /tšiyf/, piece /piys/, believe /bılíyv/, grief /griyf/	friend /frend/; also see i in long position.
*36. ie, before l	/iə/	field /fiəld/, yield /yiəld/	
*37. ie, before r	/ıə/	pier /pıər/, fierce /fıərs/	
38. o, in long position	/ow/	go /gow/, no /now/, so /sow/, ago /əgów/, alone /əlówn/, close (verb) /klowz/, home /howm/, hope /howp/, stone /stown/, those /ðowz/, whole /howl/, bone /bown/, nose /nowz/, note /nowt/, smoke /smowk/, spoke /spowk/, suppose /səpówz/	do /duw/, into /íntuw/, to /tuw/, two /tuw/, who /huw/; move /muwv/, lose /luwz/, prove /pruwv/, whose /huwz/; gone /gɔn/; does /dəz/; shoe /šuw/; above /əbə́v/, come /kəm/, done /dən/, love /ləv/, some /səm/, none /nən/; one /wən/

Letter Combination	Pronunciation	Examples	Common Exceptions
39. o, in long position, before r	/ow/²	more /mowr/, sore /sowr/, before /bɪfówr/	
*40. o, in short position, before a stop	/a/	box /baks/, drop /drap/, God /gad/, got /gat/, rock /rak/	
*41. o, in short position, before a continuant, normally	/ɔ/	across /əkrɔ́s/, along /əlɔ́ŋ/, corn /kɔrn/, cross /krɔs/, for /fɔr/, form /fɔrm/, long /lɔŋ/, lost /lɔst/, north /nɔrθ/, off /ɔf/, short /šɔrt/, soft /sɔft/, strong /strɔŋ/, born /bɔrn/, belong /bɪlɔ́ŋ/, cloth /klɔθ/, cost /kɔst/, lord /lɔrd/, loss /lɔs/, song /sɔŋ/, sort /sɔrt/, storm /stɔrm/, wrong /rɔŋ/, forth /fɔrθ/, report /rɪpɔ́rt/, morning /mɔ́rnɪŋ/, often /ɔ́fən/, order /ɔ́rdər/, corner /kɔ́rnər/, former /fɔ́rmər/, offer /ɔ́fər/, office /ɔ́fis/	woman /wúmən/; women /wímɪn/; whom /huwm/; once /wəns/; common /kámən/, follow /fáləw/, possible /pásəbəl/; word /wərd/, work /wərk/, world /wərld/, worth /wərθ/; almost /ɔ́lmowst/, both /bowθ/, most /mowst/, don't /downt/, post /powst/, only /ównlɪ/; company /kəmpənɪ/, wonder /wəndər/, tongue /təŋ/, among /əməŋ/, front /frənt/, month /mənθ/, son /sən/, another /ənəðər/, brother /brəðər/, cover /kəvər/, money /mənɪ/, mother /məðər/, nothing /nəθɪŋ/, other /əðər/, discover /dɪskəvər/, govern /gəvərn/
42. o, in short position, before l	/ow/	cold /kowld/, roll /rowl/, told /towld/, soldier /sówldžər/	
*43. oa	/ow/	boat /bowt/, coal /kowl/, coast /kowst/	broad /brɔd/

²In many parts of the United States, -ore is pronounced /ɔr/ instead of /owr/.

Spelling As an Indication of the Pronunciation of Stressed Vowels in English (continued)

Letter Combination	Pronunciation	Examples	Common Exceptions
*44. oi	/ɔy/	point /pɔynt/, voice /vɔys/, noise /nɔyz/, soil /sɔyl/	
*45. oo, final	/uw/	too /tuw/, woo /wuw/	
*46. oo, before a stop	/ʊ/	hood /hʊd/, stood /stʊd/, good /gʊd/, wood /wʊd/, book /bʊk/, brook /brʊk/, cook /kʊk/, hook /hʊk/, look /lʊk/, shook /šʊk/, took /tʊk/, foot /fʊt/, soot /sʊt/	blood /blǝd/, flood /flǝd/; food /fuwd/, mood /muwd/, droop /druwp/, loop /luwp/, stoop /stuwp/, troop /truwp/, boot /buwt/, root /ruwt/, shoot /šuwt/
*47. oo, before a continuant, normally	/uw/	room /ruwm/, school /skuwl/, soon /suwn/, moon /muwn/	
*48. oo, before r̠	/ow/	door /dowr/, floor /flowr/	poor /pʊr/
*49. ou, normally	/aw/	about /ǝbáwt/, around /ǝráwnd/, found /fawnd/, house /haws/, out /awt/, sound /sawnd/, south /sawθ/, cloud /klawd/, count /kawnt/, doubt /dawt/, loud /lawd/, mouth /mawθ/	brought /brɔt/, thought /θɔt/; though /ðow/, although /ɔlðów/; through /θruw/, you /yuw/; country /kǝ́ntrɪ/, double /dǝ́bǝl/, enough /ǝnǝ́f/, touch /tǝtš/, trouble /trǝ́bǝl/, young /yǝŋ/
*50. ou, before l̠ or r̠, normally	/ow/	soul /sowl/, shoulder /šówldǝr/, course /kowrs/, four /fowr/, court /kowrt/, pour /powr/	your /yur/, journey /džǝ́rnɪ/; our /awr/, hour /awr/
*51. ou, before final l̠d	/ʊ/	could /kʊd/, should /šʊd/, would /wʊd/	

227

	Letter Combination	Pronunciation	Examples	Common Exceptions
*52.	ow	/ow/ or /aw/	bow (weapon, or knot) /bow/, blow /blow/, flow /flow/, grow /grow/, know /now/, low /low/, own /own/, row (line, or to propel with oars) /row/, show /šow/, slow /slow/, snow /snow/, throw /θrow/, toward /towrd/; bow (point of boat, or to incline) /baw/, allow /əláw/, down /dawn/, brown /brawn/, how /haw/, now /naw/, cow /kaw/, row (disturbance) /raw/, crowd /krawd/, town /tawn/, crown /krawn/, flower /flawr/	
*53.	oy	/ɔy/	boy /bɔy/, destroy /distrɔy/, joy /džɔy/, toy /tɔy/	
54.	u, in long position	/yuw/	use /yuwz/, tune /tyuwn/, due /dyuw/, music /myuwzɪk/, mule /myuwl/	rule /ruwl/, blue /bluw/
55.	u, in long position, before r	yʊ	cure /kyʊr/, pure /pyʊr/, endure /ɛndyʊ́r/	
56.	u, in short position	/ə/ or /ər/	but /bət/, rush /rəš/, run /rən/, jump /džəmp/, dull /dəl/, burn /bərn/, hurt /hərt/, us /əs/	busy /bízɪ/; truth /truwθ/; full /fʊl/, pull /pʊl/, put /pʊt/, sugar /šʊ́gər/
*57.	y	/ay/	by /bay/, fly /flay/, cry /kray/, sky /skay/, supply /səpláy/	

sent vowel sounds with some degree of regularity. Letter combinations for
which the few examples that can be found are pronounced in various ways,
such as the u̲i̲ in *fruit* and the u̲a̲ in *guard,* are not included.

The items marked with an asterisk represent elements of regularity that
were not discussed in Lesson 17 and that should therefore be studied with
particular care in this lesson.

The third column in the table provides examples of words in which the
vowel letters in the combinations listed in the first column are pronounced as
shown in the second column. The fourth column lists common exceptions,
words in which the vowel letters *look as though they should be pronounced as
shown in the second column* but are actually not so pronounced. The words
listed as exceptions are divided by semicolons into groups, according to the
vowel sounds with which they are actually pronounced. Unfortunately, in a
few cases the total number of exceptions is almost as large as the number of
examples.

Approximately 500 words are listed either as examples or as exceptions.
Most of these 500 are among the 1,000 most commonly used English words as
identified in frequency counts such as E. L. Thorndike's *The Teacher's Word
Book.* Words that contain none of the 57 letter combinations are not included
in the table: examples would be *people* /píypəl/ and *build* /bɪəld/. Function
words, usually heard in their reduced form (*are* for example), have been transcribed only in their stressed form (/ar/); their pronunciation when unstressed
(/ər/) has, of course, been discussed in previous lessons.

You are not expected to memorize the table. The exercises at the end of
the lesson will help you to become familiar with it, and you may wish to refer
to it later. It should be a resource to you in your efforts to avoid that type of
vowel substitution which is caused by the way in which a word is spelled.

III. Exercises

A. 1. Add new examples of your own to illustrate as many as you can of the 57
        letter combinations in the preceding table.

    2. Each of the following words is an example of one of the 57 combinations.
        Give the number of the combination illustrated by each word.

a.	set	f.	cool	k.	lawn
b.	hid	g.	fold	l.	hat
c.	oats	h.	melt	m.	fill
d.	call	i.	peer	n.	cede
e.	fare	j.	shield	o.	name

p.	pierce	aa.	ale	ll.	lean
q.	seal	bb.	stew	mm.	crook
r.	toil	cc.	rain	nn.	five
s.	farm	dd.	blind	oo.	caught
t.	freight	ee.	cute	pp.	not
u.	peel	ff.	search	qq.	near
v.	proud	gg.	decéive	rr.	fourth
w.	sincére	hh.	spread	ss.	verse
x.	pair	ii.	such	tt.	piece
y.	third	jj.	meet	uu.	nail
z.	boss	kk.	may	vv.	store

B. You are probably not familiar with many of the following rather rare words, but these are the kind of words whose pronunciation you may want to try to figure out while doing your reading. The pronunciation of the stressed vowels in all of them is regularly spelled according to the table. How should each be pronounced? Remember that the table does not refer to *unstressed* vowels; you should already be thoroughly familiar with the sounds normally given to unstressed vowels. (See Lesson 3.)

1.	ábbacy	18.	hearse	35.	fiend
2.	sparse	19.	weald	36.	wield
3.	scald	20.	blear	37.	tíer
4.	smalt	21.	drear	38.	vizíer
5.	taut	22.	veer	39.	stooge
6.	paunch	23.	deign	40.	cajóle
7.	abéle	24.	skein	41.	loft
8.	subvéne	25.	askéw	42.	thong
9.	abstérge	26.	abéyance	43.	wold
10.	pert	27.	wince	44.	bólster
11.	mércurate	28.	tithe	45.	rook
12.	sere	29.	hind	46.	bourn
13.	delve	30.	rind	47.	slouch
14.	tread	31.	besmírch	48.	pounce
15.	streak	32.	dirge	49.	bulge
16.	earl	33.	filch	50.	spume
17.	yearn	34.	frieze	51.	rebúke

C. The words below all contain letter combinations that are included in our table. None of the words, however, is actually pronounced in the way indicated by its spelling. Each of them could therefore be listed in the fourth column as an exception. Be sure you know how the stressed vowels of all the words are actually pronounced, looking them up in a dictionary if necessary. Then tell both how each word is actually pronounced and how it would sound if it were pronounced as indicated by its spelling.

1.	pear	8.	foul	15.	tough
2.	realm	9.	youth	16.	scoop
3.	machíne	10.	glove	17.	Tom
4.	plead	11.	doll	18.	beard
5.	bull	12.	swamp	19.	deaf
6.	calm	13.	awárd	20.	key
7.	ninth	14.	aunt	21.	cough

D. According to our table some of the common words below are spelled regularly, some irregularly. Pick out the irregularly spelled words, and write the phonetic symbols that represent their vowel sounds. Then read the entire list several times. The hyphens in some words of more than one syllable mark syllable boundaries.

1.	do	20.	foes	39.	son
2.	go	21.	both	40.	front
3.	move	22.	cloth	41.	móth-er
4.	stove	23.	come	42.	bóth-er
5.	abóve	24.	home	43.	óth-er
6.	próve	25.	some	44.	cóv-er
7.	love	26.	dome	45.	ó-ver
8.	wove	27.	word	46.	góv-ern
9.	lose	28.	lord	47.	cló-ver
10.	those	29.	worth	48.	boat
11.	whose	30.	north	49.	broad
12.	nose	31.	most	50.	blood
13.	none	32.	cost	51.	good
14.	gone	33.	post	52.	food
15.	stone	34.	lost	53.	wood
16.	bone	35.	wónder	54.	flood
17.	done	36.	pónder	55.	boot
18.	does	37.	amóng	56.	foot
19.	shoes	38.	long	57.	soot

E. American elementary-school teachers sometimes ask pupils who are just learning to read to memorize two rhyming lines: "When two vowels go out walking, /the first one does the talking." This verse is supposed to remind the children that, when two vowel letters are written together to form a digraph such as <u>ai</u> or <u>ee</u>, the whole digraph is given the long sound of the *first* of the two letters. Thus <u>ai</u> would be pronounced as /ey/ and <u>ee</u> as /iy/. This would presumably make it possible for the children to recognize written words such as *rain* and *feet*.

Unfortunately, the verse may mislead the children. Some digraphs are not pronounced the way the verse says they should be. Our table tells us, for example, that <u>ai</u> before <u>r</u> is pronounced /ɛə/ and <u>au</u> is pronounced /ɔ/. Do you think it is wise for the teachers to ask their pupils to remember the two lines?

The class could discuss that question. This would involve going through the table and finding out how many of the digraphs listed there are regularly pronounced with the long sound of their first vowel. This exercise could alternatively be done as a small-group activity. Each group could be asked to examine the data in the table, and then to report their conclusions to the class as a whole.

F. Early in this manual a great deal of attention was paid to rhythm and intonation, because they may well be the basic elements in learning to pronounce English understandably. It therefore seems desirable to return to those elements in this final lesson in order to call your attention once more to their importance.

The sentences in each of the following groups have the same rhythm and intonation. Sentence stresses are marked. Repeat each group until you can produce that particular pattern rapidly and naturally. (This material is suitable for taping.)

1. a. To téll us to be quíet is unréasonable.

   b. The ówner is prepáred to redécorate it.

   c. I'll hélp you with your cóat when you're réady for it.

   d. I thínk he would be shócked if you ásked him for it.

   e. I néver would have thóught you would gíve it to me.

2. a. Have you stúdied your léssons?

   b. Does he spéak with an áccent?

   c. Is it wróng to get ángry?

   d. Are you wílling to téll me?

   e. Can you éver belíeve it?

3. a. I have exáms in mathemátics and chémistry.

   b. I would have thóught it was a Líncoln or a Cádillac.

   c. Was he idéntified befórehand or áfterward?

   d. You'll have to prómise me to lóve it and chérish it.

   e. Do you préfer to have it tóasted or úntoasted?

4. a. With a néw cár and enóugh tíme we could máke it.

   b. It's a lóng tíme since he léft hóme for the cíty.

    c.   If you won't go, you can write now and explain it.

    d.   When the war ends and the peace comes, we'll be happy.

    e.   There's a fine current of cool air near the window.

G.   The intonation patterns as marked in the sentences below are *not natural*. In fact, each sentence represents a type of "intonation error" often made by students. What suggestions could you make to help a person who used such patterns improve his speech?

1.   How are you, Mr. Williams?

2.   It's a beautiful day, isn't it?

3.   What do you want with a dictionary?

4.   How are you feeling this morning?

5.   I think it's better over there, John.

6.   Mr. Thomas is here, but I don't see Mrs. Thomas.

7.   Is it a boy or a girl?

8.   It's the center of our thoughts, our hopes, and our fears.

H.   **REFLECTIONS ON ENGLISH SPELLING**

         I take it you already know
         Of *tough* and *bough* and *cough* and *dough?*
         Others may stumble but not you,
         On *hiccough, thorough, laugh,* and *through.*
         Well done! And now you wish, perhaps,
         To learn of less familiar traps?

Beware of *heard,* a dreadful *word*
That looks like *beard* and sounds like *bird,*
And *dead:* it's *read* like *bed,* not *bead—*
For goodness' sake don't call it "deed"!
Watch out for *meat* and *great* and *threat.*
(They rhyme with *sweet* and *straight* and *debt.*)

A *moth* is not a moth in *mother.*
Nor *both* in *bother, broth* in *brother.*
And *here* is not a match for *there*
Nor *dear* and *fear* for *bear* and *pear.*

And then there's *dose* and *rose* and *lose—*
Just look them up—and *goose* and *choose,*
And *cork* and *work* and *card* and *ward,*
And *font* and *front* and *word* and *sword,*
And *do* and *go* and *thwart* and *cart—*
Come, come, I've hardly made a start!
A dreadful language? Man alive,
I'd mastered it when I was five!

The above verses[3] express well the frustration many speakers of English feel in regard to the way the language is spelled. This material can be quite useful to students, however, in familiarizing themselves with some of the most common and irritating inconsistencies in the spelling system.

The following activities are suggested as ways of learning something from "Reflections on English Spelling."

1. The teacher can read the material and have the students repeat it after him or her line by line.
2. The verses, or a part of them, can be given as a dictation with books closed.
3. The class can be divided into two teams for a contest. Individual team members could take turns in reading one line each. A point could be scored by a team each time a member of it read a line and pronounced all the italicized words in it correctly.

---

[3]We have been unable to identify the author of the verses definitely or to find a copy of the complete selection in print. Dwight Bolinger published part of the material in the second edition of his *Aspects of Language* (Harcourt, Brace and World, 1975). He said the verses were written by Richard Krogh, whom he did not further identify. The longer and somewhat different version that we have included here has been circulated among graduate students at the University of California, in mimeographed form, and signed with the initials T. S. W.

Accent Inventory (Copy 2)

To the Student

This "Inventory" is to be used, preferably at the very beginning of the English course, so that you may have constantly at hand a diagnosis of the elements of foreign "accent" in your own individual speech. First, your voice will be recorded as you read the "Diagnostic Passage" on the next page. The reading should be done at normal speed, in a matter-of-fact tone, without unusual care in pronunciation; in other words, it should sound as much like natural conversation as possible. Then the instructor will listen to the recording many times, and make an analysis, on the following pages, of your speech difficulties. These pages will serve as a guide to the sections of the *Manual* that are of most importance to you, and show just what phases of English pronunciation should be of most concern to you.

   The "Inventory" may be used again at the end of the course to measure the progress you have made.

SUGGESTED KEY TO CORRECTIONS

Phonetic symbols immediately under word: what you should have said. Second line of phonetic symbols under word: mispronunciation in your speech.

 ′ Over a syllable or word: you left this unstressed; it should be stressed.
(′) over a syllable or word: you stressed this; it should be unstressed.

Black line: normal intonation.
Colored line: your incorrect intonation.

 ⁄ unnatural pause you made.

Diagnostic Passage

(1) When a student from another country comes to study in the United States, he has to find out for himself the answers to many questions, and he has many problems to think about. (2) Where should he live? (3) Would it be better if he looked for a private room off campus or if he stayed in a dormitory? (4) Should he spend all of his time just studying? (5) Shouldn't he try to take advantage of the many social and cultural activities which are offered? (6) At first it is not easy for him to be casual in dress, informal in manner, and

confident in speech. (7) Little by little he learns what kind of clothing is usually worn here to be casually dressed for classes. (8) He also learns to choose the language and customs that are appropriate for informal situations. (9) Finally he begins to feel sure of himself. (10) But let me tell you, my friend, this long-awaited feeling doesn't develop suddenly, does it. (11) All of this takes will power.

Check List of Problems

I. STRESS AND RHYTHM

A. _____ Stress on wrong syllable of words of more than one syllable. (See Lesson 3, Section III, of manual.)

B. _____ Misplaced stress on nominal compounds. (L. 4, S. II.)

C. _____ Misplaced stress on two-word verbs. (L. 4, S. II.)

D. _____ Other improper sentence stress. (L. 4, S. II.)

E. _____ Improper division of sentences into thought groups. (L. 4, S. IV.)

F. _____ Failure to blend well, to make smooth transitions between words or syllables.

    1. _____ Improper insertion of /ə/ to break up difficult combinations of conso-nants. (L. 4, S. IV; L. 15, S. I.)

    2. _____ Insertion of /ə/ before initial s̲ followed by a consonant. (L. 15, S. III.)

    3. _____ Unnatural insertion of glottal stop. (L. 4, S. IV.)

II. INTONATION

A. _____ Unnatural intonation at end of statements. (L. 5, S. III.)

B. _____ In wh-questions. (L. 5, S. III.)

C. _____ In yes-no questions. (L. 6, S. I.)

D. _____ In series. (L. 6, S. II.)

E. _____ In questions with two alternatives. (L. 6, S. II.)

F. _____ In direct address. (L. 6, S. II.)

G. _____ In tag questions. (L. 6, S. II.)

H. _____ In other cases.

III. VOWELS

A. _____ Failure to obscure unstressed vowels in words of more than one syllable. (L. 3, S. II.)

B. _____ Failure to obscure the vowels of unstressed words. (L. 4, S. II and III.)

C. _____ Failure to lengthen stressed vowels before final voiced consonants. (L. 9, S. II.)

D. _____ Substitution of an improper vowel sound. (L. 2; 11; 12; 17; 18.)

1. ___ for /iy/. 5. ___ for /æ/. 9. ___ for /ʊ/. 13. ___ for /ay/.
2. ___ for /ɪ/. 6. ___ for /a/. 10. ___ for /uw/. 14. ___ for /aw/.
3. ___ for /ey/. 7. ___ for /ɔ/. 11. ___ for /ə/. 15. ___ for /ɔ/.
4. ___ for /ɛ/. 8. ___ for /ow/. 12. ___ for /ər/. 16. ___ for /yuw/.

IV. CONSONANTS

A. ___ Substitutions due to improper voicing. (L. 8, S. I.)

1. ___ /p/ for /b/. 5. ___ /ð/ for /θ/. 9. ___ /š/ for /ž/.
2. ___ /t/ for /d/. 6. ___ /f/ for /v/. 10. ___ /tš/ for /dž/.
3. ___ /k/ for /g/. 7. ___ /s/ for /z/. 11. ___ Others.
4. ___ /θ/ for /ð/. 8. ___ /z/ for /s/.

B. ___ Substitutions due to other causes, especially improper point of articulation.

1. ___ /r/ for /l/. (L. 10, S. I.)
2. ___ /l/ for /r/. (L. 10, S. I.)
3. ___ /ð/ for /d/. (L. 13, S. II.)
4. ___ /d/ for /ð/. (L. 13, S. II.)
5. ___ /z/ for /ð/. (L. 13, S. II.)
6. ___ /t/ for /θ/. (L. 13, S. II.)
7. ___ /s/ for /θ/. (L. 13, S. II.)
8. ___ /dž/ for /y/. (L. 13, S. III.)
9. ___ /y/ for /dž/. (L. 13, S. III.)
10. ___ /ž/ for /dž/. (L. 13, S. III.)
11. ___ /š/ for /tš/. (L. 13, S. IV.)
12. ___ /v/ for /b/. (L. 14, S. I.)
13. ___ /b/ for /v/. (L. 14, S. I.)
14. ___ /w/ for /v/. (L. 14, S. I.)
15. ___ /v/ for /w/. (L. 14, S. I.)
16. ___ /v/ for /hw/. (L. 14, S. I.)
17. ___ /p/ for /f/. (L. 14, S. II.)
18. ___ /hw/ for /f/. (L. 14, S. II.)
19. ___ /ŋ/ for /n/. (L. 14, S. III.)
20. ___ /n/ for /ŋ/. (L. 14, S. III.)
21. ___ /n/ for /m/. (L. 14, S. III.)
22. ___ Others.

C. _____ Improper point of articulation, resulting in abnormal sound but not substitution.

    1. _____ /d/. (L. 8, S. III.)

    2. _____ /t/. (L. 8, S. III.)

    3. _____ /r/. (L. 10, S. I.)

    4. _____ Others.

D. _____ Insufficient aspiration of initial voiceless consonants. (L. 9, S. I.)

E. _____ Excessive aspiration of final stops and voiced continuants. (L. 9, S. III.)

F. _____ Excessive aspiration of ''/d/-like'' medial /t/. (L. 9, S. I.)

G. _____ Improper addition of a consonant.

    1. _____ /ŋk/ for /ŋ/. (L. 14, S. III.)

    2. _____ /gw/ for /w/. (L. 14, S. I.)

    3. _____ /h/ inserted. (L. 14, S. IV.)

    4. _____ Others.

H. _____ Slighting or omission of a consonant.

    1. _____ /h/. (L. 14, S. IV.)

    2. _____ /s/. (L. 8, S. V.)

    3. _____ /z/. (L. 8, S. V.)

    4. _____ /t/. (L. 8, S. IV.)

    5. _____ /d/. (L. 8, S. IV.)

    6. _____ Others.

V. VOWELS AND CONSONANTS

A. _____ Confusion between the three usual ways of pronouncing the -ed ending. (L. 8, S. IV.)

B. _____ Confusion between the three usual ways of pronouncing the -s ending. (L. 8, S. V.)

C. _____ Syllabic consonants. (L. 10, S. III.)

    1. _____ Failure to pronounce the preceding consonant (for example, /wʊnt/ for /wʊdn̩t/).

    2. _____ Insertion of /ə/ (for example, /wʊdənt/ for /wʊdn̩t/).

D. _____ Failure to insert /ə/ between a front vowel and /l/ or /r/. (L. 10, S. II.)

VI. GENERAL COMMENTS

Index